VILLAGES O

C000198031

For Monica

VILLAGES OF GLASGOW

North of the Clyde

AILEEN SMART

JOHN DONALD PUBLISHERS
EDINBURGH

This revised edition published in 2002 by
John Donald Publishers
an imprint of Birlinn Ltd
West Newington House
10 Newington Road
Edinburgh EH9 1QS

www.birlinn.co.uk

First published in 1988 by
John Donald Publishers Ltd, Edinburgh

ISBN 0 85976 562 8

British Library Cataloguing-in-Publication Data
A catalogue record for this book is available
from the British Library

Typeset by Brinnoven, Livingston
Printed and bound by J W Arrowsmith Ltd, Bristol

PREFACE

It has often been said that the history of Glasgow is the history of its villages. The first edition of this volume outlined the development of ten villages which now form part of the city north of the Clyde. Three additional villages are included in this new edition – Yoker on the west and Carmyle on the east, two of Glasgow's most ancient villages, both just within the city boundary, and Grahamston, right in the centre of Glasgow, a small village with a short but colourful existence, the village which disappeared.

The author wishes to thank the many individuals who have supplied information and gratefully acknowledges the assistance received from the staffs of the Glasgow Room and other departments of the Mitchell Library, Glasgow City Archives, the Museum of Transport, Glasgow Museums Photolibrary, Clydebank Library, Glasgow University Library, Glasgow University Archives and the Map Room of the National Library of Scotland.

The following have kindly given permission to reproduce photographs:

J.G. Gillies, pp. 50, 55

Malcolm R. Hill, p. 64

R.A. Hogg, p. 107

Graham E. Langmuir, p. 143

J.A. Lynch, p. 68

Thomas M. Waugh, pp. 184, 187

Sandyhills East Community Council, p. 182 (previously published in *Shettleston From Old & New Photographs*)

T. & R. Annan & Sons, p. 4

D.C. Thomson & Co. Ltd, pp. 19, 102, 122

Scottish National Portrait Gallery, p. 33

Glasgow University Library, pp. 86, 98

Scottish Theatre Archive, Glasgow University, p. 23

Glasgow City Archives, pp. 47, 57, 88, 126, 140, 171, 175, 180, 193, 226, 228

Mitchell Library, Glasgow, pp. 73, 82, 95, 110, 120, 158, 163, 169, 173, 189, 194, 195, 202, 212, 216, 218
Glasgow Museums and Art Galleries:
   People's Palace, pp. 41, 44, 60, 67, 76, 93, 145, 150
   Museum of Transport, p. 127
West Dunbartonshire Libraries & Museums, p. 224
Other photographs by R.M. Smart

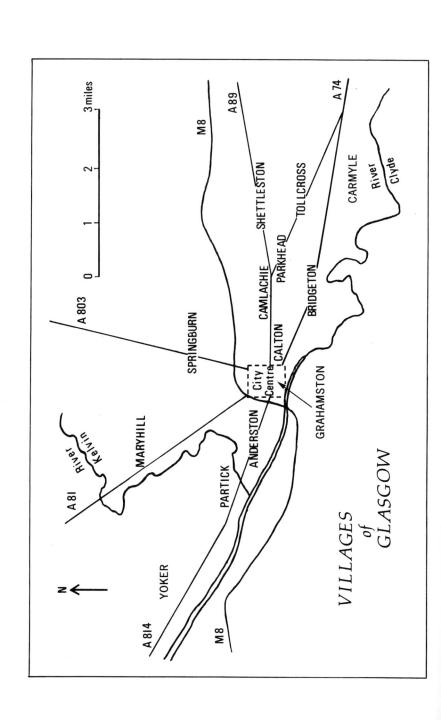

N

3 miles

A 803

A 81
River Kelvin

A 814

YOKER

PARTICK

MARYHILL

ANDERSTON

SPRINGBURN

City Centre

CALTON

GRAHAMSTON

M 8

CAMLACHIE

SHETTLESTON

PARKHEAD

TOLLCROSS

BRIDGETON

CARMYLE

River Clyde

M 8

A 89

A 74

VILLAGES of GLASGOW

CONTENTS

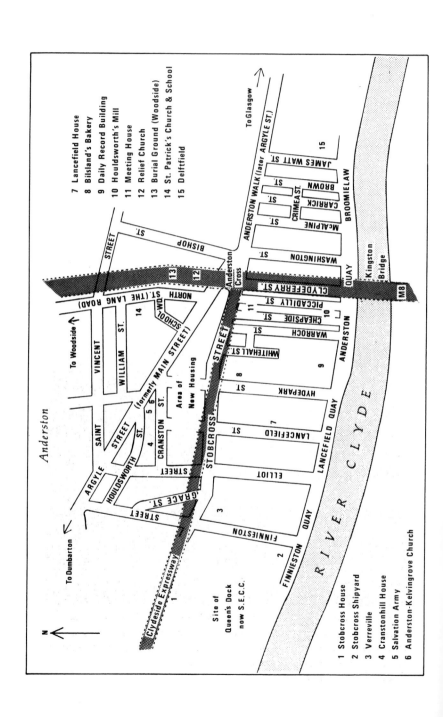

Anderston

To Dumbarton

To Woodside

To Glasgow

RIVER CLYDE

Site of Queen's Dock now S.E.C.C.

Area of New Housing

Anderston Cross

Kingston Bridge

M8

7   Lancefield House
8   Bisland's Bakery
9   Daily Record Building
10 Houldsworth's Mill
11 Meeting House
12 Relief Church
13 Burial Ground (Woodside)
14 St. Patrick's Church & School
15 Delftfield

1 Stobcross House
2 Stobcross Shipyard
3 Verreville
4 Cranstonhill House
5 Salvation Army
6 Anderston-Kelvingrove Church

ARGYLE STREET
SAINT VINCENT STREET
WILLIAM ST.
HOULDSWORTH ST.
CRANSTON ST.
SCHOOL WD.
NORTH ST. (THE LANG ROAD)
BISHOP ST.
STREET
STOBCROSS STREET (formerly MAIN STREET)
GRACE ST.
ELLIOT STREET
FINNIESTON QUAY
FINNIESTON QUAY
LANCEFIELD QUAY
HYDEPARK ST.
LANCEFIELD ST.
WARROCH ST.
CHEAPSIDE ST.
PICCADILLY ST.
WHITEHALL ST.
ANDERSTON QUAY
CLYDEFERRY ST.
WASHINGTON ST.
McALPINE ST.
CARRICK ST.
CRIMEA ST.
BROWN ST.
JAMES WATT ST.
BROOMIELAW
ANDERSTON WALK (later ARGYLE ST.)
Clydeside Expressway

1
ANDERSTON

Anderston, 'Anderson's town', began as a weavers' village in the 1720s. The first houses were laid out along Main Street, which, using modern landmarks, is that part of Argyle Street between the M8 motorway and the new Anderston–Kelvingrove Church. Each cottage was provided with a strip of land behind so that families could keep a cow and supply themselves with fresh produce. These strips ran down to Stobcross Street, now transformed into the Clydeside Expressway, but at that time the avenue to the Anderson family home at Stobcross. In the angle between Main Street and Stobcross Street was the Gushet farm, and to reach Glasgow, villagers had to make their way along a badly maintained path through the fields

Looking west along Argyle Street, formerly Main Street, Anderston. The first weavers' cottages were laid out along this stretch of road in the 1720s, and were later replaced by tenements. On the right is the savings bank building, one of the few surviving tenements in Anderston. Anderston–Kelvingrove Church is on the left.

known as Anderston Walk. In the nineteenth century the cottages and gardens gave way to streets of tenements, and Anderston Cross was laid out over the Gushet farm. The tenements were in turn pulled down in preparation for the construction of Glasgow's ring-road in the 1970s. Only two isolated buildings remain from Victorian times in this area: the Masonic building at 650 Argyle Street, now partly occupied by the Buttery Restaurant; and the Anderston branch of the Glasgow Savings Bank at number 752, now occupied by the Art House, Glasgow. This splendid red sandstone building was designed by James Salmon and opened in 1900. Above the doorway is a bust of Henry Duncan, founder of the savings bank movement, shown tapping his left forefinger against his forehead and clutching his moneybag in his right hand, presumably cautioning prudence. Since redevelopment the site of the original village has become a grassed-over area more in keeping with the rural eighteenth century than with the industrial nineteenth and early twentieth centuries. By a happy coincidence, or perhaps intentionally, the new houses built at McIntyre, Little, Grace, Port and Cranston Streets are placed close to the original village, and it must give pleasure to local residents, who feared that the heart of their community had been torn out in the 1960s, that they can again live on the spot occupied by Anderstonians for over two hundred and fifty years, first in simple thatched cottages, then in lines of tall tenements, and now in the modern flats which have seen them into the twenty-first century.

The weavers' village

Anderston takes its name from a family of Andersons who lived in the area from pre-Reformation times, when the lands belonged to the archbishops of Glasgow. James, Ninian, Jhon, Wylzem, Andro, Janat, Bessy and Violat Anderson make their appearance in the rental book of the archbishop in the time of Mary, Queen of Scots. In 1547 James Anderson is recorded as settled 'in fourty *s* a ferm land of Stob Crose'. Tradition has it that the farm took its name from a wooden cross, or 'stob', which marked the spot where a branch road, now Finnieston Street, left the main Glasgow to Dumbarton highway. The bishop was believed to take this route from his castle beside Glasgow Cathedral to his country residence at Partick. 'Stabross' was a well-enough known landmark to appear on Blaeu's map of 1654, and fifty years later the Andersons were sufficiently prosperous to build a mansion-house from which they could look down at their cattle and sheep grazing on the banks of the Clyde.

In the 1720s the head of the family, another James Anderson, decided to feu part of his land for a weavers' village – after the customary precautions of locating the artisans' dwellings as far away as possible from the mansion-house. The arrangement benefited both James, who increased his rentals, and the weavers, who were able to set up in business just outside the Glasgow boundary and so escape having to pay an entry fee to the weavers' guild of Glasgow. This chapter of history came to an end in 1735, when the last Anderson sold the estate to John Orr of Barrowfield, leaving only the family name as a reminder of former times. Stobcross House was demolished in 1875 to make way for Queen's Dock, which was itself filled in again in the 1980s with debris from the St Enoch's Hotel in the city centre to form a site for the Scottish Exhibition and Conference Centre.

The first recorded settler in the village was not a weaver, but a linen and woollen draper by the name of John Stobo. It is possible that Stobo was one of the merchants who formed the Glasgow Linen Society in the 1720s to collect locally woven cloth and send it by ship to expanding colonial markets or by packmen to England. By encouraging full-time weavers to settle in Anderston, Stobo not only had his sources of supply at hand, but was also able to ensure that the linen met the high standards demanded by London merchants. Complaints were rife at that time about the poor quality of Scottish cloth. The weavers' wives and daughters who spun the yarn produced a rather uneven and knotty thread and the men did not always bother to boil the thread before weaving to remove the dirt and saliva which their womenfolk had applied during the spinning process. Some weavers tried to improve the unattractive brown colour of the linen by bleaching it with cheap, locally available acids and alkalis such as lime and pigeon dung.

A great stimulus to linen production was given when a national 'stamp' or system of inspection for linen cloth was set up in Scotland, financed by money from the 'Equivalent'. This was money laid aside at the Union of 1707 to compensate Scots for undertaking a share in England's national debt. In 1727 it was agreed to use part of this money to encourage the linen trade, and John Stobo might even have set up in Anderston with an eighteenth-century government grant. Money was also made available for training, and the wife of a Picardy weaver was persuaded to go to Glasgow to teach the local

Anderston Cross around 1900. Stobcross Street on the left and Argyle Street on the right. Note the fine curved frontage of Anderston Cross station, designed by J.J. Burnet around 1896, for the Glasgow Central Railway. The buildings were demolished in 1967.

women how to spin cambric yarn, but unfortunately the school had to close through lack of recruits.

In 1738 the weavers of Anderston associated themselves into a 'freindly Community' with the dual purpose of controlling entry into the industry and helping those afflicted by ill health or old age. Income came from entry fees, hire of the mortcloth which was used when weavers were buried, and the sixpence fines imposed for swearing in the presence of the deacon. The names recorded on the 'Original Charter of the Weavers in Anderstoun' are: James Sym, Archibald Anderson, Michael Murdoch, John Horn, Andrew Campbell, John Jameson, Robert Hamilton, John Murray, John Paton, James Paton, Thomas Scott, James Gemmill, James Fleeming, John Kerr, James Holdin, Matthew Baird, Wm. Anderson, Wm. Scott, Jno. Taylor, Wm. Steven, Jno. Campbell, all weavers in Anderstoun and Robert Marshall, dyer there. The weavers' society owned property at the corner of Argyle Street and North Street, and when this was demolished in 1967 a lead box was found under the foundation stone containing coins, newspapers and part of a lamp and taken into the People's Palace collections. A handsome new block of flats has been erected adjoining the nineteenth-century Masonic building.

Over the entrance is a fine mosaic representing the weavers' coat of arms, depicting a man weaving and a woman spinning, with the inscriptions 'Masonic Society Anderston' and 'Philemon Housing Association, 1970'.

No weavers' cottages remain in Anderston, but the Weavers' Cottage restored by the National Trust for Scotland at Kilbarchan, built in 1723, shows that the master weaver had a comfortable house, with living accommodation upstairs and a loom shop below, or alternatively a workshop built on to a one-storey cottage. The workshop contained the weaver's loom, the most important parts of which were the beams, between which the warp yarns were stretched; the shuttle, which carried the weft threads through the warp threads; and the heddles, worked by foot-treadles, which created the space, or 'shed' between the warp threads through which the shuttle could pass. Until the invention of the flying shuttle, the shuttle was thrown from hand to hand and weaving was noisy, heavy work, carried out in an unhealthily damp atmosphere so that the threads did not break. Nevertheless, compared with other eighteenth-century artisans the weaver enjoyed a fairly high standard of living. Above all he had the freedom to work his own hours and could make time to air his radical views on politics and his dissenting opinions on religion at literary and debating societies, or stay at home to read his books or write poetry. Weavers valued education, and only two of the Anderston men on the list above could not sign their names. A few streets in the village took their names from weaving processes, but sadly Heddle Place, Dandy Row, Carding Lane, Loom Place and Warp Lane now only exist on old maps.

By the middle of the eighteenth century the Anderston weavers had a reputation for producing fine quality cambrics and lawns, using yarns imported from France and Holland. The industry was increasingly controlled by 'corks' – men who organised the supply of yarn, oversaw production and marketed the finished linen. 'Wee corks' seemed to proliferate in Anderston and were a thorn in the flesh of the weavers. One 'wee Anderston cork' with considerable business acumen was James Monteith of Bishop Street, whose family had come from Aberfoyle, and who bypassed the Glasgow merchants by importing yarn direct from a M. Mortier in Cambrai. Monteith also experimented with new yarns and methods of weaving. In 1768 his factory produced the first web of muslin to be woven in Scotland, probably from yarn imported from the East Indies. It is related that

Stobcross House, the home of the Andersons of Stobcross, who laid out the village and gave it their name, Anderson's-town. The house stood near the site of the Scottish Exhibition and Conference Centre. From MacGibbon & Ross, *The Castellated and Domestic Architecture of Scotland.*

the finished web was embroidered with gold thread and presented by Mrs Monteith to Queen Charlotte, and thereafter muslin, a very delicately woven cotton fabric, taking its name from Mosul, a town in Iraq, was renamed 'Glasgows'. Monteith later lost touch with M. Mortier when muslin drove the old staple of lawns and cambrics out of the market, and from a centre of fine linens, Anderston became a centre of fine cottons.

In 1768 Matthew Orr developed a further twenty acres of the Stobcross lands to form another weavers' village named after the family tutor, the Rev. John Finnie, and in 1774 the weavers of Anderston extended membership of their society to the weavers of 'Finniestoun'. One of the earliest residents was John Smith, who started the first circulating library in the Glasgow area in 1751. John Smith & Sons Ltd, booksellers, as the firm became, have now closed their city centre shops after two hundred and fifty years in business, and their remaining Glasgow branches are on the three university campuses.

Wealthy Glasgow citizens were given feus to build summer residences at Finnieston, but it was not long before complaints were being aired in the press. Gentlemen sending their horses to the fields for exercise were requested to stop their servants riding through the

village in crowds and at speed. 'The bleachfields, from the quantities
of dust dispersed by the horses, are almost ruined', reported the
Glasgow Journal, 'and the lives of the inhabitants, from the number
and fury of the riders, have been often in danger.' It was elsewhere
commented that the glassworks near the river would not enhance
the scene, nor would the hide and glue works of Gavin Bengo, which
stood to the east of it, improve the atmosphere. There was to be no
escape from the encroaching industry. James Barry's map of 1782
shows Anderston built up along both sides of Main Street, up part of
Bishop Street and up part of North Street, until that time called the
'Lang Road', a country lane leading north to Woodside. In 1794 the
minister of Barony parish, of which Anderston formed a part, recorded
the population of the village as 3,900. Looking to the future he gave
a gloomy forecast: 'The general character of the people', he wrote,
'as yet is that of sobriety and industry, though, from the increase
of wealth, and the number of public-houses for retailing spirituous
liquors, intemperance, with its long train of evils, is becoming more
prevalent than formerly among the labouring people.'

Potters, brewers, bleachers and print-workers

Several other industries were established in and around the early
village, including the two great potteries at Delftfield and Verreville,
which in their day rivalled not only the factories in the east of Scotland
but also the great Staffordshire potteries, exporting items to America
and elsewhere on a vast scale. First on the scene was Delftfield, so
called because it produced the popular tin-glazed delftwares first
made in Holland. The business was started in 1748 by the formidable
brothers Laurence and Robert Dinwiddie, who intended to exploit
the deposits of clay on the family estate at Germiston, to the north
of Glasgow, but these proved unsuitable and clay had to be imported
from Carrickfergus on Belfast Lough. Laurence was Provost of
Glasgow, a burgess of Edinburgh, and one of those who negotiated
with Bonnie Prince Charlie when Glasgow was threatened in 1745, and
he had twenty-one children by his two wives. Robert was Collector
of Customs in Bermuda and Governor of Virginia from 1751 to 1757.
The town and county of Dinwiddie were named in his honour, and
at one time he had the young Major George Washington under his
command during the French and Indian wars.

The Dinwiddies, who were of Dumfriesshire stock, recruited

James Watt's House in Delftfield Lane, from William Simpson's *Glasgow in the Forties*. The young James Watt is believed to have lived in this house in the early 1760s when he was employed by the Delftfield Company to advise on ways of improving their products, and to have worked on his improvements to the steam engine while staying here.

skilled workmen from England as turners and pot-painters and brought John Bird of Lambeth to Anderston to manage the pottery. The unfortunate Bird was despatched south again after one year, though he won a claim for wrongful dismissal. When the fashion changed from delft to creamware, the factory remained competitive, possibly by securing the services of the versatile young James Watt. Watt's name is not commonly linked with pottery-making, but Josiah Wedgwood, who was an acquaintance, referred to Watt as 'some years a potter in Scotland', and Watt retained his investments in Delftfield until his death. Watt seems to have been given a house in Delftfield Lane and to have been employed in an advisory capacity, perhaps through his contacts with William Cadell, one of the founders of the Carron ironworks, and owner of the important Prestonpans pottery, which had been producing creamware since 1750.

A notice in the *Glasgow Journal* in 1773 shows that more imported experts had been sent packing:

THE DELFTFIELD Company beg leave to inform the Public, that their apprentice having now learned the art of manufacturing Yellow Stone, or Cream coloured Ware, they have dismissed those strangers they were at first obliged to employ at high wages to teach them . . . The prices of their Table Plates are accordingly lowered to two shillings and six pence the dozen.

Verreville pottery was established in 1776 at Finnieston by another provost of Glasgow, Patrick Colquhoun, in partnership with Cookson & Co. of Newcastle, This firm originally manufactured fine glass, and its glass cone was a familiar sight to shipping on the Clyde. The company also owned a mill for grinding flint at North Woodside, and the ruins of this mill, demolished in the 1970s, now form a feature on the Kelvin Walkway between Belmont Street and Queen Margaret Drive Bridges. Colquhoun, a Dumbarton man, later moved into cotton and control of Verreville passed to John Geddes, best remembered as colonel of the Anderston Volunteers, otherwise known as the 'Anderston sweeps' or the 'Sugerallie corps' because of their dark uniforms and the black Arabian horse which Geddes rode. Grace Street was named after his little daughter, who died tragically after her ballgown caught fire. Grace Street originally ran between Stobcross and Finnieston Streets, but when the Clydeway Industrial Estate was built over it in the 1970s the little girl's name was transferred to one of the new streets in Anderston. Under the management of R.A. Kidston, Verreville produced china of the highest quality, with gilders and flower and landscape painters coming to work in Anderston from the celebrated Derby and Coalport works as well as artisans from France and Flanders.

The Anderston brewery was started in the 1760s by Messrs Murdoch and Warroch on the site now occupied by the *Daily Record* and *Sunday Mail* building. The Anderston brew was so successful that it was drunk by Londoners as London Porter until they were told that it was brewed at Glasgow. 'They then find Something, they cannot well tell what, that makes a small difference between it and the London-brewed.' To overcome this setback a Mr Chivers was brought from London to the brewery, but he soon left to set up a rival business in Bridgeton. Despite this defection the brewery prospered to the extent of paying one ninth of all the excise duties raised in Scotland in the 1790s.

Carrick, Brown and McAlpine Streets take their names from the partners in a bleachfield. When the land south of Stobcross Street was divided up into long strips with a river frontage, two other bleachers called McIlwham bought one of these prime sites and built a mansion-house on it, which they called Hydepark. Later this area became the centre of much heavy industry and Hydepark, Whitehall, Piccadilly and Cheapside Streets were opened up these small estates.

The last major employer in eighteenth-century Anderston was William Gillespie, whose family pioneered the printing of linen cloth at Pollokshaws. In 1772 William came north of the Clyde to begin his own bleaching and printworks on the 'Lang Road', using water from the Pinkston Burn, which he stored in two ponds in the grounds of his house, Wellfield. Barry's map shows a row of buildings in William Street which might have housed some of the three to four hundred men, women and children employed in Gillespie's Anderston works in the 1790s. William Street was called after Gillespie and Richard Street after his son.

Gillespie expanded his business by establishing Glasgow's only water-powered mill for spinning cotton in 1784 at North Woodside on the Kelvin just above Kelvinbridge – with limited success, for shortages of water meant that in summer the employees sometimes had to attend for sixteen or seventeen hours to obtain six hours' work, sitting idly by while water trickled into the dam. Gillespie's final project was a cotton spinning mill, which he set up in Cheapside Street before shaking the dust of the increasingly urbanised village from his feet and moving out to an estate in Bishopton. This was a pattern to be increasingly followed by manufacturers during the nineteenth century.

The Houldsworth empire: Alter alterius auxilio veget

Quick growth of the cotton industry and rapid population increase transformed Anderston from a rural village into an industrialised urban society. The Monteiths moved their cotton interests to Glasgow's East End, and this left the door open for a new family who were to dominate Anderston from their Cranstonhill estate for half a century as employers and leading burgesses. When Anderston became a burgh in 1824 the first provost was Henry Houldsworth. The last provost was his son John. 'It cam' wi' a Houldsworth and it'll gang wi' a Houldsworth' was an Anderston prophecy which came true in 1846 when the burgh was absorbed into Glasgow after a short life of only twenty-two years.

The business of the burgh was carried on from the Burgh Buildings in Warroch Street, and a coat of arms designed to embody the new spirit of co-operation in the burgh, with the motto *Alter alterius auxilio veget* – 'the one flourishes by the help of the other'. This bore the arms of the Anderson family slightly modified to include the head of a leopard with a spool in its mouth (the insignia of the weavers); two supporters, namely a craftsman and a merchant, symbolic of home manufacturers and commerce; and a crest, consisting of a ship in full sail, to represent foreign trade.

The first of the Houldsworths to arrive in Anderston was Henry, who was a partner with his brothers in a successful Manchester spinning firm before coming north in 1799 to manage Gillespie's Woodside mill. Houldsworth soon set up his own spinning mill at Cheapside Street, powered not by a capricious water supply, but by the newest of technology in the form of a Boulton and Watt 45 hp steam engine. A description of the mill, written in 1805 by a Belfast banker touring in Scotland, is quoted in *The Industrial Archaeology of Glasgow*:

> I saw a new Cotton Mill at Anderston near Glasgow, one half of which was built, this half was 7 stories high 30 feet wide & 14 windows in length – the floors were supported by metal pipes – which at the same time served the purpose of conveying Steam for Heating the House – the Joists are also of metal likewise the window frames & sashes, & not a piece of Timber in the House except the roof – as the floors were to be laid with tiles. I was told the expence [sic] of metal exceeded Timber 25 p ct which was saved in three years by the difference of Insurance – the pipes &c only cost 16/- per cwt.

The mill was almost certainly the first 'incombustible' mill in Scotland. It was later used as a bonded warehouse and finally demolished in 1969. The site is now occupied by Laidlaw House. The early central heating system was not for the comfort of the workers, who, on the contrary, had to endure temperatures averaging 75 °F so that the high levels of humidity needed for the spinning process could be maintained. Most spinners also needed one day off in six to clear their lungs of the dust which spinning produced and to rest from the work which required considerable exertion.

Henry Houldsworth spent his thirty years as master spinner in Anderston in a constant tussle for power with his workforce. The Glasgow Association of Operative Cotton-spinners exercised firm control over entry into the trade to ensure that pressure of numbers did not destroy the earnings of spinners as it had done those of the handloom weavers. For their part the masters were quick to employ 'nobs' or blackleg labour when the chance occurred, as during periods of strike. In 1837 matters came to a head when the masters, feeling the draught of competition from Lancashire and overseas, cut wages just after a strike the previous year had depleted union funds. In one incident a 'nob' called Arrol was pelted with stones and dirt and chased by a crowd of two to three hundred out of Anderston and despatched across the river by the police on a ferryboat for his own safety. Three months later, on 22 July, another 'new hand', John Smith, was shot in the back in Clyde Street. Smith was an unsavoury character, already convicted of committing an assault on a female, but before he died he insisted that he had been shot for being a 'nob'. A reward of £500 for information was offered by the masters. Five of the leaders of the association were arrested and collectively charged with crimes which included conspiracy for murder and murder itself. The last two charges were not proven, but the men were found guilty of being leading members of an association engaged in illegal practices and sentenced to seven years' transportation, spending three years in prison hulks on the Thames before being pardoned. Seven witnesses for the prosecution shared the £500 reward and were given free passages to Sydney or Quebec. The power of the association was broken by the struggle, but Houldsworth, realising sooner than most that King Cotton's crown, in Glasgow at any rate, was slipping, turned his back on the textile industry and Anderston, and at the age of sixty-two embarked on a new and even wore prosperous career as ironmaster and owner of the Coltness estate in Lanarkshire with its vast resources of coal and iron, the raw materials which were to power the Industrial Revolution.

Cranstonhill was the home – or rather the place of refuge – for the poor cripple Hirsling Kate, one of the 'characters of Glasgow' whose tales were told by Peter Mackenzie in the 1850s for the entertainment of Glasgow's more fortunate citizens. 'Miss Katy' is introduced as an engaging creature, in her prime about year 1812, her hair thick and wiry, hanging over her shoulders and face, but then cruelly compared in appearance to a Highland shelty newly arrived at the Broomielaw to see the world. Kate's method of locomotion is then likened to that of a paddle-steamer plying up the Clyde as, squatting on the pavement, her right hand inside an old 'bauchel' – a worthless old shoe – directing it sideways, or paddleways, her left hand revolving in the air, this human machine jerked its way along the street. But

Hirsling Kate, depicted in Peter Mackenzie's *Glasgow Characters*, was a poor cripple who 'hirsled' or slid along the street with the aid of small hand clutches. She was given a shelter on the Cranstonhill estate.

an earlier and probably less prosperous generation had shown more compassion. 'J.R.M., Glasgow', who wrote to the *Glasgow Herald* in 1863, recalls as a boy frequently seeing 'the poor cripple Hirsling Kate as she painfully dragged her body past my father's house in Anderston Walk' towards the small stone building on the western slope of Cranston Hill, just within the grounds of Cranston Hill House, given to her as her own shelter by Lady Janet Buchanan, who occupied the estate in the early nineteenth century. Kate had no legs and had to propel herself along the ground using small hand clutches. But although her face was 'coarse, masculine and haggard', continues J.R.M., and the stare of her eye like that of an enraged cat, the boys never attempted to make game of her, but gave her gifts of 'preens', or pins, to decorate her dress, and when Kate was crawling or creeping along the pavements every person gave way to her out of pity, seeing such a deplorable and defenceless piece of humanity.

Cranstonhill House, described as 'a pretty house' surrounded by well-wooded grounds with gardens, orchards and hot houses, stood near the top of the slope now occupied by Anderston Primary School. Uphill from the house was the Cranstonhill reservoir, built in 1809 to provide the village with its own water supply piped directly from the Clyde. James Baillie, who read his reminiscences of Anderston to the Old Glasgow Society in 1933, described that when the river was in spate, the water was so muddy that his mother had to stand it in a ewer till the sediment went to the bottom, and 'one day a live eel came through the kitchen pipe'. Small wonder that there were great rejoicings when, in 1863, 'the Loch Katrine water came direct to us through the main, and not through a dirty cistern'. The Baillie household had a bath, then 'a great novelty'.

During the autumn of 1837 a splendid entertainment, a kind of 'son et lumiere' entitled the 'City and Bay of Naples' was staged on the slopes of Cranstonhill. A large-scale model of the city was erected; the reservoirs of the waterworks provided the water to form the bay below; the reflections cast by the small coloured lights lining the footpaths and swinging from the trees in the grounds above twinkled and sparkled on the water; and each evening hundreds of spectators were enthralled as Vesuvius erupted in the distance, the eruption being precured by fireworks.

Fireworks displays were popular at the time and Finnieston soon had its very own expert in the business: 'T.C. Barlow, Pyrotechnic Artiste by special appointment to the Queen, and to various noblemen throughout Scotland'. Barlow made signal rockets for shipping, railway fog signals, miners' fuses and the like, but would also hire out variegated glass lamps to illuminate your ballroom, supply pitch torches for your midnight procession, put on an exhibition to commemorate a birth, marriage or coming-of-age, even hire out Gun Planks, with volleys of 12 to 100, very suitable for Regattas. Stock included squibs, crackers, pin wheels, Devil among the Tailors, Jack in Boxes, Gold Flower Pots, Roman Candles, Bengal Lights, and Slow Match-Lights to catch Rabbits.

Expansion in the nineteenth century: 'a shipload of heads and faces'

When Margaret Young, a member of the Associate Congregation of Anderston, was married to Henry Bell in 1794 in the newly-opened church in Cheapside Street, few people in Anderston that day foresaw the changes that would be brought to the village by the inventive genius of this young man. In 1812 Bell designed the *Comet*, the first vessel to be successfully propelled by steam on a navigable river in Europe – even though during her first voyage to Port Glasgow she stuck on a shoal at Renfrew and the passengers had to step over the side and push her off. In 1818 the *Rob Roy* began to make regular sea crossings from Glasgow to Belfast, and with the arrival of the *Rapid* a price war broke out which brought the cost of the passage within the reach of many Irish who migrated to Scotland first on a seasonal and then increasingly on a permanent basis. 'A shipload of heads and faces' was how one observer described the arrival of the Belfast steamer. By 1824 passengers could obtain a kind of standby fare on the *Eclipse* for threepence, and the authorities had to post up a warning notice:

> It is requested that Passengers will cease forcing themselves on board after the deck is covered for, although they may manage to 'stick in the rigging' this fine weather, a bad night might occur, when some of them might be suffocated by the crushing that will unavoidably take place.

By 1831 one quarter of the inhabitants of Anderston were Irish, but the majority of immigrants came from the Scottish Lowlands, many coming to work in the brass and iron foundries, engine shops and boiler works, rope and sailcloth works which were now filling the area between Stobcross Street and the river. One significant arrival was David Napier, who prior to coming to Anderston had made the main engine castings and boiler of the *Comet*. Napier began the Vulcan foundry between Washington and McAlpine Streets, then in 1821 opened a new workshop on the lands of Lancefield and behind this built Lancefield House as his family home. He then constructed a small tidal basin at Lancefield where he could fit his engines into wooden hulls, towed up from shipbuilding yards at Port Glasgow or his hometown of Dumbarton. The dock continued in use until 1875.

David Napier left for London in 1835 and was followed at Lancefield by his cousin, Robert. Lancefield House was the scene of a famous breakfast business meeting in 1839 between the American, Samuel Cunard, and the Scots, George Burns and Robert Napier, which led to the founding of the Cunard Line. Cunard obtained the contract with the Admiralty to carry the American mails twice monthly from Liverpool to Halifax and Boston; Burns persuaded Glasgow men to put up most of the capital; and Napier supplied the ships. To construct them he acquired a yard at Govan, where he could build, as well as engine, all his vessels. The first ship ready was the *Britannia*, a wooden paddle-steamer of 8½ knots speed, in which Charles Dickens later made his first voyage across the Atlantic.

Now that the Clyde was a deep and straight waterway, and ocean-going ships could reach the Broomielaw, more space was needed to load goods and passengers. Many ingenious proposals were made. Henry Bell suggested a dock at Glasgow Green, linked by canal to Broomielaw, but this scheme was thrown out by nineteenth-century environmentalists. Instead a chain of quays was constructed westwards from the Broomielaw. Anderston Quay was extended to Hydepark Street by 1831 and quays were constructed at Hydepark (1840), Lancefield (1844) and Finnieston (1848). The quays now extended as far as the Stobcross shipbuilding yard, the first on the upper reaches of the Clyde, which was started by John Barclay in 1818. The firm, later Barclay Curle & Co., moved to Whiteinch in 1870 to make way for Queen's Dock. A map of the 1930s shows the quays still used by the Irish boats: Belfast and Liverpool at Broomielaw; Manchester

These sheds at Lancefield Quay were used for storing cargo and have now been converted to flats. Lancefield Quay is the terminal for the *Waverley*, the world's last seagoing paddle-steamer. Behind it is the giant Finnieston crane, which was used to load Glasgow-built locomotives for shipment worldwide.

and Derry and Dublin at Anderston; Sligo at Lancefield. Nowadays the only steamer regularly berthed at Lancefield is the *Waverley*, the world's last seagoing paddle-steamer, and the cargo sheds have been mostly removed to create the Clydeside Walkway. Features of interest on the walkway at Finnieston are the ferry terminals for the high-level vehicular ferry opposite Elliot Street, which was withdrawn in 1966; and the giant crane built in 1932, 175 feet high and once the largest in Europe, used by Harland & Wolff to lift engines from their diesel engine works built on the site of Napier's house and workshops into the hulls built in their Govan shipyard across the river. Locomotives made at Springburn were drawn through the streets to Finnieston to be loaded for shipment worldwide. The harbour tunnel near the foot of Finnieston Street opened in 1895 and was used by horse-drawn carts. Animals and vehicles entered by the round entrance buildings on either side of the river and were lowered by hoist to tunnel level. The tunnel was closed to vehicles in 1940 but used until the 1980s by pedestrians willing to tackle the 138 steps. The two rotundas were restored for the Garden Festival of 1988.

Various branches of engineering other than marine were attracted to Anderston, but many were hampered by lack of space. Walter Neilson had locomotive works in Hydepark Street before he transferred to Springburn in 1861. Walter Macfarlane began business in Saracen Lane off the Gallowgate, transferred his Saracen foundry to specially designed buildings in Washington Street in 1862, and then moved on to Possilpark only seven years later. At the end of the century Anderston competed with Bridgeton as the cradle of the Scottish motor car industry, an infant which never really thrived, although the production of heavy vehicles became a major industry in less congested parts of Glasgow. The Albion Motor Car Company set up in the attics of the Clan Line repair shop in Finnieston Street in 1899. Four years later the firm moved to Scotstoun. The same premises in Finnieston were used by George Halley, who moved out to Yoker in 1907, where he specialised in the production of buses, lorries and fire engines, and then by Walter Bergius, who built the first 'Kelvin' motor car in 1904 and then developed the 'Kelvin' engine for marine use. In 1897 David Carlaw, an instrument maker from the Gorbals, opened printing works and then a garage at Cranstonhill. Carlaws became the Scottish distributors for Austin cars, and their premises have now been transformed into a block of new apartments called Minerva Court.

After the quays were built the storage and manufacture of foodstuffs became an industry which employed many men and women in Anderston. Warehouses were built along the Broomielaw and in the streets leading off it – at first mainly for the storage of grain and tea, but later also for whisky and tobacco. The first of three important flour mills in Washington Street was begun by Harvie & McGavin, the oldest part dating back to before 1845, and before closure it was used for milling rice. The Crown flour mills were owned by John Ure, and the last to close was the flour mill of J.& R. Snodgrass, which survived until the late 1990s. One of the earliest bakeries was started by the Friendly Bread Association in Bishop Street by some cotton-spinners during a period of high grain prices in 1825, and out of this bakery grew the well-known 'City Bakeries'. Some of the Anderston bakeries were spectacular buildings, especially Stevenson's Cranstonhill bakery, which was a red and white brick building in Italian palace style, used by Beatties for a biscuit factory before demolition in 1969. Bilslands' bakery, now closed, but still a landmark at the top of Hydepark Street, was begun in 1882 by four brothers who, over several years, invested £30,000 in premises which included thirty-eight ovens and a three-storey stable with sixty-three stalls for horses. William Bilsland became councillor for the Anderston ward and a Lord Provost of Glasgow, playing a leading role in the provision of health care for the poor of Anderston. James Baillie recalls the delights of entering the Crossmyloof bakery near Anderston Cross for one of the take-away specialities of his day, 'a large scone spread with treacle for a ha'penny'.

Thomas Lipton, who eventually owned a grocery empire throughout Britain, opened his first store in Anderston. Tommy was the son of Northern Irish parents who ran a grocery business in Crown Street, Gorbals. At the age of fifteen he set off for America, where he spent four years. In 1871, aged twenty-one, he set up his own 'Irish butter and ham market' at 101 Stobcross Street, selling 'choicest products shipped daily from Ireland'. Lipton's recipe for success was simple: bulk purchase of quality goods and clever advertising. Every day two pigs were driven up from the quays wearing a banner proclaiming: 'I'm on my way to Lipton's, the best place in town for bacon.' Another gimmick was the Lipton one pound note, which gave you one pound's worth of goods for fifteen shillings. These notes were so realistic that they had to be withdrawn after a court case.

Edwardian Elegance. *Left:* Sir Thomas Lipton (right) and friend set off yachting. Lipton's grocery empire began with an 'Irish butter and ham market' at 101 Stobcross Street. He entertained Edward VII on his steam-yacht *Erin* and claimed that his guest books contained the names of practically every royal personage in Europe. *Right:* Lady Bilsland, 'a gracious and generous hostess' who assisted her husband, Lord Provost William Bilsland greatly in his work. Bilsland founded the famous Hyde Park Bakery.

One Christmas the police had to be sent to the Broomielaw to control the crowds awaiting the arrival from America of a monster cheese eleven feet in circumference. Lipton placed sovereigns inside the cheese and the whole 1,375 pounds was sold out in two hours.

Lipton's chief pastime was yachting, but he never achieved his ambition of winning the America's Cup. He made his first challenge with the steam yacht *Aegusa*, which he renamed *Erin*, and repeated the challenge over a period of thirty years with Shamrocks I to V. Lipton continued to use *Erin* for cruising, sometimes in the company of King Edward VII. Built by Scott & Co. of Greenock in 1896, originally for an Italian owner, *Erin* was one of the most luxurious steam yachts ever built on the Clyde. The dining room, 200 feet long, could seat 700 people. Lipton's glittering trophies are in the Kelvingrove collections and include the gold and silver cup presented in 1930 by the citizens of America to the 'Gamest Loser in the World of Sport' after he failed to win the America's Cup for the fifth time. Lipton did not forget the city where he had started on the path to fortune, and when he died in 1931 he bequeathed a sum of nearly £1 million – almost his whole estate – for the relief of Glasgow's poor.

Churches and welfare

Until 1770 there was no church in Anderston and villagers had to travel to attend the Barony Kirk or one of the Dissenting Churches, which, although Presbyterian, no longer accepted the authority of the Established Church. James Monteith was a member of one such Dissenting congregation in the Havannah Church off High Street. Following a disagreement with this Church, he and some friends built their own Relief church in Anderston. The descendant of this congregation, Anderston Old, worshipped on the same site in Heddle Place until their church was demolished to make way for the Kingston Bridge. In 1792 a second Dissenting congregation, known as the Associate Congregation of Anderston, was formed in the village. They built a meeting house in Cheapside Street, but left in 1828 for Wellington Street in the city centre, and then built Wellington Church in University Avenue in 1884. Both congregations had burial grounds attached to their churches. Remains from both were reinterred in Linn cemetery prior to the disappearance of the original burial grounds under the M8. Also removed were the remains from even older burial grounds in North Street known as North and South Woodside. These cemeteries were the resting place of many old Partick families, and also of Alexander Findlater, supervisor of excise in Dumfries and friend of Robert Burns. The Sandyford Burns Club erected the memorial stone at Findlater's grave, now re-erected in Linn cemetery.

It was 1799 before the Established Church built a chapel of ease at the foot of Clyde Street. This church was the forerunner of St Martin's which stood, with its 100-foot spire, at the corner of Argyle and St Vincent Streets. One of the earliest ministers was Alexander Somerville, a great evangelist who, as a young minister in Larbert, 'rapped up' the miners to rouse them in time for Sabbath worship. At the Disruption in 1843 both minister and congregation 'came out' and built Anderston Free Church in Cadogen Street, before moving in 1878 to a new church at the foot of University Avenue. This church, later renamed Gilmorehill Church, is now the Gilmorehill Centre, housing Glasgow University's department of theatre, film and television studies.

In 1968 three congregations united to form a new congregation known as Anderston and for whom a new modern church was built right at the heart of the original Anderston village. In 1986 this congregation was further united with Kelvingrove. The large bells which stand outside the church were brought from Trinity Church, now the Henry Wood Hall.

The first Catholics in Anderston had to travel into Glasgow to worship in St Andrew's Cathedral until St Patrick's Church was built at Cranstonhill in 1850. The first priest at St Patrick's was Patrick Hanley, a native of Limerick, and the second was Donald McEachen, born in Arisaig. Many of the congregation also came from Ireland or the Highlands of Scotland. The first St Patrick's School was built alongside the church and included a girls' school run by the Franciscan Sisters, of whom Sister Mary Seraphina is still affectionately remembered. The foundation stone of the present church in North Street, designed by August Pugin, was laid in 1965. The centenary publication of the church contains many reminiscences of church and school life, including accounts of evacuation during the Second World War to Perth and Beith and visits to HMS *Biter,* the school's adopted ship.

Efforts to reduce Anderston's enormous social problems were made by many organisations over the last two centuries. The first known Bethel for seamen was built in Brown Street in 1825. Neglected children attracted the attention of William Quarrier, who had a shoemaker's business, and who opened the home at Bridge of Weir in 1878. A year later the Salvation Army formed its first corps in Scotland in Anderston. The Army's citadel was at 724 Argyle Street until replaced by the new centre which opened on 10 June 1972. At that time the centre was the headquarters of the Scotland territory and the administrative centre for over a hundred corps in Scotland. Emblazoned on the wall of the building is a representation of the Salvation Army's crest, bearing its motto, 'Blood and Fire'. After redevelopment of the area, many soldiers of the Anderston corps were rehoused in Scotstoun, Whiteinch and Knightswood. The centre runs activities including a charity shop, lunch club, over-sixties club, women's meeting and youth clubs for children after school and in the evening. Several youngsters are being taught to play musical instruments to carry on the fine reputation of the corps' silver band and the Songster Brigade.

Laughter and Tears

The Tivoli Theatre at Anderston Cross, opened around 1899, was a great place for Glaswegians to go for a good night out. Prices began at 4d for 'The Best Pit in Glasgow' and rose to 2s for a seat in a box. Entrance to all parts was from 85 Main Street, except for the pit, which was entered from Jamieson's Lane. In the week beginning Monday 22 January 1900 the star-studded cast included Miss Lottie Lunn, Comedienne, Burlesque Actress and Dancer; Mlle Raffin with her Troupe of Performing Monkeys; Mr Arthur Farren, the Great Female Impersonator; Young Mackenzie, Champion All-round Dancer; and Miss Mabel de Vena, Club Swinger and Axe Manipulator. After (or before) the show the audience could visit a local hostelry, such as Rorke's 'Old Anderston Houff', or Cowan's 'Favourite' Bar:

> When tae the 'Tivoli' ye gang, dinna forget tae ca'
> On Hughie Cowan, wha sells a dram tae suit baith great an' sma';
> His whusky's guid, his yill's guid, his brandy's a' three staur,
> There's nae hoose in Glesca can bate the Favourite Baur.

Those who shunned strong drink could go along the street to Alfred Annovazzi's Fish Restaurant at 97 Main Street, where Fish Suppers, 2d and 4d were Always Ready; or to A. Mocogni & Co. at 1071/2 Main Street, who sold Ice Cream and Ice Drinks and where Hot Peas were Always Ready. After 1907 the theatre changed its name to the Gaiety, then it became the Gaiety cinema, and finally housed the Scottish National Orchestra after the St Andrew's Halls were destroyed by fire in 1963. When the SNO moved into the City Halls, the Gaiety was demolished.

Three of Scotland's best-known actors had close associations with Anderston. Roddy McMillan lived at 71 Cranston Street and his teacher at Finnieston School was Duncan Macrae. The two starred together in the first TV production of Neil Munro's *The Vital Spark* in which McMillan played Dougie the Mate to Macrae's Para Handy. Another role played by McMillan was the tough Glasgow detective Daniel Pyke. Roddie McMillan also wrote plays – the finest being *All in Good Faith* and *The Bevellers*. The latter was based on his own

Roddie McMillan as the Laird and Duncan Macrae as the Presbyterian minister in Glasgow Unity's production of Robert McLellan's *The Laird of Torwatletie* at the Queen's Theatre, Glasgow in November 1946.

apprentice days in a glass mirror works. In 1979 McMillan was awarded an OBE but sadly died of a heart attack before the investiture.

Another entertainer from Anderston who has received recognition of his talents as actor and comedian is Billy Connolly, who was awarded the honorary degree of Doctor of Letters as part of the 550th centenary celebrations at the University of Glasgow in 2001. Billy Connolly was born in Dover Street, Anderston, brought up in Partick, and served his apprenticeship at Stephen's Linthouse shipyard.

There were other moments in Anderston when real-life drama and tragedy struck. At six o'clock on a cold November evening in 1864 the Clyde Street ferry was swamped by the wash from the paddle-steamer *Inverary Castle*. The ferry was licensed to carry twenty-four passengers, but was possibly overloaded. It overturned, trapping several passengers, and floated bottom upwards down the stream with several of them clinging to the keel and gunwale. A few people swam ashore or were rescued, but nineteen, including John Roger, the ferryman in charge, were drowned.

In May 1941 several buildings in Finnieston Street, Hill Street, Hydepark Street and Lancefield Street were destroyed in air-raids.

But Anderston's darkest hour came in the 1960s as a result of two disastrous fires. The first was in March 1960, when a whisky bond in Cheapside Street went on fire about 7.30 p.m. and exploded about 9 p.m. Parts of the building collapsed on top of three fire engines and a turntable ladder, trapping the firemen beneath the rubble. The death toll was fourteen firemen and five salvage corps workers. In the James Watt Street fire November 1968 twenty-two factory workers were trapped behind the barred windows of a building formerly used as a bonded warehouse.

One of the most talented of all Anderstonians was the painter William Simpson, who was born in 1823 in Carrick Street. Simpson was the world's first professional war artist and his first assignment was to record the events of the Crimean War. He became known as 'Crimean Simpson', and Crimea Street was named in his honour. Shortly before his death in 1899 he returned home to compile the much admired series of drawings for *Glasgow in the Forties* now in the possession of the Mitchell Library. He wrote:

> What spot could compare to the place in which one has been born and grown up . . . to that dear friend I now dedicate these drawings with the well known words – 'Let Glasgow Flourish'.

Progress, therefore, is not an accident, but a necessity

A newspaper report of around 1900 describes the thousand of carts passing along the Broomielaw every day in the week laden with German pianos, American cheeses, Irish hams, Australian mutton, Danish butter, Spanish onions, Norwegian ice, Baltic grain and Mediterranean fruit coming in; Glasgow girders, boilers, locomotives and whisky going out; the ship's chandlers, restaurants, whisky shops and lodging houses crowded with foreign seamen. A century later, redevelopment in Anderston is being centred on the quaysides and adjacent streets. Broomielaw has been renamed Atlantic Quay and is almost entirely given over to the provision of services, particularly in the financial and telecommunications sector, housed in ultramodern buildings and converted warehouses. The Clyde Navigation Trust's headquarters (now Clydeport), one of Glasgow's most important and impressive buildings, is a rare twentieth-century survivor.

Washington Street is a microcosm of three centuries of change in Anderston. At the north end McGavin's flour and rice mill has been transformed into the luxury Milton Hotel and leisure centre, with additional accommodation in the former Washington Street School, built on the site of a powerloom cotton factory. Next to the school is the Pentagon business centre, where the German Consul occupies the former offices of the Customs and Excise. This building was previously Buchanan's bonded warehouse, which was built on the site of the famous eighteenth-century Saracen and Globe foundries. Ure's mill now houses a bathroom showroom and Snodgrass's mill is to be converted into flats. Across the street is a tropical fish and reptile wholesaler and one old established business, R.M. Easdale & Co., metal merchants. Further up, the old building with three crow-stepped gables to the street continues as the premises of the Royal Scottish Pipe Band Association.

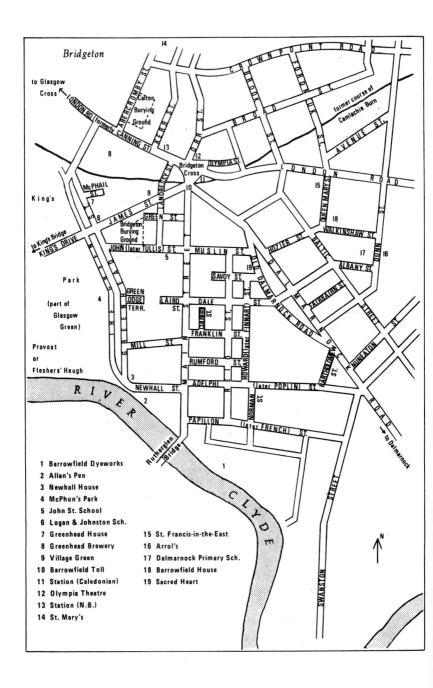

Bridgeton

to Glasgow
Cross

former course of
Camlachie Burn

King's

to Kings Bridge

Park

(part of

Glasgow

Green)

Provost
or
Fleshers' Haugh

1 Barrowfield Dyeworks
2 Allan's Pen
3 Newhall House
4 McPhun's Park
5 John St. School
6 Logan & Johnston Sch.
7 Greenhead House   15 St. Francis-in-the-East
8 Greenhead Brewery   16 Arrol's
9 Village Green   17 Dalmarnock Primary Sch.
10 Barrowfield Toll   18 Barrowfield House
11 Station (Caledonian)   19 Sacred Heart
12 Olympia Theatre
13 Station (N.B.)
14 St. Mary's

2
BRIDGETON

In 1765, when the magistrates of Glasgow decided that the Old Bridge over the Clyde at the Briggait was in such a state of disrepair that 'carts loaden or unloaden' should be banned and only passengers on foot or 'gentlemen and others in coaches and chaises' allowed to cross, they could hardly have foreseen that this decision would lead twelve years later to the creation of a new village on the eastern doorstep of their city. The ban on carts was such a hindrance to the people of Rutherglen that they decided to build their own bridge about one mile upriver. Rutherglen Bridge was completed in 1776 – the present bridge is a replacement of 1896 – and a new road constructed to take the traffic into Glasgow through the part of the Barrowfield estate known as Goosefauld. Within two years this new road had become Main Street, Bridgetown. McArthur's map of 1778 shows the village already laid out on a regular grid plan, suitable for the flat terrain and in keeping with the fashion of the day. There are about twenty-four feus marked on either side of Main Street and additional feus along John Street as far as Glasgow Green. The first four houses in the village are shown on the east side of Main Street between Muslin Street and Dalmarnock Road.

Bridgeton has been extensively rebuilt with new houses as part of the Glasgow Eastern Area Renewal (GEAR) project, established in 1976. The main thoroughfares, London Road, James Street, Greenhead Street, Main Street, Dalmarnock Road, Poplin Street and Dunn Street remain largely as originally laid out. Elsewhere street patterns no longer follow the rigid grid plan, but most street names have been retained to preserve continuity with Bridgeton's rich, varied and colourful past. Much of the renewal has been achieved by the demolition of old industrial buildings, but not without the loss of some fine public buildings.

The growing village: chimney-top of the neighbouring city

Bridgetown rapidly developed as an industrial village after David Dale, George Mackintosh and others set up the Barrowfield dyeworks and began calico printing just to the east of Rutherglen Bridge in 1785. The firm was taken over by Henry Monteith in 1805. To house the workforce additional streets were laid out and named after men whose inventions and reforms had supposedly improved the lot of mankind: Howard, Franklin, Rumford and Colbert. Did Dale perhaps intend to create at Bridgeton a model workers' village on the lines of New Lanark, where industry would bring not only material prosperity but also moral improvement to the workforce? It is gratifying that so many of the original street names have survived in the areas of new housing, some in a modernised form, as for example, Dale Path. Papillon Street, called after the native of Rouen brought to Barrowfield to reveal the secrets of the dyeing process, was later renamed French Street; and Landressy Street is said to be called after a village in France where some of the Turkey red workers originated.

The rapid transformation of the green fields of Barrowfield into a centre of textile manufacture continued in the early years of the nineteenth century with the appearance of a line of cotton spinning and weaving mills along the Camlachie Burn. Another mill was built beside a small burn on the line of the present Bartholomew Street, which also formed the boundary between the Barrowfield and Dalmarnock estates. By the middle of the century powerloom weaving factories had sprung up on the west side of the village which until then had kept its rural character. Bridgeton was now encircled by factories, forcing the ever-growing population into crowded, insanitary back lands. The change in the village over this period is vividly summed up by the Rev. J. Logan Aikman, writing in 1875:

> The population of Bridgeton would not at that time (1805) be more than two or three thousand, chiefly employed as handloom weavers or in connection with the establishment of Henry Monteith & Co. at Barrowfield – then commencing those operations in calico printing and turkey red dyeing which have since made the works there one of the most extensive factories in Scotland. From that time Bridgeton has gone on increasing in the number of its inhabitants and public works, until the population of the present registration district has reached, at this date, 64,000; and its crowded factories and workshops of all kinds may be counted by scores, covering acres of what, a few years ago, were waving corn fields, and pouring forth, through forests of tall, grimy, furnace stalks, at all hours of the day, volumes of dense black smoke, giving the district now very much the appearance of the chimney-top of the neighbouring city.

The 'Umbrella' at Bridgeton Cross. This cast-iron pavilion, a well-known landmark in the East End of Glasgow, was the gift of Messrs George Smith & Co. of the Sun Foundry. The Olympia Theatre on the right has served as music hall, cinema and bingo hall.

In these early days Bridgeton was governed by the Bridgeton feuars' court, whose minute book has unfortunately not survived. The villagers operated their own bakery, fleshing and victualling societies in Main Street, and supported a public library in Muslin Street. In 1846 the village was absorbed into Glasgow and spilled over eastwards into the lands of Dalmarnock, where engineering became an important industry. The small village of Mile-end, which stretched from Bridgeton Cross towards Camlachie with Broad Street as its main artery, also became a centre for a variety of industries including potteries, carpet weaving, food processing, ironfounding, chemical works and engineering. Bridgeton now entered into its industrial heyday. Although cotton spinning declined, thread making continued and Bridgeton became a centre for the weaving of fine-quality fabrics. The firm of D. & J. Anderson, for example, exported worldwide from their Atlantic Mills in Baltic Street until taken over by the House of Fraser group in 1959 and subsequently closed. John Lean & Sons of Reid Street supplied the Middle Eastern market with Arab head-dresses, only losing out to Japanese competition in the 1960s. W. & J. Martin of the Albion leather works kitted out the British Army with boots made from their chrome leather uppers, and Hillary and Tensing conquered Everest wearing boots made from the same firm's high-quality ZUG grain leathers. The firm of Andrew Muirhead & Son tanned, finished and dyed the leather for Air Force One, the American presidential plane, and still uphold the Bridgeton tradition of quality in their Dunn Street works. Singer sewing machines were made in James Street before the firm moved to Clydebank, and the Bridgeton workers had to be transported morning and evening on a train known as 'Singers special'. The first Argyll motor cars were produced in Hozier Street by Alexander Govan before he moved to Alexandria in 1906. Not many people realise that the second Tay Bridge, the Forth Rail Bridge, the Forth Road Bridge, Tower Bridge in London, the North Bridge in Edinburgh and the Humber Bridge were all built by Sir William Arrol, whose Dalmarnock ironworks were established in Dunn Street in 1872, occupying a twenty-acre site and employing at times from four to five thousand men. These and other bridges, cranes and workshops built by the company throughout the world are the permanent symbols of the outstanding skills of the engineers of Bridgeton. The firm ceased operation at Dunn Street on 3 October 1986. Glasgow East Industrial Village now occupies the site.

Barrowfield, Clemintina Walkinshaw and the '45

Although Bridgeton is a comparatively recent village, the lands of Barrowfield on which it is built are mentioned in records at least as far back as the sixteenth century. In 1513 the spelling 'Bowrrowfield' appears, and also found are Borrwfeld, Borowfeyld, Burrowfeild and Burrowfield. A rent roll of 1587 uses the spelling Barrowfield. The name may mean land belonging to the town or borough, or alternatively it may indicate arable land laid out for cultivation in 'burrel' or barrel-shaped ridges.

After the annexation of temporalities to the Crown in 1587, the lands of Barrowfield passed through several hands and eventually came into the ownership of John Walkinshaw, an influential Glasgow merchant, shortly after he bought the adjacent Camlachie estate in 1669. Walkinshaw's grandson, also named John, came to grief as a result of supporting the Jacobite cause in 1715. Walkinshaw had the dubious honour of having his name printed in the second issue of the *Glasgow Courant*, Glasgow's oldest newspaper, after the Battle of Sheriffmuir:

> Stirling Bridge, 13th Nov. at 9 at night, 1715.
>
> We are still confirmed, that the Duke of Argyle is master of the field; and for a proof of it, he has sent in sixty prisoners, whereof eight or nine are Gentlemen. About an hour ago, I am informed by one of the Guard, that Borrowfield is one of them.

Walkinshaw later escaped from Stirling Castle by the unoriginal but effective device of walking out dressed in his wife's clothes during a visit. In 1723 he was obliged to agree to the sale of his manor-house and lands to the magistrates of Glasgow. This transaction required the consent of his wife, Ketherine Paterson, and after obtaining the lady's signature, it is recorded that the provost showed his appreciation of her cooperation by giving her and her daughter 'ane hundred tuenty five guineas, being £131 5s of compliment'. A trustee was allowed to operate the coal workings on certain parts of the estate for the benefit

Barrowfield House, the home of the Walkinshaws of Barrowfield. The family lost their estates through their support of the Jacobite cause in 1715. The house stood in the vicinity of Walkinshaw Street and Albany Street. From *Glasghu Facies*.

of the family for a period of nineteen years, and Lady Barrowfield was allowed to keep a small house at Camlachie for her own use.

It is not known when the manor-house of Barrowfield was built, but when sold it had office-houses, biggings, a dovecot, a summer-house, a well, a nursery, two 'firr parks', avenues and three parks called the middle, south and north parks, which indicates a substantial estate. The town sold off the estate again in 1730 to another city merchant, John Orr, whose family kept ownership until 1788, by which time the Orr family fortunes had also been dissipated in another abortive attempt to work the Barrowfield coal. Even David Dale and William Dixon, normally level-headed businessmen, lost money trying to mine coal at Barrowfield. Barrowfield House is shown on Roy's map of 1755, with the driveway following the line of the present Hozier Street. Mr Hozier, owner of Newlands estate to the east, is shown as the owner of Barrowfield on Richardson's map of 1795. In 1844 stone from the house was used to build a farmhouse known as Queen Mary's Farm, entered from London Road, along the line of the present Queen Mary Street. According to local legend, after her defeat at Langside, Mary sought help from the people of Barrowfield who, however, advised her to recross the river and flee to England. There was an equally good case for having a Moray Street, since the regent, Mary's half-brother, camped at Barrowfield on the eve of the battle.

Albany Street commemorates the liaison of Clementina Walkinshaw, youngest of the ten daughters of John Walkinshaw and Katherine Paterson, with Prince Charles Edward, the Young Pretender. They met at Bannockburn House, home of her uncle, Sir Hugh Paterson, where Charles stayed in January 1746, after spending ten days in Glasgow. Charles was twenty-five at the time and Clementina nineteen. She joined the prince in exile in 1752 and bore him a daughter named Charlotte. Clementina was regarded with much suspicion in Charles' household because her sister Katherine held an influential position in the household of the Princess Dowager of Wales, mother of George III. The association between Charles and Clemintina ended in 1760 when Clementina, with the title of Comtesse d'Albestroff, retired to a convent. When her long life ended at Fribourg in Switzerland in 1802, she left twelve pounds sterling, six silver spoons, a geographical dictionary and three books of piety, bequeathing a louis apiece to each of her relatives, 'should any of them still remain, as a means of discovering them'. In the last years of his life Charles invited his daughter to live with him in Rome,

Left: This portrait of Clementina Walkinshaw, by an unknown artist, is in the collections of the Scottish National Portrait Gallery. Clementina joined Prince Charles Edward in exile in 1752 and bore him a daughter named Charlotte. *Right:* Also in the Scottish National Portrait Gallery is this portrait of Charlotte, Duchess of Albany, by H.D. Hamilton. Prince Charles Edward legitimised his daughter shortly before his death in 1788 and created her Duchess of Albany. She is celebrated in a poem by Robert Burns as 'The Bonny Lass o' Albany'.

legitimised her, and created her Duchess of Albany, using the ancient Scottish title for the second son of the monarch. A letter survives written by Charles to a lady shortly before his death on the last day of January 1788, in which he refers to Charlotte, 'ma chère Fille la Duchesse d'Albanie . . . qui fait le bonheur de ma vie et que j'aime de tout mon coeur'. Charlotte inherited her father's estate but survived him by less than two years, dying at Bologna after a fall from her horse in apparently mysterious circumstances. She is celebrated by Burns in 'The Bonnie Lass of Albany':

> We'll daily pray, we'll nightly pray,
> On bended knees most fervently,
> The time may come, with pipe and drum,
> We'll welcome hame fair Albany.

During his stay in Glasgow the prince reviewed his army on the Provost Haugh, now part of Glasgow Green. Many years later

a Jacobite who took part wrote of a triumphant army marching to
the ground with drums beating, colours flying, bagpipes playing and
watched by multitudes of people who had come from all parts to see
them, especially the ladies, who greeted the prince with the most
enthusiastic loyalty. A very different account is given by Provost
Andrew Cochrane in a letter written at the time:

> The Prince appeared four times publickly in our streets, without the
> smallest respect being paid him; no bells rung, no huzzas, nor did the
> meanest inhabitant so much as take off their hats . . . our ladys had not
> the curiosity to go near him, or to a ball held by some of the leaders.

Provost Cochrane walked a political tightrope for six months to bring
Glasgow relatively unscathed through the rebellion. On their way
south the Jacobites forced the Glasgow authorities to pay over £5,500.
The defenceless citizens were terrified of the MacGregors and other
clansmen hovering around the northern outskirts of the town. '[The
rebels] have 6 or 800 Camerons and McDonalds still lying at the Frow,
waiting to join the Athol men who are still behind. This body they
threaten to march in by Glasgow, in case we refuse their demands,'
wrote the provost to the authorities in Edinburgh, asking for a supply
of arms. This only brought the unsympathetic reply: 'I only beg you
would pull up your spirits; the worst it can come to is breaking your
looking glasses and china: for plundering or burning you need be
in no pain.' The Jacobites were doubly exasperated against Glasgow:
not only had the town failed to send men to join the prince, but it
had raised a battalion for the government. On their return north the
Jacobites ordered Glasgow to supply them with '6,000 cloth short
coats, 12,000 linnen shirts, 6,000 pairs of shoes, and as many pairs
of tartan hose and blue bonnets'. The craftsmen of Glasgow, used
to supplying large quantities of shoes and clothing to America, met
the order within three weeks. Provost Cochrane's final duty was to
spend three months in London, bowing, fawning and cringing at
court, before Glasgow's losses were repaid in full.

Life in nineteenth-century Bridgeton: three views

In May 1833 Sir David Barry arrived in Bridgeton. The purpose of
his visit was to inspect various factories and make an official report
on the health and working conditions of the employees, especially
the children. Barry's first visit was to the Barrowfield dyeworks

then owned by Henry Monteith & Co. The firm had five hundred employees and printed cotton cloth for a worldwide market. Barry noted that the printers worked in temperatures of 80 °F, sometimes assisted by children of nine years upwards, but most children seemed to be outdoors attending to the drying and bleaching grounds round the factory. According to Barry, the most remarkable persons in this splendid establishment were the stove-girls, twenty young women whose job it was to go into the stoves, kept at 140 °F, to hang up the webs to dry and afterwards go back to take them down, constantly passing through the open air as they went from one stove to another. Tall and rather thin girls were preferred for this work. The girls were provided with fine flannel chemises by the proprietors, worked barefoot, and often had leisure to sit. They appeared as healthy as any girls in the establishment, and as Mr Rodger, 'the benevolent manager of the works', explained, 'when any of them happens to catch cold, they are very soon cured by going into the stove again'. The stove girls were paid 7s 6d per week, the children from 2s to 2s 6d, and the printers earned very good wages, from 25s to 30s.

Sir David then inspected several spinning mills, including Oswald's mill which stood on the site of the now closed Bridgeton Central Station. This was a six-storey building, employing 461 operatives, 202 males and 259 females, of whom 105 were Irish. Most mills at the time worked twelve hours daily from Monday to Friday, and nine hours on Saturday. At Oswald's mill the working day was from six in the morning to seven-thirty at night, with forty-minute meal breaks at nine and two. All the spinners were men from eighteen to fifty, on piece work, and earned at least as much as the printers and much more than a tradesman. Each spinner had two or three assistants who were paid by himself and were usually his own children or relatives. Most of the children were from ten to fifteen years old. The older ones were outside piecers, earning 6s 6d per week. The younger ones were inside piecers and scavengers, crawling under the looms to mend the broken threads or sweep up fluff, and earning around 4s and 3s respectively. Living standards could fall through accident, ill health or unemployment. Barry noted that 'all the adult male spinners are pale and thin'. Standing on the mill floor all day in temperatures of 80 °F could lead to general debilitation and lack of resistance to disease. Women often developed lung illnesses from breathing in fluff.

Barry was then taken to meet some of the spinners' families in their homes. For the most part these were two-apartment houses with a rental of about £4 per annum. Even a widow could be comfortably off if she had children in a factory. Widow Keith, for example, owned the status symbols of a mahogany bedstead, a well-stocked china cupboard and a handsome clockcase, but unfortunately the works were at the pawn as her twenty-year-old son, a spinner, was out of employment. However, enough money was coming into the house from her eighteen-year-old daughter, a powerloom worker, and from the lodger, a 25-year-old spinner, to enable them to eat flesh meat three times a week and Sundays. The widow believed that factory work was likely to shorten the lives of her children, since their father, after working in a factory as a card-master for twenty years, had died at the age of thirty-nine, 'stuffed in his chest'.

Barry then visited some handloom weavers' homes and found this a distressing experience. In the 1830s there were over two thousand handloom weavers in Bridgeton struggling to keep their families on little more than what a teenager could earn in the mill, eating porridge, potatoes and sour milk, occasionally herring, and very, very seldom meat; working all the hours of daylight in damp cellars for one-fifth of the rate paid twenty years previously, in the halcyon days before soldiers returning from the Napoleonic Wars, and immigrants from the Lowlands, the Highlands and Ireland had glutted the market with cheap labour, and before the introduction of powerloom weaving which gave employment to many girls, but to few men. The dilemma was well summed up by William Grierson, a Bridgeton man of forty-five, bred to the loom:

> Considers that his wages for the last 7 years average not more than 5s 6d per week and that requires him to work 14 hours clear. If he was in his young days, he would go into the mill, on account of the wages; but he considers a weaver much freer, who can go out and come in of his own wishes, 'without any man tyrannizing over him'.

Even harder times lay ahead for the weavers before alternative employment became widely available in the 1840s.

Thirty years later Bridgeton schools were included in a report on the state of education in Glasgow, published six years before the passing of the Education Act of 1872, which made schooling compulsory for all children between the ages of five and twelve. The district was noted as 'not overrun with poverty' but was nevertheless an educational blackspot, where only one child in four attended school, the worst figure for anywhere in Glasgow. Even though the

This sculpture was placed on Greenhead House when it became the Buchanan Institution for orphan and destitute boys. The boys were taught the three Rs and a trade, as symbolised by the slate and the plane. The building has now been converted into flats.

parents were mostly skilled artisans and small shopkeepers, not one of them would think of refusing an offer of a few shillings for a child's labour, 'although the penalty may be a lifetime of ignorance'. The teaching in the sessional schools run by the churches was good, the staff sufficient and efficient, but the education was limited to spelling, writing, arithmetic, grammar and geography, and many of the 'better sort of children' went to schools beyond the district – such as St James' in Calton – the master of which was formerly at the head of Bridgeton sessional school.

Similar complaints about children being taken away from school too early were made by the Marist Brothers and Sisters of Mercy, who taught in St Mary's Boys' and Girls' schools in Abercromby Street, each with a roll of about three hundred. There was also an infant school attended by 140 children, a few under three years old, and about eighty of them between three and six. The mistress frankly admitted that 'most of them were sent, because their mothers were out working, to keep them from mischief and danger'. St Mary's also ran two residential schools for children under sentence of a magistrate in two adjacent buildings, the orphanage, where girls learned domestic subjects, and the industrial school, where boys were taught tailoring, shoemaking and carpentry.

As well as these well-run schools, two schools attached to mills and eight 'adventure' schools operated in Bridgeton. At this time children between the ages of eight and thirteen employed in factories had to attend school for three hours during the working day. In one mill school the teacher was struggling on his own against the odds with a hundred children huddled in a corner of the mill beside the 'foul and offensive' Camlachie Burn. Conditions in this school, however, were nothing compared to those in the private or 'adventure' schools, conducted in low-roofed, badly ventilated, disused dwelling-houses, crowded with 'ragged, dirty-faced little mudlarks'. The very worst school in the whole of Glasgow, 'an academical monstrosity', was held in a dirty close near the Barrowfield toll-bar. The master was well-known in the district in connection with the issue of education certificates, for which he charged sixpence apiece. These certified that a child had attended school for at least thirty days and not less than 150 hours, and had to be produced before a child could be employed in a printfield. The proprietor was in some trouble, as 'his certificates had fallen into disrepute through persons who had been ill-natured enough to assert that he issued many more than he had scholars to represent'. The inspectors made their way into the dank cellar, a few steps under the gutter-run, in which thirty-five children were assembled, but stayed only long enough to compile this report:

> The smell was hot, foul, and oppressive, and contact with any part of the hovel, its furniture or occupants, was pollution. A drunken fellow, apparently a seaman, a friend of the master, was lying asleep across one of the benches at which the children were seated, waited for at the door by some dissolute young women. We gave up the idea of examining the school as too absurd to be seriously entertained.

Reminiscences of sixty years as a general practitioner in Bridgeton were the subject of an interview given by Dr John Burns, Scotland's eldest practising physician, to a *Weekly News* reporter in December 1905. At the age of ninety-one, the Grand Old Man of Glasgow Medicine still came down from his home in Fitzroy Place in the West End to attend his consulting rooms in Bridgeton five days in the week, and such was his reputation that since the beginning of 1905 no fewer than 3,630 people had come from far and near to consult him, and half of these had never seen him before in their lives. The doctor remembered that in a previous year he had once treated as many as ten thousand patients.

Dr Burns came to Bridgeton from his native Perth in 1848 and the same year narrowly escaped death when the man he was talking to on the doorstep of his surgery in John Street was fatally wounded by a shot during a bread riot. He endeared himself to his patients by remaining in the village during a typhus epidemic in the 1850s which nearly claimed his own life. Dr Burns recalled how in the 1850s he had visited a room-and-kitchen house where five people were lying sick with smallpox and the husband came home to his meals and returned again to his work in a factory. Dr Burns considered the general health of the people had much improved after Sir William Gairdner was appointed Glasgow's first Medical Officer of Health in 1863. Before that he had as many as forty cases of typhus fever under his care at one time and about four hundred cholera cases.

The doctor, however, saw no improvement in the morals of the villagers. In his opinion, drink, gambling, and an excessive love of sport were the giant evils of the day, killing the churchgoing habits and quiet, respectable ways of a former generation. 'I disapprove of football,' stated the doctor. 'I have never seen a football match, although I have often driven past when one was in progress. But I can judge of results, and I have had many cases of very severe injuries caused by football. A big match is to me a perfect pandemonium.'

Another sign of the evil of the times were the fifty or so drunks who could be seen sleeping on Sunday mornings on Glasgow Green. Above all, the doctor deplored the decline of family life. We leave Dr Burns with this commentary on moral backsliding in Bridgeton in 1905:

> In Bridgeton it is no uncommon thing for 3, 4 and 6 young girls to leave their houses, take a two roomed house, and form a makeshift home for themselves, taking turn about with the cooking and household duties. I need not say that that is a bad agreement.

Bridgeton's West End: John Street and Greenhead Street

John Street is the second oldest street in Bridgeton, linking Main Street with Glasgow Green. It was renamed Tullis Street in 1926 in honour of one of Bridgeton's firms of 'Leather Barons' which became

a world leader in the production of belting for industry. The family
came from Arbroath and named their factory the 'St Ann's Works'
in memory of their mother. The site is now occupied by new houses
and is called Tullis Court.

The oldest place of interest in the street is Bridgeton burying-
ground, where Brigtonians were laid to rest from 1811 to 1869.
The ground has been restored but only a few stones have legible
inscriptions. The best preserved is against the wall just inside the John
Street entrance, and has the inscription 'The Burying Place of James
Black Baker Calton and Cecilia Brown his wife and their Children
1827'. A list of forty-four inscriptions copied from stones is held in
the Mitchell Library.

Two churches formerly stood in John Street; Bridgeton Free
Church, built in 1849, stood to the east of the burying-ground, but
the honour of being the first church in the village went to the Relief
church, built in 1809 on the site later occupied by John Street School.
The congregation were reminded at their centenary celebrations in
1905 that from 1805 to 1809 their predecessors worshipped in the open
air on Bridgeton village green – on land granted in 1785 to the feuars
and inhabitants of the village 'for the sole purpose of a Common
Green for Washing, Bleaching and Drying Cloathes, and in no other
way whatever'. The green lay on the south side of the Camlachie
Burn and was reached from Green Street, now McKeith Street. The
green became the property of the City Improvement Trust in 1866
and James Street was formed across it and the burn filled in. The
Relief church was the only church in Bridgeton for thirty years until
the Established Church granted a chapel of ease in the village and
built a church in Dale Street in 1837, which became Bridgeton Parish
Church in 1853. After the union with St Francis-in-the-East in 1987,
the church in Dale Street was demolished, but the name of the first
minister of the parish is remembered in Fairbairn Path.

John Street Secondary School began in 1883 as the higher-grade
school for the East End, and in 1900 it was reported that 'the
admirably equipped physical and chemical laboratories are now
complete and the school fairly entered upon that work of science
teaching for which it was principally designed'. The success of the
school was due in large part to Mr Robert Paterson, who retired
in 1908 after forty-five years' service in Bridgeton, twenty-five of
these as headmaster of John Street. The school logs record the ups
and downs of school life. Janet Bain won the gold medal in the

The smartly turned out office staff of Steel Coulson & Co, of the Greenhead Brewery in the 1890s. The site was later occupied by the aerated water manufacturer, Dunn & Moore.

Burns competition; a pupil of great promise, Edward Crossley, was drowned in the Clyde; and A. Goodfellow, the assistant janitor, was disciplined after a week's absence 'through sickness occasioned by his exertions on the football field the previous Saturday' as a result of which the school shivered for a week in temperatures of under 51°F. John Street School is now closed and the buildings demolished. The pupils now attend Whitehill Secondary School and Eastbank Academy.

Greenhead, the part of Bridgeton north of John Street and intersected by the Camlachie Burn, was an early centre of industry, one of the earliest businesses being the Greenhead brewery, established by the Struthers family and later owned by Steel Coulson & Co. Dunn & Moore, the soft drinks firm, were the last business to occupy the site before redevelopment for housing. On the south side of the burn is Greenhead House, which was the private residence of Dugald and Duncan McPhail, two brothers from Ardnamurchan who built a spinning mill behind the house in 1824 and brought their workforce to live in the area immediately to the north, Silvergrove, which immediately became known as 'The Hielands'. In the 1850s

A girl bottling Solripe lemonade at Dunn & Moore's factory in 1977. The business closed in the 1990s. The name 'Silvergrove' has been given to the new housing on the site.

the McPhails employed around 250 men and 850 women as well as 400 outworkers. The house was sold in the late 1850s and became the Buchanan Institution, a home for fatherless boys. One of the destitute boys is portrayed in sculpture on the front of the building. The Logan and Johnston School of Domestic Economy at the corner of James Street was founded in 1890 by William Logan and his wife Jean Johnston to fulfil a similar need for girls, particularly those with either surname. The Beehive of Industry can be seen sculpted on the west front of the building. Both buildings have been converted into flats.

Originally Greenhead Street extended only as far south as John Street. All the land beyond that as far as the Clyde was the grounds of Newhall House, the home of Alexander Allan, a manufacturer with sugar plantations in the West Indies. From McArthur's map it appears that in 1778 he was using the ground between his garden and the river as a printfield. In order to maintain his privacy, Allan enclosed an ancient right of way along the riverside within a tunnel or 'pen' covered over with turfs, thereby antagonising the villagers who refused to work for him. The dispute was settled when ice from the river got into the tunnel during severe weather and the whole structure collapsed, never to be rebuilt. The spot is now marked with the simple inscription 'Site of Allan's Pen'. Part of the grounds of Newhall House was used later for a cotton mill and powerloom factory. Facing the Green, halfway between Newhall House and John Street was a house called Green Lodge. This was a double cottage of unusual shape, known locally as 'The Piano' or 'The Sideboard'. One half was occupied by Archibald Templeton, who had come from Campbeltown to go into business as a carpet manufacturer with his brother James. Archibald moved to London in the 1850s to take charge of the London office and warehouse. Green Lodge was demolished in the early years of last century. After Newhall House was demolished in the 1860s good-quality tenements were erected on the site. 'At this end of Main Street,' wrote a commentator in the 1920s, 'the predominant note is fur coats, not fish suppers.'

The residents of Greenhead Street enjoy a fine outlook over King's Park and the Provost Haugh, the last areas of land to be incorporated into Glasgow Green. King's Park was sold to Glasgow in 1773 by John King, deacon of the fleshers, who also gave his name to King's Drive, which was opened as a highway through the Green in the early 1900s, and leads to King's Bridge, which carries the road over the Clyde into Gorbals. Around the same time the little ornamental garden known as McPhun's Park, or the Dassy Green, was laid out through the generosity of a local wood turner, Robert McPhun, owner of the Greenhead sawmill in Mill Street. McPhun's Park contains a fine Celtic cross inscribed to the memory of the officers and men of the 7th (Blythswood) Battalion of the Highland Light Infantry who fell in the Great War. Another feature of the garden is a stone statue of James Watt, now in poor condition, brought from the Atlantic Mills, a reminder that it was in Glasgow Green that the idea of the separate steam condenser was worked out in Watt's mind, during his famous Sunday walk in 1765, and a tribute to the importance of steam power in the development of Bridgeton.

The Provost Haugh was a low-lying area of land beside the river reserved for their own use by the provosts of Glasgow and later owned by the Incorporation of Fleshers and renamed Fleshers' Haugh. The land was sold to Glasgow in 1792. During improvements to the haugh in 1876 a workman uncovered a complete and unbroken samian

The Rangers Team 1876–77. *Back row:* George Gillespie, W.D. McNeil, James Watt, Sam Ricketts. *Second row:* W. Dunlop, David Hill, Tom Valance, Peter Campbell, Moses McNeil. *Front row:* James Watson, A. Marshall. Rangers' first games were played on Glasgow Green.

bowl of the fourth century AD, and decorated with raised figures of animals and mythological figures. The bowl is now in the care of the People's Palace.

The chief claim to fame of the Fleshers' Haugh is not as the place where a rare Roman bowl was found, nor even where Bonnie Prince Charlie stood under a thorn tree to review his army, but as the birthplace of Glasgow Rangers Football Club. The story of how the club began was told by the club's first historian, John Allan, in *The Story of Rangers, 1873–1923*. According to Allan, on summer evenings in 1873 a number of lads keen on rowing used to finish off the evening by coming ashore at the Fleshers' Haugh, where a football team called the Eastern played on a pitch 'abutting a small plantation or shrubbery, which served as dressing quarters'. The rowers, mostly natives of the Gareloch, formed themselves into a team which they named Rangers, and played on this pitch until 1875. The leading members of the team were three brothers called McNeil. Moses McNeil was the captain and became the first Rangers player to play for Scotland. Rangers joined the Scottish Football Association in time to compete for the Scottish Cup in 1874–75 and first won the cup in 1894. This area of Glasgow Green is still used for football.

Bridgeton Literati and the Bridgeton Burns Club

By the end of the nineteenth century people had more leisure than previously, and large numbers of Brigtonians are reported as turning out to hear the Rev. Somerville give a lecture on 'Some of the East End Poets' as part of the Glasgow Public Libraries series in 1909, when the speaker dealt with the life and works of no fewer than fifteen local bards: Sandy Rodger, William Miller, Dr John Graham, Hugh Macdonald, William Freeland, James Macfarlane, Robert Ford, Dr Findlay (George Umber), Alex. G. Murdoch, John Brackenbridge, William Cameron, Rev. Robert Campbell, ex-Bailie Willox, Hugh Muir and Tommy Johnston.

Hugh Macdonald was born in Rumford Street and lived at 92 John Street. His *Rambles round Glasgow*, published in 1854, are still enjoyed today, and first appeared serialised under the signature of Caleb in the *Evening Citizen*, of which the author later became a sub-editor, The *Rambles* describe places of interest within a circle of eight to ten miles round Glasgow, from Blantyre and Bothwell in the south-east to New Kilpatrick and the Whangie in the north-west, and were based on actual Sunday excursions made by Macdonald and some friends who formed themselves into a club called 'The Eccentrics'.

The first ramble is round Glasgow Green, starting at the west end, where the trees have a doleful, black and melancholy look and are dying off year by year. This is where the children of misery and vice have sneaked forth for a breath of clearer air from the 'reeky and noisome haunts' of the Saltmarket. The theme of smoke and noise was repeated in a fine poem composed by Macdonald's friend, Alexander Wilson, entitled *Glasgow*, the final words of which, 'noise and smoky breath', have been used for the title of an anthology of Glasgow poetry. At the Bridgeton end of the Green, however, sixty species of wild plant could still be found on the gently sloping banks 'spangled with the daisy, the dandelion and the buttercup'. Macdonald's special interest was botany and he describes how shamrocks are still gathered here on Saint Patrick's Day, and how the girls of Bridgeton and Calton come in hundreds to pluck 'the mystic Yarrow' as a love-charm 'between the gloamin' and the murk of May eve'.

After Macdonald's death in 1860 a fountain was erected to his memory on the Gleniffer Braes. The fountain was later removed to Glasgow Green. It is inscribed with a verse of his own poetry:

> The bonnie wee well on the breist ol the brae
> Where the hare steals to drink in the gloamin' sae grey,
> Where the wild moorlan' birds dip their nebs and tak' wing,
> And the lark weets his whistle ere mounting to sing.

Alexander Rodger was another well-known Bridgeton poet who sang his own songs at Saturday evening concerts. A great favourite was his own composition, 'The Mucking of Geordie's Byre'. Rodger was buried in the Necropolis and a monument was erected there to his memory by public subscription.

With this literary tradition behind them, it comes as no surprise that the Bridgeton Burns Club, instituted in 1870, was once the largest in the world. A former president was William Freeland, who, like Macdonald and Rodger, was a 'printer-poet', all being at one time employed at the Barrowfield dyeworks. Freeland became the editor of the *Evening Times*. He was largely responsible for introducing the annual Burns competition into schools. Choirs in East End schools compete for the Silver Shield of the Bridgeton Burns Club, a handsome piece of silver engraved with a portrait of the poet surrounded by scenes representing the Cottage, Tam o' Shanter, Cottar's Saturday Night, Poosie Nancie's and the Auld Brig.

Around Bridgeton Cross

Bridgeton Cross was formed by the City Improvement Trust in the 1870s as a result of clearance of old properties, of which unfortunately no photographic record was made. The Cross stands at the junction of seven streets and is one of the best-known landmarks in the East End of the city. In 1875 its appearance was enhanced by the gift of a cast-iron pavilion designed and erected by Messrs George Smith & Co. of the Sun foundry, which soon became known as 'the Umbrella'. It is an elegant structure, fifty feet high, with ten slender columns supporting the roof, above which rises a clock tower with four faces. The area round about is now pedestrianised and provided with seating but the drinking fountains have been removed.

The Premier Cafe stood in Main Street, Bridgeton, and was owned by the Crolla family, well-known manufacturers of ice-cream and owners of cafes and fish and chip shops in Glasgow since the 1930s.

The first tenements at Bridgeton Cross were the building at the north corner of Dalmarnock Road with 'Bridgeton Cross' cut into the stone at roof level, and the building at the north corner of James Street which is dated 1873. These tenements were built using the local honey-coloured sandstone. Building then slowed down, mainly because the Improvement Trust was underfunded, even though it had powers to levy a rate of 6d in the pound, an unpopular charge which cost Lord Provost John Blackie, one of the chief promoters of the scheme, his seat on the council. The collapse of the City of Glasgow Bank in 1878 also held up building.

The ground floor of these buildings was occupied by shops, public houses and banks. Until recent closure Vernal Brothers traded at no. 128 for over a century as gentlemen's outfitters and manufacturers of regalia.

The Cross was not completed until around 1900 by a group of tenements built of red sandstone brought from Locharbriggs as the local stone was by then exhausted. This group includes Bridgeton Cross Mansions, a fine tenement with a tower at the corner of Main Street and Dalmarnock Road, and the exuberant Glasgow Savings Bank building at the corner of Landressy Street, designed by John

Gordon, with its lion rampant crouching over Bridgeton Cross at roof level, and decorated with the old royal arms of Scotland, bearing two unicorns and the motto, *Nemo me impune lacessit* – 'Wha' daur meddle wi' me' – overlooked by a smiling cherub. The building is now occupied by William Hill, the bookmaker. John Gordon also designed the Bridgeton Working Men's Club, which stood round the corner in Landressy Street. The club had a bowling alley in the basement, a reading room, chess room, library and facilities for bagatelle, dominoes and summer ice on the ground floor, and a billiard room with clerestorey lighting on the upper floor. Its demolition in the 1980s was a great loss.

The North British Railway Company erected a row of red sandstone tenements on either side of the entrance to their now disused Bridgeton Central Station on the north side of London Road in 1897. When the revived Argyle line, which links Glasgow Central with Motherwell, was recently reopened, the entrance to the new Bridgeton Cross station was sited on the east side of the Cross, and Dalmarnock station was also reopened. The now vacant building on the east corner of Orr Street started life in 1911 as the Olympia Theatre of Varieties, was operated as a cinema between 1923 and 1974, and then became a bingo hall. The theatre, billed as 'the clean and comfortable family resort', was a great favourite with pantomime audiences who could enjoy old favourites like *Babes in the Wood*, *Aladdin* and *Sinbad the Sailor*, secure in the knowledge that the building had been 'disinfected throughout with Jeyes Fluid in the Interests of Public Health'. Around 1920 Harry McKelvie, later the proprietor of the Princess's Theatre, the forerunner of the Citizens', produced several pantomimes at the Olympia, including a 'new and up-to-date panto' *Peter Wilkins*, and another called *Tommy Toddles*, which later reappeared at the Princess's as *Tommy Troddles* to conform to the thirteen-letter titles favoured by McKelvie for his productions, because he had thirteen letters in his own name.

North of Bridgeton Cross, in Abercromby Street, is the Church of St Mary, the second oldest Catholic church in Glasgow, built in 1842. A headstone from St Mary's burying-ground is preserved on the north side of the church. This was a private place of burial for the clergy, a few paupers and children from the orphan house. Sacred Heart was formed as a separate parish in 1873, and the present large church was erected in Dalmarnock Road in 1910. The first head of the Marist teaching order at Sacred Heart was Brother Walfrid, who brought leading football teams of the day such as Clyde and Dundee Harp to play exhibition games – not on Glasgow Green, but at the former Barrowfield ground at the south-west end of Dalmarnock Road – for the benefit of his school's 'Dinner Table and Clothing' scheme, and is best remembered for his part in the founding of Celtic FC, whose story is told in the chapter on Parkhead.

Into the twentieth century: the bad times of idleness and boredom

Tenements like Bridgeton Cross Mansions represented a great advance in housing standards. Although the houses had still only one or two apartments, each had its own WC and a few even had a bathroom. A single-end in these circumstances could be a perfectly comfortable house even for a small family. Unfortunately most Bridgeton families were large or took in lodgers, and although legislation passed in 1892 made sanitation compulsory inside every tenement, for most families this meant a shared WC on the landing. Better housing was one of the issues on which the ILP fought the 1922 general election, in which James Maxton won the Bridgeton seat which he held until his death in 1946.

James Maxton, born in Pollokshaws in 1885, educated at Hutchesons' Grammar School, arts graduate of Glasgow University, teacher in several Glasgow primary schools including St James', Calton from 1909 to 1912, good athlete, devotee of golf and fervent supporter of Celtic, joined the ILP in 1904 and at the outbreak of war held firm to his pacifist principles. In 1916 he served twelve months in Calton Jail in Edinburgh for his part in calling a general strike on Clydeside. The following year he stood unsuccessfully as MP for Bridgeton. As the 1922 election approached, it became clear that support for Maxton was growing. Bridgeton Branch of the ILP became the strongest in Scotland. The Olympia Theatre was packed every Sunday evening with audiences eager to hear the Socialist message. With the support of the Catholic vote, the result was an ILP landslide. Maxton was returned to Westminster with a majority of 7,698 in the company of John Wheatley, David Kirkwood, Tom Johnston and others. Their support helped Ramsay MacDonald to the premiership in the first minority Labour Government of 1924. Maxton was the Chairman of the ILP from 1926 to 1931 and again from 1934 to 1939, but its disaffiliation from the Labour Party on the insistence of Maxton in 1932, and its association with the Communist cause reduced the ILP

Plaque in St James' School to James Maxton, MP for Bridgeton from 1922 until his death in 1946. Maxton taught at St James' from 1909 to 1912.

to only three MPs Personal popularity – Churchill called him 'the greatest gentleman in the House of Commons' – kept Maxton secure in his Bridgeton seat for a quarter-century.

The decade that saw the departure of the Red Clydesiders to Westminster also saw the flourishing of the Glasgow gangs. *No Mean City*, a novel cobbled together by an unemployed Gorbals barber and a journalist from London, did much to sully Glasgow's image in the 1930s and is supposedly based on the exploits of a Bridgeton gang, the Billy Boys. Sir Percy Sillitoe, appointed Chief Constable of the city in 1931, mentions Bridgeton frequently in the chapter of his memoirs, *Cloak without Dagger*, which relates how he smashed the Glasgow gangs. Another reason for the notoriety of the Billy Boys might simply be that they sang louder than everyone else, the highlight of their repertoire being 'Hello! hello! we are the Billy Boys', sung to the tune of 'Marching through Georgia'. It was customary to conclude an evening's loafing round Bridgeton Cross by standing to attention to sing 'God save the King'.

The leader of the gang was Billy Fullerton, who had the misfortune to kick the winning goal against Kent Star, a Catholic gang from Calton, during a friendly game on Glasgow Green in 1924. After recovering from the hammer attack which followed, Fullerton raised a gang eight hundred strong, recruited from as far afield as Airdrie, Coatbridge and Cambuslang. The gang shunned housebreaking but raised the funds necessary to pay fines and other expenses by ambushing rival gangs on their way home with their 'buroo' money, or kicking in the plate glass windows of shopkeepers who declined to contribute to the cause. Their deadly enemies were the Norman Conks (Conquerors), whom they taunted by marching every Sunday morning up Poplin Street and down French Street (on either side of Norman Street and therefore in the heart of enemy territory) on their way to the Church of Scotland (attendance at service not required). On saints' days and holy days the parade went straight through Norman Street. Sillitoe's description can hardly be bettered:

> As soon as the distant strains of his offensive music were heard by the Conks, they manned all upper windows, and even the roofs in their street, and when the Billy Boys' band tried to march past, it was met with a downpour of bricks, missiles, buckets of filth, and broken glass. If the Norman Conks could have made boiling lead, I am sure they would not have hesitated to use that too. It was certainly all that would have been needed to complete the picture of a medieval siege.

Other Bridgeton gangs were the Stickit, the Bluebell, who specialised in disrupting dance halls, the Nunnie from Nuneaton Street and the Baltic Fleet from Baltic Street. (Gangs were very fond of rhyming slang.) Baltic Street was called after the Baltic Jute Company, a Dundee firm which had a fleeting existence in Bridgeton.

In later years several people claimed to have worked towards breaking up the gangs: Sillietoe with the strong arm of the law; the Rev. J. Cameron Peddie of Hutchesontown Parish Church by setting up clubs where boys were taught plumbing, carpentry and joinery; and R.M.L. Walkinshaw, the governor of Barlinnie, who took an interest in gang members on their regular visits. Many former prisoners attended his funeral when he died after a fall from the Glasgow to Stranraer train.

During the general strike of 1926 some of the gang members came down on the side of law and order and carefully preserved the certificates they were given at the end. Fullerton later commanded a Fascist unit of two hundred which was used to break up Communist marches. Many former gang members finished the Second World War with good records, and William Fullerton died peacefully at home in 1962 at the age of fifty-six. A crowd of one thousand escorted his cortege from Brook Street by way of Crownpoint Road to Riddrie Cemetery, and Edwin Morgan wrote a poem:

Bareheaded, in dark suits, with flutes
and drums, they brought him here, in procession
seriously, King Billy of Brigton, dead,
from Bridgeton Cross: a memory of violence

*

No, but it isn't the violence they remember
but the legend of a violent man
born poor, gang-leader in the bad times
of idleness and boredom, lost in better days,
a bouncer in a betting club, a quiet man at last, dying
alone in Bridgeton in a box bed.

Into the twenty-first century: rural quietness and amenity

The dispersal of part of Bridgeton's population to new council estates
in the inter-war years made little difference to the appearance of the
area. The story has been very different in the last quarter-century as
tenements, factories and many public buildings have been demolished
and replaced with modern housing, some services and a little industry,
now mostly located south of French Street and at Dalmarnock and
Mile-end. One of the areas redeveloped for housing has a plaque on
a building at the corner of Laird Place and Main Street:

The Lord Provost of Glasgow
    Dr Michael Kelly
Laid this brick on August 25th 1983
    to mark the first phase of this
Bridgeton redevelopment.

In 1905 a Bridgeton minister reminded his congregation, in the
presence of Lord Provost Sir John Ure Primrose, that a century
before, Bridgeton had been a village by itself, 'with a rural quietness
and amenity which had its own restfulness and charm'. A century
later, the landscaping, pedestrianised areas, house gardens and open
play areas of Bridgeton's twenty-first century neighbourhoods would
most certainly meet with his approval.

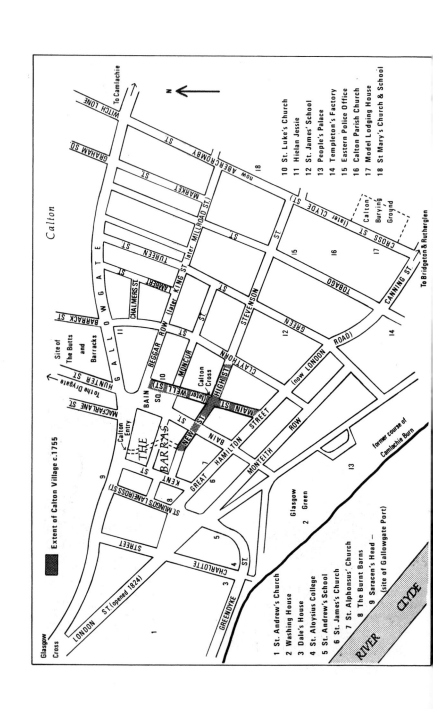

Calton

Glasgow
Cross

■ Extent of Calton Village c.1755

To Camlachie

WITCH LONE

GRAHAM SQ

now ABERCROMBY ST

MARKET ST

ST

later MILLROAD ST

ST

(later CLYDE ST)

Calton
Burying
Ground

CROSS ST

To Bridgeton & Rutherglen

TOBAGO ST

CANNING ST

TUREEN ST

ST

ST

STEVENSON ST

GREEN ST

Site of
The Butts
and
Barracks

BARRACK ST

G A L L O W G A T E

CHALMERS ST

LAMBERT ST

BEGGAR ROW (later KING ST)

MONCUR ST

CLAYTHORN ST

(now LONDON ROAD)

To the Drygate

HUNTER ST

MACFARLANE ST

BAIN SQ

WELL ST (later)

HIGH ST

MAIN ST

Calton
Cross

12

15

16

17

14

THE
BARRAS

Calton
Entry

BAIN ST

NEW ST

ST

HAMILTON STREET

MONTEITH ROW

former course of
Camlachie Burn

GREAT HAMILTON ST

KENT ST

ST MUNGO'S LANE (CROSS ST)

Glasgow
Green

13

CHARLOTTE STREET

GREENDYKE ST

LONDON ST (opened 1824)

1

RIVER CLYDE

1 St. Andrew's Church
2 Washing House
3 Dale's House
4 St. Aloysius College
5 St. Andrew's School
6 St. James's Church
7 St. Alphonsus' Church
8 The Burnt Barns
9 Saracen's Head –
    (site of Gallowgate Port)

10 St. Luke's Church
11 Hielan Jessie
12 St. James' School
13 People's Palace
14 Templeton's Factory
15 Eastern Police Office
16 Calton Parish Church
17 Model Lodging House
18 St Mary's Church & School

3
CALTON

Ye canny whack thi Calton
fur noise and durt and smell.
The streets ur full u bizzies,
wae plenti tales tae tell.
Aw thi wimen grass oan ye,
thi men kin slag ye tae.
Ye canny whack thi Calton
An ats aw ave tae sae.

Calton, whose indomitable community spirit is so splendidly summed up in this song, written by the pupils of St James' Primary School, lies about half a mile east of Glasgow Cross, between the Gallowgate and Glasgow Green. It began as a weavers' village in the early eighteenth century, became a burgh in 1817 and was absorbed by Glasgow in 1846. Weaving continued in the area into the twentieth

Pupils of St James' Primary School in 1977 sing the Calton song.

century. Since the song was written in 1976 most of the site of the original village has been rebuilt with attractive red or yellow brick houses with well-kept gardens as part of the project to regenerate the East End of the city. The west part of the Calton ('a' pronounced as in 'cat') is the site of the famous 'Barrowland' market, known to all Glaswegians simply as 'the Barras'.

Weavers' village and industrial suburb: 'mutuall love and good neighbourhead'

Calton has kept a separate identity within Glasgow for reasons going back to Reformation times. The land on which the village was built was once part of the old Gallowmuir of Glasgow, an area of common land to the east of the town, where the townsfolk could pasture their cattle and cut their peats. As the name implies, it also served as a place of execution. After the departure of Archbishop Beaton to France, the magistrates of Glasgow took possession of the common lands and proceeded to dispose of them in lots. This outrage turned white the hair of William Walker, the archbishop's steward, who had been left behind to collect rentals on his master's behalf. Walker wrote to France that he had been 'in great trublis, as is knawin utuartlie be the changeing of the colouris of my hair qlk was blak and now is quhyte'. Although these sales were later stopped, some desirable parts of the common lands had passed completely outwith the town's ownership. One of these was an enclave of land between the Gallowgate and the Green, just beyond the East or Gallowgate Port. A century later this land came into the possession of the Walkinshaws of Barrowfield and part was feued out by John Walkinshaw in 1705 as a weavers' village, ideally placed within easy reach of the Glasgow markets, but outwith the control of the Glasgow guilds.

The new village was laid out very simply, with two streets intersecting at Calton Cross. The street which ran north and south was called Main Street. Before recent development this was Well Street, and is now Claythorn Avenue. The south end of Main Street joined the Barrowfield Road (now, after several changes of name, London Road), which led to Dalmarnock and Rutherglen. The street which ran eastwards from Calton Cross was called High Street (later Kirk Street and now Stevenson Street). New Street (now Stevenson Street West) ran westwards and stopped abruptly at the Glasgow boundary. At this point Calton was linked with the Gallowgate by Calton Entry,

John McDowell and 'Wee Maggie', 1916. When this picture was taken, McDowell was the last working handloom weaver in the Calton district. He started work in 1846 as a ten-year-old apprentice. Maggie was John's niece.

part of which can still be seen at the Gallowgate between Baird's Bar and the Barrowland Ballroom.

The village was originally called Blackfauld, a name applied to the surrounding area where the ground was blackened by the refuse left by primitive coal workings. The alternative name of 'Calton' was introduced when Glasgow took its chance of buying back Walkinshaw's land in 1723, mainly in order to protect the trading privileges of the citizens. Blackfauld village now became a suburb known as 'the Calton of Glasgow'. No satisfactory explanation of the name 'Calton' has been found, but it seems to have been applied to pockets of industry on the outskirts of towns, in the same way that villages had their Kirktons which grew up round the church, and their Miltons round the mill. The name may have arisen because many early industries depended on a good supply of water from a 'cauld' or weir. Various spellings of the name occur: Caldton on Roy's map (1755); Calton (Barry, 1770); Caltoun (McArthur, 1778 and Barry, 1782); and generally Calton thereafter.

At this time special laws were in force against the exercise of crafts in suburbs adjacent to royal burghs, and so agreements had to be drawn up in 1725 between the weavers of Calton and their opposite numbers in Glasgow 'for mentaining mutuall love and good neighbourhead'. The cordiners also agreed 'that no stranger professing himself to be a cordiner or shoemaker' could settle in the village of Blackfauld 'whill [until] first he make good and thankfull payment of twelve pound Scots money, whereof one half to the poor of the cordeners of Glasgow and the other half to the poor of the cordeners of Blackfauld'. Work in the village was to be inspected every Tuesday afternoon, the day preceding the Glasgow market, 'to try if their work be sufficient to serve his Majestie's lieges'. Substandard work was to be confiscated and given to the poor of Blackfauld. One spirited Calton feuar stood out for independence, protecting that by this capitulation Calton people might be brought under a 'groundless servitude and imposition', but he was supported by only six inhabitants.

In 1730 Glasgow again sold the land on which Calton was built, this time to John Orr, a merchant who now owned the Barrowfield estate. The estate was made into a barony, which gave Orr the right to impose law and punish wrongdoers. Calton now spread eastwards, and the new village was added to the old one. An additional entry was made from the Gallowgate leading into what is now Bain Square. This was called Calton Mouth. Calton Mouth joined up with a lane known as the Beggar Row, which formed the northern boundary of the expanded village. The eastern boundary was the Witch Lone, now Abercromby Street, an old drove road leading from the north to Rutherglen, and the only road across the Gallowmuir from north to south. The southern boundary of the village was the Barrowfield Road.

Pottery-making is an ancient industry in the Calton area because of the large 'Mount Blue' clay bed which stretches from Glasgow Cross through Claythorn and on to Camlachie and Parkhead. The earliest potter in Calton whose name is known to us is William Maxwell, who gave in a petition in 1722 'craving that the councill would be pleased to allow him to build a little house without the Gallowgate, on or near where the old pighouse was, for working and making of earthen pigs, potts and other earthen vessell, for the service of the inhabitants'. 'Pig' was a term used for all domestic earthenware and included such items as a 'hot pig' to warm the bed. A pottery-ware chimney-can was also a 'pig', so that in stormy weather you had to beware of pigs falling off the lums!

Several other potteries were started in the Tureen Street area, including those of John Anderson and Michael Bogle, who supplied building materials for Calton's distinctive brick cottages with their whitewashed walls, red pantiled roofs and red chimneys, which made Calton unique among Glasgow villages. These old cottages can be seen in many of the photographs taken around 1913 by Glasgow's chief sanitary inspector, Peter Fyfe.

Several potters came into the district from the east of Scotland. Cubie Street was called after a family from Prestonpans, and Williamson Street after their son-in-law. Potters also arrived from Staffordshire, and St Thomas's Wesleyan Chapel, known as 'the Potters' kirk', was built for them in Wesleyan Street. These three streets ran off the Gallowgate just east of Abercromby Street. John Wesley preached on Glasgow Green in 1751, presumably with success, because by 1789 the *Glasgow Mercury* was reporting that 'the increase of Methodists is much complained of'. St James's Church in London Road was originally built as a Methodist chapel.

Another religious minority who were beginning to attract criticism were the Catholics. In Calton the home and warehouse of a potter named Robert Bagnall were attacked in 1779 when anti-Catholic feelings were running high. Bagnall seems to have given offence by allowing his workmen to work on one of the Kirk's fast days, but it is probable that business rivalry also played a part. Three Presbyterian clergymen reportedly gave the family food and lodging 'in an unobtrusive manner'.

Bagnall's output included medallions, crucifixes and plaques. He is something of an enigma, having come to Calton via the east of Scotland. Bagnall is a common name in Staffordshire, but Robert Bagnall was believed by some to be a Frenchman who named Tureen Street after the French Admiral Turenne. Others derive the name from the French 'terrine', literally an earthen vessel. Bagnall was certainly an astute business man. While in Calton he successfully sued his partners in the firm of Thomson Anderson & Co. for £500 plus £100 expenses over a business dispute, then sued Glasgow Council over the riot and won compensation of £1,429, before finally disappearing from the Calton scene in the 1780s.

The Calton weavers: 'they are unworthy of freedom who expect it from hands other than their own'

The best known event in the history of Calton is the weavers' strike,

This portrait, one of a series drawn by Alasdair Gray for the People's Palace, shows Harry McShane, Red Clydesider, beside the Calton weavers' memorial in 1977. Abercromby Street model lodging house, now demolished, is shown behind.

which took place in the summer of 1787. Three of the six weavers who died are interred in the Calton burying-ground. They are commemorated by two stones, erected in 1836 and renewed by Glasgow Trades Council in 1931 and 1957, particularly through the efforts of Harry McShane, a leading 'Red Clydesider'. A portrait of McShane standing beside the stones was drawn in 1977 by artist Alasdair Gray and is now in the People's Palace. Also on view is a mural, one of a series of eight commissioned to depict the history of labour in Glasgow, in which the artist, Ken Currie, has vividly portrayed the scene at the Drygate Bridge immediately after the shooting of the weavers.

The background to the strike was the steady decline in the bargaining power of the weavers after 1751 when an Act of Parliament broke the power of the incorporations by removing entry fees. This opened the door to a flood of new entrants who wished to share in the prosperity of the weavers, but who were prepared to take low wages to get work. The 1787 strike began on 30 June, when 7,000 of the 20,000 men who had united to form the Clyde Valley Weavers'

General Association held a meeting on Glasgow Green and agreed not to work at reduced prices. The manufacturers retaliated with a lock-out, and the stoppage continued for the unusually long period of two months.

Matters came to a head on the morning of Monday 3 September, when a group of weavers set upon three weavers in Camlachie who had continued to work, smashed their looms, seized their webs and returned along the Gallowgate to Glasgow, intending to take the webs back to the Glasgow manufacturers. Their way was barred by the provost and magistrates, who were pelted with bricks and stones and pursued towards Glasgow Cross. A detachment of the 39th Regiment arrived to the rescue and chased the weavers back out of the city. All remained quiet until four o'clock, when the weavers came back along the Gallowgate and up what is now Hunter Street, intending to enter Glasgow by the Drygate. This led to the fatal encounter with the military at the Drygate Bridge, near where Tennent's brewery now stands in Duke Street. According to some reports, while James Granger, one of the leaders, was arguing that it was unreasonable to reduce wages during a period of rising costs, the crowd began to stone the troops. The town clerk read the Riot Act, but before he had finished, the first shots were fired, killing three weavers. Three others died later. As a conclusion to the day's events, 'a number of respectable burgesses were summoned to attend the magistrates during the night, and every method taken to secure the peace of the city, which was effected'. Next day notices in the paper confirmed the determination of the authorities that no threat to security from these 'daring combinations' would be tolerated. Colonel Kellet was given the freedom of Glasgow, the officers a dinner in the Tontine, and every soldier employed in quelling the mob a pair of stockings and a pair of shoes.

James Granger was brought to trial on charges of inciting to mobbing and rioting, found guilty and banished for seven years. He returned to take part in the great weavers' strike of 1812, and when he died in 1825 he was buried in the weavers' lair. The inscription on the right-hand stone reads:

> This is the Property of the Weaving Body under charge of the five districts of Calton, erected by them to the memory of John Page, Alexander Miller, and James Ainsley who at a Meeting of that body for resisting a reduction of their wages were upon the 2nd Sep 1787. Martyred by the Military under orders of the Civic Authorities of Glasgow firing upon

the Multitude. Also to the memory of their brethern in trade, viz. James Granger, James Gray, Alexander Megget, Duncan Cherry, James Morton, Thomas, Miller, John Jaffray, the first four highly distinguished for zeal on behalf of their trade.

The date on the stone is incorrect. The left-hand stone, erected by Glasgow Trades Council, has the lines:

We'll never swerve. We'll steadfast be.
We'll have our rights. We will be free.

They are unworthy of freedom who expect it
from hands other than their own.

Along the Gallowgate

The northern boundary of the Calton is the Gallowgate, an ancient thoroughfare first mentioned in 1325, the high road to Edinburgh and England, and still one of Glasgow's great streets. Travellers entered and left the town by the East Port, also known as the Gallowgate Port. With the passing of the Jacobite threat after Culloden, however, Provost Andrew Cochrane felt that the time had come to open Glasgow's doors to the world, and the port, by then 'a complete rickle', was demolished and replaced by a fine new inn – the Saracen's Head. Its successor of the same name, built in the early twentieth century, still occupies that site today. The signboard, with its picture of a ferocious scimitar-wielding Saracen, no longer exists, but displayed on the exterior walls of the present public house are three pictures, one depicting a stage coach leaving the inn in 1755, another showing the old college in the High Street in 1855, and the third, undated, showing the Trongate in its former splendour. On display inside the pub are the blunderbuss carried for protection on the London coach and a cleaned and polished skull found during digging operations on the site. The latter is a gruesome reminder that this spot was once the kirkyard of Little St Mungo's Chapel, where lepers were buried, and tradition has it that the legendary meeting between St Mungo and St Columba took place here. As 'Senex', the Glasgow historian, put it, 'It was certainly rather a queer idea to plant an inn in a kirkyard, converting the graves into wine cellars and kitchens as was actually the case.' When the opening of the inn was announced in the *Glasgow Courant* for October 1755, the proprietor, Robert Tennent, was careful to stress the modern comforts of the thirty-six-room inn:

The bed-chambers are all separate, none of them entering through another, and so contrived that there is no need of going out of doors to get to them. The beds are all very good, clean and free from bugs.

The second keeper of the inn was James Graham, who gave his name to Graham Square. After his death his widow remarried and became Mrs Buchanan. The inn then became known as one of the most spacious and elegant in Scotland. Merchants' daughters were sent for 'lessons in the culinary arts', each paying the head cook five shillings to see how the different dishes were prepared and served up. At one 'great county dinner' the appearance of fifteen or sixteen elegant young cooks with white aprons placing the dishes on the dinner-table made such an impression on the gentlemen present that

the younger and more sprightly county gentlemen immediately set about joking and flirting with these handsome cooks, and were greatly more entertained by this sport than with their dinner, for some of them went down to the kitchen and assisted the young ladies to hand up the dishes.

Like all inns of any standing, the Saracen's Head had its own punch-bowl, made at the Delftfield pottery near Anderston, with a capacity of almost four gallons. Punch made with sugar and rum brought to Glasgow from the West Indies was much appreciated by chilled travellers, who liked to linger over a bowl of steaming punch and smoke a clay pipe. The manufacture of clay pipes became a great industry in Calton. In 1891 William White's Bain Street works were producing 14,000 pipes per day. White's business was the oldest clay pipe manufactury in Britain, originally carried on by the Corporation of Tobacco Spinners of Glasgow. The premises are now part of the Barrows market.

Many illustrious visitors stayed at the inn. Johnson and Boswell arrived on horseback on their return from their Hebridean tour in 1773. Robert Burns paid a visit in 1788, the same year as the first coach arrived from London. Dorothy Wordsworth arrived in 1803 in an Irish jaunting car, her head beating with the noise of carts. She was moderately impressed by the inn: 'quiet and tolerably cheap, a new building', she noted in her journal. Walking with William along the Trongate after dinner, she found the stone buildings of the New Town superior even to those of London streets. If Dorothy and William had turned in the opposite direction and walked a short distance eastwards, they could have admired two fine three-storey tenements

Villages of Glasgow

Evening chat. Tenement life in Market Street in the hot summer of 1976. The tenements have been replaced by houses with gardens as part of the GEAR scheme.

which still stand in Gallowgate, at the top of Claythorn Street. Both were built in 1771 in Scots vernacular style, with crow-stepped gables and a round staircase at the back. No. 394 was restored by the Scottish Special Housing Association, and to mark the occasion the queen unveiled a plaque on 1 July 1983. The artist Horatio McCulloch was born in this building in 1805. The ground floor of no. 374 is occupied by the Hielan Jessie public house. Claythorn was an estate owned by the Lukes, a family of prosperous goldsmiths and jewellers.

Hielan Jessie's was reputedly the favourite tavern of Highland soldiers billeted in the barracks which formerly stood between Barrack Street and Hunter Street. It may also have been frequented by Highlanders brought by George Mackintosh to work in his chemical works in Duke Street. Mackintosh, a native of Dunchattan in Ross-shire, was so intent on keeping his processes secret that he surrounded his works with a ten-foot wall, housed all the unmarried men in his entirely Gaelic-speaking workforce on the premises and held a roll-call every evening. Mackintosh began work in Glasgow in a tannery in the Gallowgate and his son Charles invented the waterproof 'mac'.

The barracks stood on land which in medieval times was used for 'wappinshaws', periodical days of muster, when the men of Glasgow had to turn out with their weapons and perform military duties. 'Buttis' were set up 'for exerceis of schutting' and the area became known as 'the Butts'. In 1540 the Scottish Parliament decided that the only weapons permitted were 'speares, pikes, starke and lang, six elnes of length, Leith axes, halbardes, hand-bowes and arrows, croce-bowes, culverings, two-handed swordes'. The Battle of the Butts was a particularly bloody skirmish fought in the area during the minority of Mary, Queen of Scots. On one side were the supporters of the Stewart Earl of Lennox, a family with close associations with Glasgow, and on the other was a force led by the then regent, the Earl of Arran, head of the Hamilton family. Arran won the day and Glasgow, whose citizens had supported Lennox, was turned over to pillage and narrowly escaped being burnt to the ground.

In 1795 it was decided to build infantry barracks on the Butts. A central block facing the Gallowgate was erected for officers, with a block on either side at right angles for soldiers. Tradition has it that at the battle of Vittoria against the French in northern Spain, Lt-Col. Henry Cadogan spurred on the men of the 71st or Glasgow Regiment with the cry: 'Huzza boys, down the Gallowgate with them!' In the 1870s the troops were moved to Maryhill because of the smoke from nearby factories and because, as Lord Provost Peter Clouston worded it, 'the men were exposed to temptation of no ordinary character by coming in contact with the most dissolute and profligate portion of the population'. The site was then used as a railway depot. But although many parts of the Calton were undoubtedly overcrowded and disease-ridden, the entire population of the area by no means belonged to what the Victorians termed 'the lower orders'. Living in the part of the Gallowgate just east of Calton Entry was a bank agent and notary public occupying a six-room house, and several houses of three and four apartments were occupied by master drapers, a mason, a saddler, a pottery foreman, a customs officer and two rag and waste merchants employing five and six workers respectively. There was one gentleman who combined the occupations of hairdresser with ale and porter bottler, and another who described himself as chemist, druggist and dentist. All these persons were Scots, but among the Irish residents were a butcher and a cattle dealer, probably in business at the cattle market in Graham Square. The police station in Calton Entry was manned by an inspector (Irish), a detective constable (English), two officers (one Irish, one Scots) and two constables (Scots). Two of the Scots were called McAlpine and McLauchlan, and no doubt had enough Gaelic to keep the customers of Hielan Jessie's well under control if necessary.

The Green, Charlotte Street and Monteith Row

Glasgow Green underwent two stages of development to reach its present form: the first in the seventeenth century, when several crofts were consolidated for the use of the townsfolk, and the second early in the nineteenth century, when the Green was drained and levelled, and driveways and paths were laid out. The name of one of the crofts, Crapnestock, survives in Craignestock Mansions, a tenement at the corner of Green Street and London Road.

As the name suggests, the Green was a place where women came to wash and bleach their linen. The sight of hundreds of women and girls working at the 'boins', as the tubs were called, was a spectacle guaranteed to attrack English tourists, who were always writing about 'Scotch washing' in their travelogues. The lid of a snuff-box which belonged to the manager of the public wash-house built in 1732 on the banks of the Camlachie Burn shows the women with skirts and petticoats hitched high, trampling their blankets. 'Scotch washing', scandalised the Victorians who transferred operations to a 'steamie' beside Templeton's carpet factory. Till recently Calton women pegged out their washing on the poles which still stand just to the east of the People's Palace.

While the washerwomen were hard at work, some of the local merchants and gentry were to be seen down on the Green enjoying a round of golf. Glasgow's first known golfer is Patrick Bogle, who asked the Council in 1760 for permission to extend 'the present lodge in the Green' on behalf of those 'who use the exercise of the golf'. By 1787 the golfers had formed themselves into the Glasgow Golf Club. Jones's Directory for that year lists twenty-two members.

It seems that the golfers were early risers, for according to 'Senex':

> At 9 a.m. the cows were brought to the turnstile at the west entrance to be milked, and I have seen our gentlemen golfers after a morning's sport, stop short here, and with great gusto swig off a tinful of milk to give them appetite for breakfast.

Scotch washing

Early English travellers in Glasgow made a point of visiting Glasgow Green to see 'Scotch washing'. This illustration is taken from the lid of a snuff-box owned by the manager of the Washing House on the Green. An inquisitive gentleman is being splashed and chased away by one of the washer girls. The box is in the People's Palace collections.

There appear to have been seven holes, and a match was three rounds, twenty-one holes in all. Two of the holes were called 'the monument hole' and 'the Humane Society hole'. After 1836 nothing is heard of the club until 1870, when it was reconstituted and play began in Queen's Park, moving to Alexandra Park in 1874, then Blackhill in 1895, and to its present home at Killermont in 1903. As part of the bicentenary celebrations in 1987 the club captain, dressed in period costume, played four holes specially laid out on the Green with 'featherie' balls and wooden clubs.

For refreshment of a different kind golfers could call in at the Burnt Barns tavern, established in 1679 and believed to be Glasgow's oldest public house. Its modern successor, the Old Barns, occupies the same spot at the corner of Ross Street and London Road. The name is a reminder of a great fire in 1668 which destroyed the grain stored in the many barns which stood in the area. As a result each burgess had to 'mak and provyd ane sufficient lether buckit, and put their awine names therwpong and to have them in reddines at all occasiounes in their awine houssis'.

A residence overlooking the Green was just the place for Glasgow professional and business men, and Charlotte Street and Monteith

The Old Burnt Barns, established in 1679, is believed to be Glasgow's oldest public house. It took its name from a fire which swept the area a few years before. Its modern successor, the Old Barns, occupies the same site at the corner of Ross Street and London Road.

Row were laid out on the south-west edge of Calton to attract such feuars. Charlotte Street was the earlier, laid out in 1779 in an area previously known as Merkdaily, used for a fruit and vegetable market. The best-known resident was David Dale, who secured a prime site at the south-west corner of the street in 1780. At that time, Dale, aged forty, was a successful importer of linen yarns, which he gave out for weaving to large numbers of weavers working at home through the west of Scotland. He was also an agent for the Royal Bank of Scotland, and could well afford £6,000 for a fine mansion facing the Green. While resident in this house Dale became a partner in the Turkey red dyeworks at Dalmarnock and in the large cotton spinning mills at New Lanark. Dale's daughter, Anne Carolina, was married in the house to Robert Owen, who took over the mills in 1800. However, Charlotte Street was not without its inconveniences. On one occasion Dale had arranged to entertain to dinner the directors

Two Calton worthies as depicted in Peter Mackenzie's *Glasgow Characters*. *Left:* Hawkie, an early Glasgow street hawker and 'patter merchant'. *Right:* David Dale, a pillar of Glasgow society.

of the Royal Bank, who were coming from Edinburgh to Glasgow for the day in coaches, but the Camlachie Burn overflowed and the kitchen flooded. The good Calton neighbours rallied round to cook the food, but only wine from Dale's own bins was considered good enough for the distinguished guests. The problem was solved when a 'sea-faring man' was fetched in, and, with Miss Carolina on his shoulders to advise, descended to the cellars to select the proper vintages. Much more troublesome was the smell from the tan pits, glue works and tripe houses situated near the slaughter house at the west end of the Green. Dale left Charlotte Street in 1800 to reside at Rosebank in Cambuslang, where his unmarried daughters continued to live after his death in 1806. The house in Charlotte Street became the premises of the Glasgow Eye Infirmary in the 1850s. The famous oculist, Dr William McKenzie, carried out eye operations in Dale's octagonal library, with its fine domed roof. Among later occupants were the Salvation Army. Dale's house was demolished in 1954 amidst

much controversy to make way for an extension to Our Lady and
St Francis' School.

Our Lady and St Francis' dates from 1847 when the first Franciscan
Sisters to come to Glasgow settled in Charlotte Street and opened a
girls' school attached to their convent. The school had a particularly
good reputation for teaching French by conversational methods far
ahead of the times. In the 1900s the girls were reported as speaking
and understanding French with exceptional fluency and correctness,
but on the inspectors' recommendation the girls of class III were
introduced also to Sonntag's French grammar and Moliere's *Le
Médeoin malgré lui*. In 1899 new school buildings were completed. Our
Lady and St Francis' became a comprehensive school for the girls of
the East End until closure in the 1990s and subsequent demolition
of the buildings.

Another well-known Glasgow School, St Aloysius College, also
began in Charlotte Street. The college occupied the site at the south-
east corner of the street, and was a grammar school managed by the
Jesuits on behalf of the board for the education of boys aged seven
and upwards from all parts of Scotland. Its academic standing was
high. According to an inspector who visited the school in the 1860s, it
could bear comparison with the High School or St Mungo's Academy.
At fourteen the boys were reading Homer, Xenophon, Euripides and
Thucydides in Greek; Virgil, Horace and Livy in Latin; Voltaire in
French; and an Italian and German 'reader'. Boys were encouraged
to point out each other's mistakes by acting as 'censors'. In 1866 the
school left Charlotte Street and eventually moved to its present site
in Garnethill in 1885. The original site was later occupied by Camp
Coffee, one of Glasgow's oldest food-processing firms.

Only one original Georgian house remains in Charlotte Street,
at the north end. This has been restored and converted to six self-
catering flats which visitors to Glasgow are invited to rent. The
area to the west of Charlotte Street was developed for housing in
1999 when Glasgow was nominated UK City of Architecture and
Design. A range of flats overlooking Glasgow Green was designed
by different architects and the bold designs of these 'Houses for the
Future' attracts much interest and, as expected, varied responses from
Glaswegians and visitors from outwith the city.

The second fashionable street to be built on the south side of
Calton was Monteith Row, laid out in 1820 on part of the Green
following improvements begun in 1814 under the direction of James

Cleland, Superintendent of Public Works and statistician of Glasgow. Much of the landscaping was the work of unemployed weavers during a period of depression in 1820. Greendyke Street was opened to give access from the Saltmarket to the Calton Green, joining with Great Hamilton Street on the north. Monteith Row was one of the finest Regency terraces in Scotland, designed by David Hamilton, and called after Henry Monteith of the Anderston family, then Lord Provost of Glasgow. A few years after it was built, Monteith Row was in danger of losing its open outlook when work began on London Street, which was intended to connect Glasgow Cross directly with Bridgeton Cross and form a new route for coaches to London, so as to avoid the tortuous Gallowgate. London Street reached Greendyke Street in 1824, but the influential residents of Monteith Row prevented the street continuing across the Green in front of their houses. As a result traffic had to make the awkward turn into Great Hamilton Street, as it still has to do to this day at the Old Barns. A proposal in 1847 to bring a railway through the Green was also resisted, but the biggest threat came eleven years later when the Council approved a plan to lease the Green for coal mining, as a means of paying off the £100,000 debt it had run up by purchasing the McLellan Galleries and land for the Kelvingrove and Queen's Parks. A contemporary song, 'Airn John', rediscovered by the folk singer, Adam McNaughton, sums up exactly the feelings of the East-enders:

Wi' sticks an' stanes, we'll come John,
An' fecht while we've a spark;
Ye'll never get the Glasgow green
To pay the west-end park.

The Green survived these threats, but by the 1860s smoke from the mills and factories in Calton and Bridgeton had caused many residents of Monteith Row to depart for the now fashionable West End. Readers of Guy McCrone's novel, *Antimacassar City*, set in Glasgow in the 1870s, will recall how Bel Moorhouse, proud owner of an elegant new house in Grosvenor Terrace in Kelvinside, deplored her mother's stubborn refusal to leave her 'much betasselled and upholstered flat' in Monteith Row. Mrs Barrowfield, for her part, had no wish to move 'to the very edge of the town to sit among the hoity-toities from Park Circus and Royal Crescent'.

Life in the Row can never have been dull. Residents had a grandstand view of the many military reviews, religious and temperance meetings, political demonstrations in favour of burgh reform and the extension of the franchise, and May Day rallies, which continued until moved to the Queen's Park in the 1950s. A few eyebrows must have been raised behind the lace curtains when Dr Elizabeth Chalmers Smith, wife of the minister of Calton Parish Church, took part in suffragette demonstrations and was sent to prison for setting fire to a house in Park Circus.

New buildings were regularly erected on the Green, most spectacular of all Templeton's carpet works, designed by William Leiper to resemble the Doge's Palace in Venice. Tragedy struck when a wall collapsed in 1889 during construction, killing twenty-nine women and girls in the temporary weaving sheds beneath. For nearly a century the factory produced carpets for palaces, luxury liners and government buildings throughout the world, until it closed in 1979. It is now used as a centre for small businesses. The People's Palace was built in 1893 to provide reading and recreation rooms, a museum and a picture gallery for the people of the East End.

Only one house of the original Monteith Row remains, and this is used as a model lodging house. The site is now mostly occupied by a Barratt housing development which was begun in 1981. Monteith Row has been renamed Weavers' Court as a fitting tribute to the weavers of the Calton.

Calton burgh

In the early nineteenth century Calton was faced with the twofold task of maintaining law and order among a rapidly growing population and encouraging manufactures to recover from the depression which followed the end of the Napoleonic wars. To this end Calton became a burgh of barony in 1817. The eighty-one persons who had paid £2 2s each to help defray the expenses of setting up the burgh met in Calton's chapel of ease and elected Robert Struthers, owner of the Greenhead brewery, as provost, James Parker, James Kerr and John Clark as bailies, and Robert Shaw as treasurer. Eleven men were elected 'counsellors and birleymen'. 'Birleyman' was the old Scots term for persons chosen to arbitrate in disputes between neighbours. A coat of arms was designed which combined the arms of Glasgow, the arms of Provost Struthers, and the insignia of the weavers, surmounted by a crest depicting bees busily swarming round a hive with the motto 'By Industry we Prosper'. Provost Struthers resigned in 1819 and was succeeded by Nathaniel Stevenson, owner of the Barrowfield cotton mill, who held office for the next twenty years. The last two provosts, before Calton was absorbed into Glasgow in 1846, were Robert Bartholomew and William Bankier.

A police force was set up in 1819, and since duty in the Calton was reckoned to be particularly dangerous the men were issued with cutlasses. As a result they cleared the district of resurrectionists, nearly amputating the arm of a body-snatcher caught robbing a grave in Calton burying-ground. This was generally approved of as a 'wholesome blood-letting'. After 1846 the Calton police, under Assistant Superintendent James Smart, became the eastern division of the Glasgow force. One of their first duties was to quell a bread riot in John Street, Bridgeton, in 1848. In circumstances not unlike those of 1787, stones were thrown at the police, who fired on the crowd, killing a collier, David Carruth, and fatally wounding two other men. The chief of the Glasgow police resigned after an enquiry, his replacement died shortly after, and James Smart was appointed to the post which he held until 1870, becoming the first officer to hold the title of Chief Constable of Glasgow. In 1869 a new police station was opened in Tobago Street. The main building contained the court

This shop and public house were photographed in 1904 at what was then the corner of Canning Street and Clyde Street, now London Road and Abercromby Street.

room, mortuary, muster hall and other offices with thirty cells at the back. The two single-storey wings at either side were occupied by the fire brigade, cleansing and lighting departments. The building was vacated in 1981, when the new police headquarters for the eastern division were opened in London Road.

Another social problem which was energetically tackled after Calton became part of Glasgow was the clearance of overcrowded housing. In 1849 the city was seized with a 'dinging-doun' fever as the result of the collapse of a house in Gorbals during an Irish wake. The Dean of Guild began to inspect all premises liable to collapse and his chief target in the Calton was the notorious 'Whisky Close' at 32 New Street. This was a long, narrow close, five feet in width, occupied by seventy families, mostly Irish, occupying a four-storey brick tenement on one side and a lower house on the other. The occupants earned their living as weavers, labourers, and hawkers of china, hardwear, sponges, fish, fruit and onions. It was considered by the authorities in the eastern district as the greatest plague-spot within their bounds. The 'Whisky Close' was finally demolished by the City Improvement Trust shortly after 1866. A wide new street was laid out on its 'foul surface' and named after the lord provost, Sir James Bain. Bain Square was laid out in 1874 and was used as a children's playground until the area was recently landscaped.

One result of the 'dinging-doun' was to reduce the amount of accommodation available and drive the homeless into lodging-houses. The best-known chronicler of the common Glasgow lodging-house was a half-literate street hawker called William Cameron, better known as 'Hawkie', whose autobiograghy was published in 1888, thirty-seven years after his death. Despite the basis of reality on which his stories are founded, Hawkie's much-quoted accounts of the squads of rats which moved whole eggs by ingenious teamwork and ate the corpse in the next bed are rather too much to swallow. 'Hawkie' was not a native of the Calton, but of the Plean, a village in Stirlingshire. One of Hawkie's stances was Calton Cross, where he scraped a living by spinning tall yarns to draw a crowd, exchanging repartee with onlookers, then selling off his stock of chapbooks or cheap novelettes to his audience in the same way that patter-merchants do their 'shericking' at 'the Barras' today.

The first group to seriously tackle the problem of housing homeless people was the Model Lodging Association, whose members bought a property in Greendyke Street in 1849 with the aim of providing an alternative to the squalid common lodging-houses of the type described by Hawkie. After 1866 the town council built seven model lodging-houses at a cost of £90,000. One of these, in Abercromby Street, remained in use until 1981, when it went on fire and was demolished. One of its cubicles, with bed, stool, coat hooks, lockable cupboard and mirror was formerly on display in the People's Palace.

Two women of the Calton: 'the best people in the world'

As a plaque outside 244 Gallowgate announces, Glasgow's famous weekend street market, 'the Barras', was established by Mr and Mrs James McIver in 1921. The best-known member of the family was Mrs McIver, who became known as Maggie McIver, the Barrows Queen. Maggie was brought up in Bridgeton and started in business selling fruit from her own barrow at the Scotch Fruit Bazaar in the Gallowgate, and then from a shop. After the First World War the McIvers hit on the idea of renting out barrows to the clothes hawkers who until this time had operated from the old clothes market in Greendyke Street. The barrows were made and repaired at a yard in Marshall Lane, and the McIvers were soon hiring out 300 barrows at 1s 6d per week. Around 1920, when a number of tenements were demolished in the Gallowgate, they bought ground as a permanent site for a market, build stalls, then roofed and enclosed the market in 1928.

The next business venture was the opening of the Barrowland Ballroom above the market on Christmas Eve 1934. The hall was licensed to hold 1,250 dancers, but the first night the hawkers were the guests of honour. The resident band was Billy McGregor and his Barrowland Gaybirds, and for many years Lena Martell was resident vocalist, singing under her own name of Ellen Thomson. Another local girl, Lulu, has performed many times at Barrowland. The people of the Calton have recorded their memories of 'the Barras' and these have been published in an entertaining and informative book called *Barrapatter.* 'The Barras' also provided inspiration for the late Matt McGinn, writer and singer of popular ballads, whose songs have been published under the title *McGinn of the Calton.*

Betty McAllister is another distinguished Calton woman, whose campaign for better housing, jobs, community facilities and a better environment has brought her a MBE. Mrs McAllister was born in Bankier Street, and when she set up a residents' association in the

A bare-footed boy at the Barrows. This is one of the photographs taken by Peter Fyfe, Glasgow's chief sanitary inspector, just before the First World War to illustrate poverty in the Calton area.

1970s, five hundred people turned up at St James' School. She was also the recipient of the rosebowl awarded in 1984 to the *Evening Times* Scotswoman of the Year for the part she played in reviving the community spirit which has always been a feature of life in the Calton, and which is summed up in her own words: 'I love the Calton and I think the people in the East End are the best people in the world . . . therefore they deserve the best.'

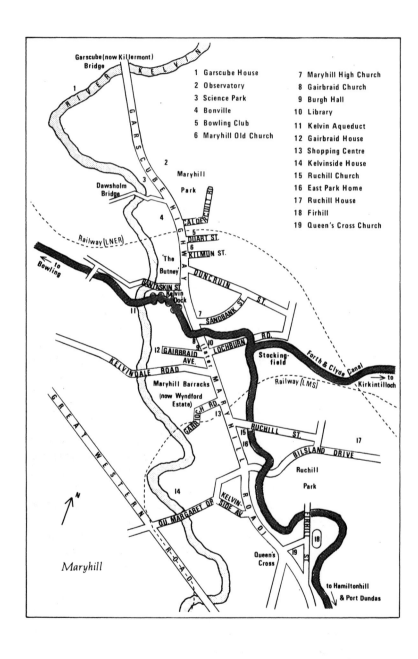

Garscube (now Killermont) Bridge

1 Garscube House
2 Observatory
3 Science Park
4 Bonville
5 Bowling Club
6 Maryhill Old Church
7 Maryhill High Church
8 Gairbraid Church
9 Burgh Hall
10 Library
11 Kelvin Aqueduct
12 Gairbraid House
13 Shopping Centre
14 Kelvinside House
15 Ruchill Church
16 East Park Home
17 Ruchill House
18 Firhill
19 Queen's Cross Church

RIVER KELVIN

GARSCUBE HIGHWAY

Maryhill Park

Dawsholm Bridge

Railway (LNER)

to Bowling

The Butney

RANTASKIN ST.
Kelvin Dock

CALDES

DUART ST.
KILMUN ST.

DUNCRUIN ST.

SANDBANK ST.

LOCHBURN RD.

GAIRBRAID AVE.

KELVINDALE ROAD

Stockingfield

Forth & Clyde Canal

Railway (LMS)

to Kirkintilloch

Maryhill Barracks (now Wyndford Estate)

GARRIOCH RD.

MARYHILL ROAD

RUCHILL ST.

BILSLAND DRIVE

Ruchill Park

GREAT WESTERN ROAD

QU MARGARET OR SIDE AV.

KELVIN ROAD

FIRHILL ST.

Queen's Cross

N

Maryhill

to Hamiltonhill & Port Dundas

4
MARYHILL

Maryhill originated as an industrial village laid out on the north part of the Gairbraid estate by the owner, Mary Hill, and her husband, Robert Graham, of Kilmanan, at the end of the eighteenth century. Mary and Robert never did fulfil their grandiose scheme for a town 'which is to extend from Glasgow to Garscube Bridge', but by granting feus only on condition that buildings should 'in all time coming be called Maryhill', the proprietrice of the estate achieved her own kind of immortality. The Grahams were imitating gentility like Sir James Colquhoun of Luss, who named Helensburgh for his wife, or the Earl of Eglinton, who had the streets of Eaglesham laid out in the form of an 'A', because that was the initial letter of his wife's name.

Maryhill village was laid out some time after the Forth and Clyde Canal reached Stockingfield in 1775. The canal was subsequently extended in two directions: along the Glasgow branch to Port Dundas; and towards the Clyde estuary at Bowling. Bleachfields, printfields, weaving mills and paper mills grew up along the Kelvin, followed by sawmills, boatyards and iron foundries along the canal. By 1856 the village had grown sufficiently to be granted burgh status, although gentlemen's estates still lay along either side of the Garscube Highway, as Maryhill Road was then known. It was not until heavy industries brought an even greater influx of population into the district in the last quarter of the nineteenth century that the green fields were sold off to property developers and disappeared under tenements, leaving only street names such as Gairbraid Avenue, Ruchill Street, Kelvinside Avenue and Garrioch Road as reminders of their origin.

In 1912, when Maryhill was absorbed into Glasgow, the burgh became one of the city's largest suburbs, extending northwards, as Mary Hill had foreseen, from Queen's Cross to the city boundary at Killermont. Today Maryhill is a blend of these nineteenth- and twentieth-century tenements which survived the wholesale demolition of the 1950s, new houses of imaginative design which are gradually filling the ugly gaps, council estates, including the first corporation houses to be built in Glasgow just after the First World War at Duncruin Street, and the award-winning Wyndford estate, with its 26-storey flats on the site of the former Maryhill barracks, and a few old cottages scattered here and there along the banks of the canal and in the north of the village.

A place in the country: Gairbraid, Ruchill and Garscube

The first inhabitants of Maryhill whose names are known to us were a family of Hutchesons who held the lands of Gairbraid as rentallers of the Archbishop of Glasgow. In 1600 Gairbraid was purchased by George Hutcheson, one of the two brothers who founded Hutchesons' Hospital, and who belonged to the Lambhill branch of the family. Both brothers died childless and Gairbraid passed to their nephew, Ninian Hill, and then eventually to Ninian's granddaughter, Mary Hill, who inherited the estate on the death of her father, Hew. A 'Plan of Laigh Gairbraid Farm' drawn by Charles Ross shows how the estate looked in 1759. It includes a sketch of the farmhouse, built in 1688, a substantial dwelling on two floors, with offices, gardens, a Laigh Park, a Cow Park and an East Park. The farmhouse appears to be on the same site as the later mansion-house, that is, where the Kelvindale Laundry once stood to the west of Gairbraid Place.

Robert Graham, who married the Gairbraid heiress in 1763, was variously known as 'of Dalsholm', 'of Barley Mills', and 'of Kilmanan'. He was a figure of romance, having been captured and enslaved by Algerian pirates. Having no income from trade like some of their Glasgow merchant neighbours, the Grahams could not improve their estate until they found some way of creating wealth from it. Robert seems to have attempted to extract some income from sinking coal pits, but despite his reputation as a 'bold and energetic speculator', he failed to make a profit. Portions on the north of his wife's estate were sold off to adjoining proprietors. The part of Maryhill known as Acre was once the acre of ground which Graham held back from a sale in order to 'big colliers' houses'. Acre House, a nineteenth-century villa, is now owned by Glasgow University and the grounds are shared by the observatory and buildings of the department of physics and astronomy, the hydrodynamics laboratory and the department of naval architecture and ocean engineering. Another coal speculator who failed was Robert Walker, who built Bonville, and whose son gifted the Walker Art Gallery to Liverpool. The Maryhill coal was of good quality, but the pits were wet and pumping was too expensive.

The Grahams' ship finally came home when it was decided to take the Forth and Clyde Canal through the Gairbraid estate. A new mansion-house was built in 1789 and the north part of the estate was laid out in feus for an industrial village. This house, as well as the mansions of Ruchill, Kelvinside and Garscube, is illustrated in *Old Country Houses of the Old Glasgow Gentry*.

Robert Graham died in 1804, aged eighty-two, and Mary Hill died in 1809, aged seventy-nine. Both are buried in the grounds of Glasgow Cathedral. The stone built into the south wall of the churchyard includes the name of their daughter Lilias, who continued to live at Gairbraid until her death in 1836. The estate then passed to her sister's son, John Dunlop, who acquired a bad reputation in Maryhill as an absentee landlord who reneged on his promises to give land free to the burgh for recreational purposes. Dunlop was so horrified by the scenes of drunkenness that he saw around him on a visit to Gairbraid in 1829 that he returned home to Greenock and founded the first temperance society in Great Britain, but not before he had persuaded his aunt and her companion to sign the pledge. In November 1829 a men's temperance society was formed in Maryhill Free Church, with the minister and ninety others, mainly tradesmen, as signatories. At this time there was one licensed house to every fifty-nine Maryhill residents. In his temperance work Dunlop was assisted by Edward Collins of the Kelvindale paper mills and the celebrated bible-printing firm. The first abstainers refused 'the scorching brandy, the burning rum, the fiery whisky and the stinging gin', but did not refuse ale or wine, sales of which increased. Edward Morris, a clerk in the canal Swift boat passenger office at Port Dundas, was active in the later campaign, which demanded total abstinence and laws to bring drinking under control.

The Gairbraid family seems to have had its full quota of eccentrics. Mary Hill's other grandson, William, was the 'Tiger Dunlop' who settled in Ontario, built a highway 'through the thickest of bush and swamp' from Toronto to Goderich on Lake Huron, and called his Canadian home 'Gairbraid'. His will contained the following bequests:

> I leave my silver tankard to the eldest son of Old John, as the representative of the family. I would have left it to Old John himself, but he would have melted it down to make temperance medals, and that would have been a sacrilege. However, I have left him my big horn snuff-box; he can only make temperance spoons out of that.

The author of *Old Country Houses of the Old Glasgow Gentry*, writing of Gairbraid in 1878, laments the passing of a whole way of life:

> The old house now stands naked and forlorn amidst a wilderness of 'free coups', broken bottles and bricks, pools of dirty water, clothes lines fluttering with part-coloured rags and all the abominations of a new suburb. Instead of the singing of birds and the music of the soft flowing Kelvin, which of yore pleased and refreshed the passer-by, the air is now vocal with the discordant voices of rough men, scolding women, and 'greeting bairns', with the clang of machinery and the hiss of the steam engine.

The Industrial Revolution had reached Maryhill!

Ruchill estate was purchased early in the eighteenth century by James Peadie, a sugar merchant and Provost of Glasgow, who moved out of the city to what was then called 'Roughill'. In 1749 Ruchill passed to Allan Dreghorn, one of the first men to start up the trade in tobacco with Virginia, and owner of the famous Dreghorn Mansion in Clyde Street. This Dreghorn was succeeded by his nephew Robert, the notorious 'Bob Dragon' a tall, thin, gaunt figure, the ugliest and

Garscube House, built in 1827 to a design by William Burn for Sir Archibald Campbell of Succoth. Part of the estate was made into Dawsholm Park in 1921 and the remainder purchased by the University of Glasgow, who demolished the house in 1954 because of dry rot.

most profligate man in Glasgow, with a bent nose and squint eyes and his face deeply pitted by small-pox.

Part of Ruchill was detached at an early date to form an estate first called 'Bankhead', then later renamed 'Kelvinside'. Kelvinside House, built in 1750, stood near the top of Botanic Crescent, and is claimed as the birthplace of the Liberal prime minister, Sir Henry Campbell-Bannerman. The estate was sold around 1870 by the last owner, Matthew Montgomerie, and then built over with tenements. Garrioch was also detached from the Ruchill estate and sold in 1869 to the government for barracks. The boundaries of Garrioch estate are represented today by the barracks wall which was retained round the Wyndford housing estate.

The last owner of Ruchill was William James Davidson, an East India merchant, who sold the estate to the city of Glasgow, which reserved the eastern portion for Ruchill Hospital, laid out Ruchill Park and the Glasgow North-Western (now Ruchill) golf courses and used the remainder for housing. The artificial summit of Ruchill Park, known as 'Ben Whitton' after the Director of Cleansing who built it, was created by taking the earth excavated from the foundations of the hospital and adding it to the top of the existing hill to form the present fine viewpoint.

The only estate which has survived almost intact is Garscube, which forms a welcome green belt between Maryhill and the housing estates at Killermont beyond the Glasgow city boundary. The Garscube estate came into the hands of the Campbells of Succoth in 1687. The most distinguished member of this legal family was Sir Ilay, the first baronet, who rose to be Lord President in 1789. A memoir written by the butler, Mr Robb, describes the life-style at Garscube during the time of the second baronet, Sir Archibald, a judge of the Court of Session. Sir Archibald and Lady Campbell spent the winter in the capital, returning to Glasgow in early March 'to escape the east winds in Edinburgh'. The family travelled by large family coach, their luggage went by road on two hay waggons and the servants went by the Forth and Clyde canal 'on boats drawn by horses'. Lady Campbell's passion was planting wild flowers to beautify the estate grounds. 'Always at 3 p.m. her pony [called Cumlodden] was ready and the odd man with his barrow she claimed till 5 or 6 o'clock and one of the journeymen gardners she had with his tools and seeds.' Sir Archibald, on the other hand, 'being very fond of a good dinner and good cooking was always consulted about the Bill of Fare, and paid generally a daily visit to the kitchen. Sir Archibald got often presents of turtle from the shipping firms in Glasgow, turtle soup was a great favourite with him. Sometimes they were kept alive in the bathroom, fed on lettuce leaves and killed when wanted.'

When Sir Archibald died in 1846 an inventory was made of his effects at Garscube. He owned a considerable collection of paintings and books, including 338 volumes in the study and 2,803 volumes in the library. Of the total estate of £6,582, silver plate accounted for £2,585 and the contents of the wine cellar £1,043. This included 202 dozen bottles of sherry, 42 dozen bottles of Madeira, 103 dozen bottles of claret, but only 1 dozen 9 bottles of whisky (value £1.15s) and 1 dozen 11 bottles of brandy (value £5.15s).

In 1921 seventy-two acres of Garscube estate were made into Dawsholm Park by Glasgow Corporation. The University of Glasgow purchased much of the remainder for use by the department of veterinary science. Part is now occupied by the Wolfson Hall of Residence, built in 1964 and by the West of Scotland Science Park, and other ground is given over to outdoor and indoor sports. Garscube House was made into flats for lecturers, but dry rot meant that it had to be demolished in 1954.

The grounds of Garscube House afforded an unrivalled setting for a great historical pageant, the 'Story of the West', performed each evening during the last week of June 1928, covering the broad sweep of history from the time of St Mungo to the coming of Prince Charlie to Glasgow at Christmas 1745. The purpose was to raise funds for a new dental hospital in Glasgow to replace the outdated building at the corner of Renfrew and Dalhousie Streets, where the accommodation was altogether inadequate – chairs in the operating room packed so closely that there was scarcely room to move, laboratories and classrooms anything but hygenic, a crowded, badly ventilated waiting room and people queuing outside in the rain waiting for the only free dental treatment in Glasgow.

The spot chosen was a wooded part of the estate with the Kelvin in the background where a level grassy haugh, half-circled by a sloping bank, formed a large natural arena. This area is now part of the university playing fields. The pageant was presented by a cast of 7,000 performers, singers and dancers in four episodes: the Legend of Languoreth; the Invasion of Somerled; the Story of Glasgow's Trade; Prince Charles Edward in Glasgow. The programme tells us that among the performers are knights, squires and and ladies on

One of the knights taking part in the great historical pageant at Garscube in 1928 takes time off to quench his thirst with a glass of the local Castle Ale produced at Maclachlan's brewery at Maryhill.

horseback, monks and bishops, tobacco lords, Glasgow bailies and councillors. Sailors sing sea-shanties as they roll barrels down to the quays, and the washerwomen on the Green, armed with wet clothes and soap-suds set about impudent students and apprentices. There are old-fashioned country dances and a mystery play is presented from the top of three wagons by the School of Art Dramatic Society. A dragon-ship is dragged up the river by a hundred Viking warriors, and the great battle of Renfrew is enacted on the green haugh beside the Kelvin at Garscube. Somerled, the mighty Lord of the Isles is slain, his ships (lent by Yarrows) captured, his forces utterly routed. The pageant ends as the Highland army, numbering 150 horse and 1,500 foot, is played on by 150 pipers, led by the prince on a white horse, and ends as, with a bow and wave of the hand to Clementina Walkinshaw, Prince Charlie and his army march off to Culloden.

The Forth and Clyde Canal: 'a ditch, a gutter, a mere puddle'

The Forth and Clyde Canal was surveyed and planned in 1763 by John Smeaton, but it took five years of heated debate before a route was finally agreed. Glasgow merchants, displeased that the proposed route would bypass the city, engaged Robert Mackell and James Watt to draw up an alternative scheme for a canal which would enter the Clyde at Glasgow where the river was then only four feet deep. This alternative plan was immediately attacked in the Edinburgh press, being described as 'a ditch, a gutter, a mere puddle', which might serve the purposes of trade, but not those of 'magnificence and national honour, which was the sort of thing that men of Enlightenment in Edinburgh expected. 'What is commerce to the city of Edinburgh?' it

An engraving of the Kelvin Aqueduct made about 1825. The 400-ft aqueduct, which carries the Forth and Clyde Canal across the River Kelvin at a height of 70 ft, was considered lone of the most stupendous works of the kind perhaps in the world when it was completed in 1790.

was asked. 'Edinburgh, Sir, is the metropolis of this ancient kingdom, the seat of Law, the rendezvous of Politeness, the abode of Taste, and the winter quarters of all our nobility who cannot afford to live in London; and for these and other reasons equally cogent Edinburgh ought to have the lead upon all occasions. The fools of the west must wait for the Wise Men of the East.'

Eventually a compromise was reached by the promise of a collateral cut to Glasgow city centre, and work got underway at Grangemouth in 1768. In 1773 the canal was navigable from the Forth to Kirkintilloch; in 1775 it was extended to Stockingfield; and in 1777 the Glasgow branch was completed as far as Hamiltonhill, which 'immediately became a busier port than the Broomielaw' and a focus for industrial growth. Wyndford takes its name from Wyndford Bridge at lock 20, seventeen miles to the east at the other end of the summit stretch near Castlecary.

By this time the canal company had run out of funds, and no work took place for nine years. In 1784 the company received from the government an advance of £50,000 out of the monies realised by the sale of estates forfeited after the 45 Rising. In 1786 work began again at Stockingfield under a new superintendent, Robert Whitworth, and four years later the canal reached Bowling and was opened for traffic, with appropriate ceremony, on 28 July 1790. The Glasgow branch was extended to Port Dundas in 1790 and in 1791 a cut of junction was made to the Monkland Canal, which served the dual purpose of improving the water supply and extending the trade routes.

Maryhill became something of a tourist mecca at this time with visitors flocking to view the locks and the great aqueduct, described with pride by the Rev. John Burns, minister of the Barony parish of which Maryhill then formed part:

> The great bridge over Kelvin was begun in June 1787 and finished in April 1791. It is carried over a valley 400 feet long, and 65 deep. It consists of four very large arches of excellent masonry work; is in height about 83 feet from the bed of the river to the top of the bridge and is one of the most stupendous works of the kind perhaps in the world.

A committee, which included Sir Ilay Campbell, met every month to award contracts, make appointments and deal with the day-to-day problems of running the canal. Contracts were awarded to Walter Johnstone, mason in Govan, to build two bridges to carry the canal over Lochburn Road and the Garscube Highway, and to William

Gibb and John Moir to build locks nos. 24 and 25 (the two most westerly of the five locks at Maryhill), 'provided they will agree to execute the same at Seven pounds per rood'. The committee accepted Mr Whitworth's plans for a graving dock on the north side of the basin between locks 22 and 23, where 'Nature seems almost to have formed the proposed situation for such a purpose'. The old wooden locks have since been replaced by steel ones and a lock built at the basin as part of the Millennium Link project to refurbish the canal. So that the canal could cross the Garscube highway at a right angle, the old road had to be realigned between the present Gairbraid Avenue and Bantaskin Street. The old road lay further east, passing round behind the present public library and along Aray Street. Seventy years after it was built, alterations had to be made to the bridge to enable the water pipes from Loch Katrine to Glasgow to pass underneath, and in 1881 Johnstone's bridge was replaced by a new bridge just to the south which gave more space and headroom to the horse trams. The bridge over Lochburn Road is still Johnstone's original 'pen' or 'pend' bridge.

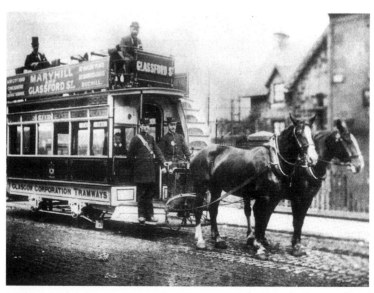

A horse-drawn tram at the Maryhill terminus at Duart Street. Horse-trams were a common sight on Glasgow roads from 1872 until electrification of the whole tramway system was completed in 1901.

It is worth walking on along the canal from Stockingfield to Glasgow to see the remaining canal structures such as the aqueduct at Bilsland Drive (built 1879) and the timber basin at Firhill (built 1788, extended 1849) and the canal cottages at the Old Basin at Hamiltonhill beside the offices of the British Waterways Board, which took over responsibility for the canal after it closed in 1963. The standard Forth and Clyde wooden bascule bridges at Firhill Street and Baird's Brae have been replaced by fixed bridges, but the original bascule bridge at Port Dundas is still intact.

As well as opening up the Maryhill area for industry, the canal created a new means of travel across central Scotland. In 1809 travellers could sail on the *Charlotte* or the *Margaret* between Port Dundas and Camelon, with coach connections to Glasgow and Edinburgh. Cabins were heated with stoves, meals and drinks served, and passengers could while away the five and a half hour journey with books and games or by listening to fiddle music. Twenty years later, light iron passage boats called 'swifts' were introduced, drawn by two horses with a liveried postillion on the second horse. On straight stretches the horses galloped at nine miles per hour and the journey was cut down to three hours. The swifts were soon restricted to night use only when they could race along without upsetting other traffic, blazing their headlights and blowing their horns. They became known as 'hoolets'. After the Edinburgh–Glasgow railway opened in 1842 there was little demand for passenger transport on the canal.

The last era of canal sailing was that of the pleasure steamers which began operating in the last decades of the nineteenth century and continued until World War Two. These much loved steamers were the *Rockvilla Castle*, the two *Fairy Queens*, the *May Queen* and the *Gipsy Queen*, which picked up Maryhill passengers at Ruchill Bridge. In its latter years the only boats to pass through the locks at Maryhill were pleasure craft and east coast fishing boats taking a short cut to the west coast herring fishing. One surprise visitor was the midget submarine XE IX in June 1952, which was going through from the Clyde to the Forth.

The canal was finally closed on 1 January 1963, but in recognition of a renewed interest in canal use for leisure and recreation, the Forth and Clyde Canal Society was formed in 1980. With much co-operation between local communities along the canal banks and the British Waterways Board, the canal was finally re-opened on 26 May

2001, when a flottila of over forty boats made the three-day journey from lock 16 at Falkirk to the Clyde at Bowling.

From industrial village to police burgh

One of the oldest industries on the Kelvin was paper-making, which was begun at Woodside in the 1680s. A century later William Macarthur started a paper mill on the west side of the Kelvin just below Dawsholm Bridge. The paper-making firm always used the spelling 'Dalsholm' although the Campbells of Garscube insisted that 'Dawsholm' was correct. Around 1830 the Collins family took over another paper mill a little further downstream at Balgray, built a mansion alongside, and changed the name to Kelvindale. In 1960 Kelvindale had 400 employees and Dalsholm had 70. Both works are now closed. The site at Dalsholm has been landscaped and incorporated into the Kelvin Walkway. At Kelvindale a few firm's houses remain, although the site has been used for modern housing. Kelvindale Buildings is a two-storey red brick building with decorative bands of yellow brick. Two similar villas on Kelvindale Road may be a manager's and a foreman's house.

Another early industry at Dawsholm was calico printing, begun by William Stirling, who moved in 1770 to a larger site at Cordale in the Vale of Leven. These printworks were demolished by Glasgow Corporation in 1872 to make way for some gas works, now also demolished. A second printworks was begun on the Maryhill side of the river in the 1830s. This was the Maryhill printworks, operated at one time by Messrs Reid and Whiteman, who introduced cylinder printing by machine to replace hand block printing. The partners also owned an adjacent handloom weaving factory which in its heyday employed two hundred hands, but was superseded by the 1850s by a powerloom factory using steam power erected in Wyndford by a Fife manufacturer, Robert Jeffrey. This factory was demolished in the 1890s to make way for Messrs Maclauchlan's Castle Brewery. The site is now occupied by the Maryhill division of Strathclyde Police.

The opening of the canal brought boat-building, sawmilling and iron founding to Maryhill. The first tenant of the graving dock planned by Whitworth was Thomas Morrison, and the district quickly became known as 'the Dock', 'Drydock' or 'Kelvindock'. David Swan, who married Morrison's granddaughter, took over the business in 1837 and the Swan family carried on shipbuilding until 1893. The Swans built iron ships in sections which were sent to Bowling for assembly, and also built the first custom-built screw lighter, the *Glasgow*, in 1857. This type of vessel soon acquired the nickname 'puffer' from the noise of its exhaust exiting through the funnel. More than sixty puffers were built at Kelvindock between the 1860s and 1921 – both 'inside' puffers for canal use and sea-going 'outside' puffers. The Swans also had a sawmill alongside the dock, but could not compete with larger sawmills at Firhill and Ruchill. The Swans lived in Collina Cottage, 'a superior cottage commanding a view of the whole of Maryhill'. The same fine view is enjoyed today by the residents of the high flats at Collina Place.

Several foundries and ironworks were started along the canal by young men from Falkirk, where Carron Works had begun in 1759. These included Messrs Aitken and Allan, who founded the Kelvin foundry between the canal and Lochburn Road in 1838, James Shaw's Maryhill foundry on the Glasgow branch behind Lochburn Park, and Thomas Allan's large Springbank ironworks at Queen's Cross. These once large enterprises have long disappeared, but the Firhill ironworks, started by Shaw & McInnes in 1866, continued in business on their original site at Firhill Road until 2000. Several of the ironmasters brought their own labour force of 'Falkirk bairns' to work as skilled iron and sand moulders, iron dressers, stocktakers, smiths and wrights. Nineteen of the thirty-seven families living in 'Allan's Land' near the Springbank ironworks came from the Falkirk area. The remainder, employed mostly as foundry labourers, were Irish, plus a few West Highlanders, notably from Islay, who have left us with the names of Dunard, Bonawe and Dalmally Streets.

The Glasgow branch of the canal remained largely undeveloped for industry between Stockingfield and Firhill until the 1870s, when the Glasgow lead and colour works was built for Alexander Fergusson & Co. on a site at rural Ruchill, where no-one would be troubled by the pungent smells given off by the paint manufacturing process. This business is now closed, but their neighbours, McLellan & Co., whose works date from the same decade, still manufacture industrial rubber components. Later arrivals on the stretch of canal between Bilsland aqueduct and Firhill Basin were the Ruchill oil works, the Caledonian glass bottle works, the Glasgow glass works and the Firhill glass bottle works. Not surprisingly the street of tenement houses above these works was named Murano Street, a reference to the famous Venetian glass works. This industrial site was cleared in the 1970s and developed for student accommodation in modern flats.

As factories grew up along river and canal, the feus offered by Mary Hill were gradually taken up and built over by 'lands', the buildings erected by tradesmen or manufacturers for their workers and sometimes for their own families as well. For example, Scott's land was occupied by Scott, a builder, and masons and joiners who were his employees. A 'Plan of Gairbraid and Maryhill Village', dating from the early nineteenth century, shows the original village extending from the canal to Duart Street, with feus laid out on both sides of the Garscube highway. Whitelaw, Reid, Kelvin and Walker Streets are laid out on a grid pattern (later Whitelaw, Cowal, Lochgilp and Glencloy Streets) with the words TOWN OF MARYHILL written across them and the feus to the north. Two rows of feus near the canal are named as 'Mary's Hill Feu's' on ground now occupied by nos. 1668–1698 Maryhill Road, and 'Botany Feu's' at the foot of Bantaskine Street, where a new road has been constructed. A story was devised that 'the Butney', as the area became known, was named after the penal colony begun at Botany Bay in Australia in 1787. One version of the story is that the canal was built by convicts who were given the choice: Maryhill or exile. Another is that conditions for the workers on the canal or in the printfield were akin to penal servitude. The area has now been redeveloped with modern housing.

By 1850 the population of Maryhill village had risen to around three thousand. Half of the families were Irish, with the proportion in 'the Butney' being three-quarters. In the next few years there was an influx of labourers into the district to build the Glasgow to Helensburgh railway line on the north of the village and to lay the water pipes from Loch Katrine to Glasgow under Maryhill Road. A favourite muster point for ruffians at this time was the top of Kelvin Street, 'from which spot pedestrians would be saluted with a shower of stones or receive a blow from a half brick shied at them'. Clearly this state of affairs could not continue, and a petition signed by the requisite number of inhabitants was presented to the sheriff of Lanarkshire and the necessary formalities gone through to create Maryhill a police burgh in 1856. It is said that the last straw for the long-suffering villagers was the refusal of Glasgow to lend them two constables, even though they offered to pay their salaries! One of the first appointments was George Anderson as superintendent of police and fiscal and the first burgh building was built in 1857 on the northernmost of the 'Mary's Hill

feu's', with accommodation for police officers and offenders, A coat
of arms was designed in the form of a shield with a representation of
the aqueduct with a ship on top and symbols of engineering, founding
and saw-milling beneath and the motto 'Vires acquirit eundo' ('We
gather strength in our cause').

In 1878, with forty-five different manufactories now in the burgh,
the police commissioners embarked on a programme of public
building. The centrepiece were the municipal buildings designed
by Duncan McNaughton in French Renaissance style. One of the
features of the hall were twenty stained glass windows representing
various trades and manufactures carried on in the burgh. These
splendid windows, produced by the firm of Stephen Adam, the
leading stained glass artist of the time in Scotland, are now preserved
in the People's Palace. By the time the public library was opened

The glass blower. One of twenty stained-glass windows produced for
Maryhill Burgh Hall by Stephen Adam depicting typical industes carried
on in the burgh. There were several glassworks along the canal bank from
Bilsland Drive to Firhill Basin.

in 1905, Maryhill had become part of the city of Glasgow. During its thirty-five years as a burgh, from 1856 to 1891, Maryhill had six provosts: David Swan, James Shaw, James Robertson, John Murray, John Craig and James Stirrat.

Many Maryhill men became leading figures in Glasgow affairs. Sir Charles Cleland, who lived all his life at Bonville, was the first chairman of Glasgow Education Authority. Robert Jeffrey, proprietor of Wyndford mill, left his reference library of over four thousand volumes to the city in 1902, many of high value and great rarity. The collection contains many illustrated volumes on natural history, travel, antiquaries and art, and includes Audubon's great *Birds of America*. The 'Jeffrey Room' in the Mitchell Library was used for many years for public lectures and then as a public search room for users of Strathclyde Regional Archives, but is no longer open to the public. The handsome bookcases round the walls were the work of Laird of Kelvinbridge and are decorated with fine carvings of the Jeffrey crest of the sun rising out of clouds.

Maryhill Barracks

The long saga of finding a site for new barracks in Glasgow began in the 1850s when the town council drew the attention of the government to 'the inadequate provision now made for the preservation of the Public Peace in this City and Neighbourhood', particularly 'on those occasions of Riot and Tumult which too frequently occur in the manufacturing and populous districts of the Country produced it may be by temporary stagnation in trade and want of employment among the Labouring Classes'. It was pointed out that in 1795, when the population of Glasgow was 73,000, the military accommodation was for one regiment of infantry and a detachment of cavalry, whereas in 1866, when the population was half a million, there was accommodation for only half a regiment of infantry and no detachment of cavalry. Smoke and squalor had made the infantry barracks in the Gallowgate unsuitable, and the cavalry barracks in Eglinton Street had been sold to the Parochial Board of Govan to be converted into a workhouse for the poor.

At first the military authorities favoured a site at Cowlairs as having most of the advantages required for new barracks – good elevation, good supply of water, free access by rail to all parts of the country and ready access by rail or road to the centre of the town. However,

A group of gunners, with mascot, at Maryhill Barracks in 1894. The barracks were demolished in the 1960s and the site is now the Wyndford housing estate. The barracks wall and picket-house were preserved.

the site was discounted because it was 'with certain winds under the influence of smoke from the tall chimneys of Chemical Works'. Hyndland was then considered as a possible site, but rejected because 'the lands of Hyndlands . . . are entirely exposed to the view of the Inhabitants of the Asylum [Gartnavel] which would be prejudicial to the latter' and also the land was too expensive. Eventually the government purchased thirty acres of the Garrioch estate from Davidson of Ruchill in 1869, and accepted estimates of £100,000 for the erection of the new barracks. A dispute with the contractor stopped all work from 1871 to 1873, when the War Office purchased an additional twenty-seven acres and had the work completed by the Royal Engineers. When the buildings were completed in 1876 there was accommodation for a regiment of infantry, a squadron of cavalry and a battery of field artillery. The barracks also contained stables, a chapel, a hospital for sixty patients, accommodation for fourteen sick horses, a prison with cells for twenty-one offenders and recreational facilities. One third of the site, nearest the Kelvin, was used for exercise ground.

Over the years the barracks were occupied by various regiments

stationed in Glasgow. In 1920 part of the barracks became the depot of
the Highland Light Infantry, which in 1923 officially became the City
of Glasgow Regiment. The Elephant and Bugle pub near the barracks'
gate takes its name from the badge of the HLI which included a bugle-
horn (a Light Infantry badge) and the elephant (the old badge of the
74th Highlanders). The insignia of the elephant was awarded to the
74th Highlanders (2nd Battalion HLI) for its epic stand at the Battle of
Assaye in India in 1803. This famous victory also brought the regiment
the unusual distinction of the third colour, known as the Assaye
Colour, now laid up in the chapter-house of Glasgow Cathedral. The
Highland Light Infantry vacated the barracks in 1958 and moved to
Ayr where they amalgamated with the Royal Scots Fusiliers to form
the Royal Highland Fusiliers. Rudolph Hess was put into the charge
of the Cameronians at Maryhill after he was captured in 1940 before
being transferred to the Tower of London.

The site was then taken over by Glasgow Corporation, who
removed the barracks and built the Wyndford housing estate: four
blocks of twenty-six stories, five blocks of fifteen stories, one block of
nine stories, and also blocks of eight, four and three stories, making a
total of 1898 houses of one, two, three and four apartments for 5,493
people. The scheme was completed in 1968 and won an award from
the Saltire Society for good design. The infantry parade was retained
as a grassed-over area, as well as the barracks wall round the estate
and the picket-house. A plan to demolish the wall in order to widen
Maryhill was dropped in the face of local opposition, and the historic
landmark remains. Maryhill shopping centre and car park stand on
the site of the former barracks station (later Maryhill Central). Traces
of the railway can be seen disappearing eastwards under the canal
and into a tunnel beneath Ruchill golf course. Westwards the line
crossed the Kelvin over a bridge which stands at the foot of Garrioch
Quadrant.

The veterans' homes at Prince of Wales Gardens off Caldercuilt
Road were opened by the prince just after the First World War. The
Walcheren barracks at the corner of Shakespeare Street and Garrioch
Road is the HQ of the 1st Battalion 52nd Lowland Regiment, formed
in 1967 from the infantry battalions of the old 52nd Lowland Division.
The name commemorates the action in 1944 when the division
invaded and captured the strategic island of Walcheren off the coast
of Holland. The regimental museum of the Royal Highland Fusiliers
is now at 518 Sauchiehall Street.

Churches, schools and social welfare

Until 1850 Maryhill formed part of Barony parish. In 1824 the church later known as Maryhill Old was erected as a chapel of ease on ground gifted by Miss Lilias Graham of Gairbraid. The minister was Robert McNair Wilson, who left the Established Church in 1843 with the bulk of the congregation to form Maryhill Free Church. The first ministers seem to have resided at Eastbank until a manse was built at the north end of the village in 1851. The church was closed in 1981 but has only recently been demolished, and the future of the surrounding churchyard and its monuments is unclear. Many of these recorded the names of Maryhill families, including Allan, Baird, Morrison and Russell. Also in the churchyard, though now removed, was the memorial to George Miller, a calico worker stabbed to death in the Butney in 1834 by a 'nob' or strike-breaker, during a dispute in the printfields over union membership. The congregation of Maryhill Parish Church mow worship in the former church hall, which was built a short distance to the north in 1930 on the site of the old parish school and the schoolmaster's house.

After the minister and his congregation 'came out' at the Disruption, they were obliged to vacate the church and worship for some time in David Swan's sawmill, which became known as 'Maryhill Cathedral'. A site for a new church at Aray Street was gifted by Sir Archibald Hay Campbell of Garscube, and Maryhill Free church was opened in 1848, followed shortly by a school, a teacher's house and a manse. The congregation carried on mission work at Eastpark and appointed a young Gaelic-speaking divinity student 1871 to work among the Highland labourers engaged in the construction of railways in and around the village. The church was later known as Maryhill High and was linked in 1986 with Maryhill Old to form Maryhill Parish Church. Maryhill High Church has now been converted into flats.

The congregation of Gairbraid Church of Scotland have their roots in a United Presbyterian congregation formed in 1856 under the Rev. Robert Niven, for whom the present church was built in 1859 and the manse added in 1868. Records show the members coming to worship from a wide area, from Killermont to Partick.

Two churches in the south of Maryhill parish are noteworthy for their connections with the distinguished architect, Charles Rennie Mackintosh. Mackintosh designed the hall of Ruchill Church, but did not receive the commission for the church. He did, however, design

Charles Rennie Mackintosh's perspective drawing of St Matthew's Church (now Queen's Cross Church). The architect has skillfully overcome the difficulties created by an awkwardly shaped and cramped corner plot.

Queen's Cross Church, opened in 1899. When the congregation amalgamated in 1977 with Ruchill, the Charles Rennie Mackintosh Society negotiated a 21-year lease with the Church of Scotland and in 1999 they were able to purchase the church thanks to a generous bequest by Dr Tom Howarth, Professor Emeritus at the University of Toronto. The church has been extensively restored and is visited by admirers of the architect's work from all over the world. It is the only church designed by Mackintosh which was actually built. The style is Art Nouveau Gothic of a very original variety, with a tower developed from a medieval one which the architect saw at Meriot in Somerset. In the interior Mackintosh's mastery is apparent in his use of the steel ties which cross the nave and the sense of spaciousness given by the high arched ceiling.

Very little is known of the Roman Catholic community in the early village except that it was attached to St Andrew's Cathedral in

Clyde Street. A traditional story relates that an organised procession made its way there from Maryhill each Sunday, headed by a piper, Archie Daroch. In 1851 the foundation stone of a church was laid and the church dedicated in honour of the Immaculate Conception of the Blessed Virgin Mary, the first church in Scotland to be given this title since the Reformation. The church stood for a century between Duncruin Street and Kilmun Street. In 1900 the 'Donegal Side' or aisle was added; this took its name from the many young Donegal men employed in the gas works who favoured that side of the church. The church was badly damaged by the blast of a landmine in 1941. In the log book of the adjacent school is the entry: 'School badly damaged by Air Raid on 14th March 1941, at 11.40 p.m. To all appearances the building is beyond repair.' In Kilmun Street 107 people were killed. St Mary's Primary School was rebuilt on the scene of the disaster, and a new church built on the site of Bonville at the north end of the village. Because of structural problems, this church had to be demolished in the 1980s, but a new Church of the Immaculate Conception has been built on the same site. St Gregory's Church in Kelvindale Road is another place of Catholic worship in Maryhill.

In the middle of the nineteenth century there were schools connected with the parish church, the Free Church and the Catholic Church. Maryhill also had an infant school supported by J.D. Colquhoun of Killermont, and several 'adventure' schools. Shortly after the setting up of the Maryhill School Board in 1873, the parish and Free Church schools were almagamated as Maryhill Public School. The headmaster, Mr John Miller, wrote up his log book in a forthright manner: 'Both Miss Forfar and Mr Cook off today – ill(?).' 'Mr Cook still "non est".' 'Had to dun several of the pupils for their fees. Result unsatisfactory, but "Better an empty house than a bad tenant".' When the unfortunate Mr Miller fell from a tramcar and was killed, the school did not close because the annual inspection, on the results of which the following year's funds depended, was so near, but 'all were so unhinged that little effective work could be done'. In 1884 the school moved to Gilshochill, where it continues today as Maryhill Primary School. Two new primary schools, Wyndford and St Gregory's, have been built side by side on the Wyndford estate.

East Park Home for Infirm Children was begun in 1874 by William Mitchell. In its early years the home was overcrowded with children crippled by rickets, tuberculous joints and various other muscular diseases. The number of children suffering severe physical disabilities

The children of East Park Home cheer on the runners in the Maryhill Mini Marathon of 1987.

has gradually declined and more mentally handicapped children are now being catered for.

In the 1870s East Park was a small hamlet of a dozen houses, almost the only habitation between Springbank and Maryhill. Two old cottages are incorporated into the home. East Park Cottage can be made out at the front, right in the centre. An older cottage, Chapelside, is incorporated into the rear of the building. Both cottages were at one time occupied by David Caughie, who became master at the first model school opened by the Glasgow Infant School Society in the Drygate in 1827 and later taught at the Free Church Normal Seminary at Cowcaddens. Infants memorised little verses to help them learn parsing:

> Three little words we often see
> Are articles – 'a', 'an' and 'the',
> A noun's the name of anything
> As 'school' or 'garden', 'hoop' or 'swing'.

East Park Home has always had a special place in the hearts of Maryhill people and the children play as full a part as possible in the life of the community. The home has been visited by royalty, 'show biz' and TV personalities and receives donations from the general public and businesses large and small. In former years 'treats' for the children included tea parties, concerts, cinematographs, strawberry feasts and an annual tramcar drive. Nowadays the annual outing is in beribboned and ballooned taxi cabs organised by the taxi owners' association.

The Maryhill Bowling Club, the 'Jags' and the Harriers

At least four local sports clubs have already celebrated their centenaries: The Maryhill Bowling Club, Partick Thistle Football Club, Maryhill Football Club, and Maryhill Harriers.

Maryhill Bowling Club began when a meeting was held in 1861 to decide on a suitable piece of ground for playing bowls. A site was selected at Duart Street and the first clubhouse built. Various replacements and extensions have been made over the years, and the present clubhouse was rebuilt and completely renovated in the 1980s. An interesting addition to the premises is an old cottage to the rear, which started life as a 'penny school' and then became the parish officer's house. The cottage is now used as a bowls-house and also contains the directors' room. One of the earliest bowling enthusiasts in the village was Police Superintendent George Anderson, and many leading players have been policemen. The 'James Hay' trophy is played for annually between the club and Strathclyde Police to commemorate the name of Constable Hay, who died on duty in the Maryhill area. In 1962 the club altered its name to The Maryhill Bowling Club.

Partick Thistle Football Club was thirty-three years old when it moved to its present home at Maryhill, having started life in 1876 and playing on various grounds in Partick before moving to Firhill. The first major win for the 'Jags' was the Scottish Cup Final in 1921, remembered not only for the 1–0 victory over Glasgow Rangers, but also for the boycott of the game by the Rangers fans, a circumstance brought about by a combination of the bizarre choice of Celtic Park for the venue plus a doubling of the admission price to 2s. The *Evening News* editorial column of the day reported: 'The big clubs cannot have it all their own way. The winning of the Scottish Cup by the Partick Thistle has restored to professional sport the essential ingredient of the unexpected.'

Maryhill Harrier 'Dunkie' Wright (extreme left) leads the field. at the start of the 22-mile Perth to Dundee race in 1946, just ahead of W. Connor, Shettleston, wearing no. 8.

Half a century later it was again Firhill for thrills when the Thistle won the Scottish League Cup in 1971, this time defeating Celtic 4-1 at Hampden. To the delight of their supporters, Partick Thistle will play in the Premier League in the season 2002–03 after finishing top of the first division in 2002.

Maryhill Football Club, one of the oldest junior clubs in Scotland, was formed in 1884. In 1897 the club moved to Lochburn Park on the site of an old quarry, where the Kelvindock Curling Club used to play, and this is still their home ground. Maryhill won the Scottish Junior Cup in the season 1899–1900, and again in 1939–40. Famous former players include Davie Meiklejohn, who played in the 1920s and later joined Glasgow Rangers, and Danny McGrain, Tommy Burns, Pat McClusky of Celtic and Scotland.

Maryhill Harriers, formed in 1888, is the second oldest athletic club in Scotland – only Clydesdale being older. The first Harriers trained around two farms north of Lochburn Road, then met at Maryhill Baths in Gairbraid Avenue, and now meet at John Paul Academy. Maryhill Harriers wear a distinctive royal blue vest with a gold badge showing a red deer jumping over a gate and the motif 'Fortis'. Three Maryhill Harriers have competed in Olympics: Robert Graham, Donald Robertson and Duncan (Dunkie) Wright, who won marathon gold for Scotland at the inaugural Empire Games in 1930 at Hamilton, Ontario.

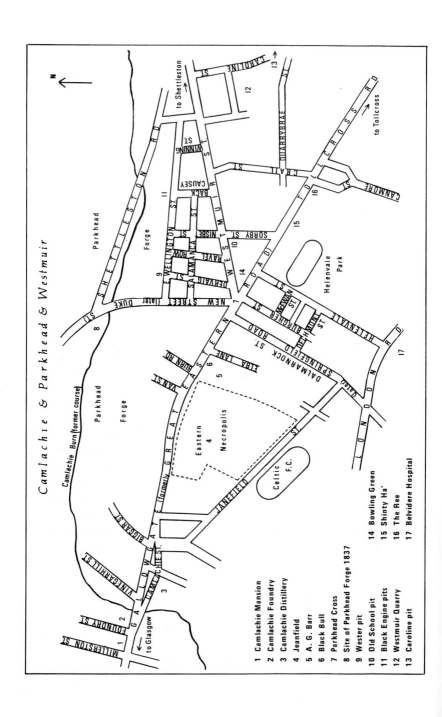

Camlachie & Parkhead & Westmuir

1 Camlachie Mansion
2 Camlachie Foundry
3 Camlachie Distillery
4 Jeanfield
5 A. G. Barr
6 Black Bull
7 Parkhead Cross
8 Site of Parkhead Forge 1837
9 Wester pit
10 Old School pit
11 Black Engine pits
12 Westmuir Quarry
13 Caroline pit
14 Bowling Green
15 Shinty Ha'
16 The Ree
17 Belvidere Hospital

5
PARKHEAD

Until the eighteenth century Camlachie, Parkhead and Westmuir were little more than hamlets strung along the main highway from Glasgow to the east. Camlachie was inhabited mostly by weavers, Westmuir by colliers, and Parkhead, about three miles from Glasgow Cross, consisted of an inn and a few cottages at the 'Sheddens', later Parkhead Cross, where the roads divided to lead to Shettleston, Airdrie and Falkirk in one direction and to Tollcross, Edinburgh and London in the other. In 1794 the population of the combined villages of Parkhead and Westmuir was 678, and that of the neighbouring village of Camlachie 977. Population increased as people came into the villages from country districts to work as weavers or carters transporting food, fuel and building materials into the ever-expanding and increasingly prosperous city. Pigot, in his *Directory* for 1821, noted 'the immense quantity of coaches, carriages and conveyances of every description which are incessantly traversing the great road between Glasgow and Edinburgh, the number of which is scarcely exceeded upon any road in the United Kingdom'. Pigot gives the combined population of Parkhead and Camlachie as 3,000.

The next generation found employment in the iron and chemical works then springing up along the Camlachie Burn. Parkhead forge became the major employer in the district and transformed the area into a centre of heavy industry. 'Even at night', wrote a commentator towards the end of the nineteenth century, 'when the last light has blinked into darkness, the lurid glare from the surrounding forges darts dreadfully about, transforming men into giant silhouettes which seem to dance and fight alternately. Such is the eastern gate to the city: by day in clouds of smoke, by night in shafts of fire.' The last lights went out for good when the forge closed in 1983.

Although Westmuir remains an identifiable part of Parkhead, it did not develop separate institutions. Camlachie, however, retained separate identity, with its own churches, schools and public buildings. After the demolition of the last tenements in 1986, little remains of Camlachie except a name going far back into history. Parkhead has fared better, with the handsome buildings at Parkhead Cross preserved and the Forge shopping centre development complete. Mrs Susan Baird, who was born and brought up in Parkhead, carried out her first tree-planting ceremony as Lord Provost of Glasgow at the Forge shortly after taking up office in May 1988.

David Willox's Parkhead

David Willox belonged to an old Parkhead family. As a boy he was taught weaving, then worked in the Forge and finally started up on his own manufacturing washing powder. He became bailie for Whitevale Ward. In 1920 Willox wrote his memoirs for his son Charles in America and entitled them *The Place, the People and the Pastimes of Parkhead, as far back as I can remember, say about 1850.*

From his starting place at the Sheddens, Willox takes us on a tour along each of the five main streets of Parkhead, describing each as it was in his youth. He starts with the short stretch of the Great Eastern Road called 'the West End'. Elba Lane, Reid's Lane and Stewart's Lane lay on the south side, and Burn Road (later Invernairn Street) on the north side. Dalrymple's Home Brewery was in Burn Street. The favourite west end shop was 'Old Brody's', which supplied the younger members of the community with half-penny keek shows, 'bools' of various colours, tops, peeries, false faces and valentines.

Dalmarnock Street was always called 'dry thrapple' by the older people. On the west side was a wide and deep goat or ditch, with a fairly high hedge, beyond which were little patches of garden ground, then the houses and larger garden spaces behind. Off this street, near the site of 'the present palatial Newlands school', was one of the finest wells in the whole neighbourhood, called 'Carrick's Well'. This was a private well in one of the gardens, and outsiders had to pay a small sum for a supply. On the east side of Dalmarnock Street was 'the Stiles' – now Dechmont Street – a nice little rural pathway that led through hawthorn hedges to Burgher Street, where Willox was born in a place called 'Nae Place'. He later owned a little property at number 48 Burgher Street. At the top of Burgher Street on the west corner stood 'a decent two storey building' occupied by Dr William Young. Dr Young was the only doctor in the place and had a predilection for the company of old 'Rubble', the local scavenger, especially when they were both 'in maut'. 'Old Rubble' was the great grandfather of David Kirkwood, chief shop steward at Beardmore's, later MP for Dumbarton Burghs. In his entertaining

Parkhead Cross around 1900. This postcard shows the Shettleston–Parkhead–Paisley tramcar passing Wilson's bakery at the corner of Westmuir Street and Great Eastern Road, now Tollcross Road.

Parkhead Cross. The same corner in 1988. This junction was traditionally known as the Sheddens. The Royal Bank of Scotland on the corner has relocated in the Forge shopping centre.

biography, *My Life in Revolt* – to which Winston Churchill wrote
the foreword – Kirkwood explains that 'Rubble' got his name from
carting rubble from Parkhead to Glasgow Green to fill up the cavern
of Nelson's Monument.

Willox now takes us along Duke Street, then called the New Road.
On the west side was the 'Gushet House' owned by George Honeyman,
who, besides being a liquor merchant, was a water merchant as well,
and sent carts through the village with large water butts, retailing the
precious article at so much a 'stoup'. After this came Agnes Paterson's
grocer's shop (a favourite one with the Forge labourers because she
gave 'tick'), then a low broken-down dyke running right down to the
old Forge gate. On the east side of New Street was a school called
'Corkey's school' because the schoolmaster, Mr McAuley, was said to
have a cork leg, which did not stop him being a strict disciplinarian.
The building at the corner of New Street and Westmuir Street was
occupied by Jock Arbuckle as a barber's shop. Mrs Arbuckle on
busy occasions did the 'soaping' and Jock did the shaving. Charges
were a halfpenny for shaving and one penny for haircutting. This
building was replaced by the fine range of four-storey tenements
built by Messrs Watson, an old Parkhead family, who had heads of
the members of the family sculpted on the façade. The Watsons had
their house and grocery business in a building at the corner of Gray's
Lane, but the monogram WHW on the present building stands for
W.H. Wyllie, who took over the business from the Watsons in 1924.
'Rab' Watson started off selling all kinds of grocery goods as well as
grain and feeding stuffs for horses and cattle and Willox reckoned
that he had left his family a business with a turnover in 1920 of not
less than £600 per week. One of Watson's best-selling lines were their
large range of soaps. In 1885 Best Brown and Best White were selling at
5½d per 2 lb or 1s per bar, and X Pale, Primrose and London Mottled
cost 3½d per 2 lb or 8d per bar.

Before continuing down Westmuir Street, Willox takes us down
Gray's Lane (now Dervaig Street) to East Wellington Street, on the
north side of which stood the old 'Wester' coal pit – called 'Waster'
by Willox – of considerable antiquity even in those days. The coal
was once brought to the surface in baskets by hand, and women used
to work there, but Willox had never seen any women working and
only recollected the coal being raised by mechanical means. The pits
in this area formed part of the extensive Westmuir colliery owned
by Robert Gray of Carntyne. Some of the first streets in Westmuir

were laid out by Robert Gray, who named Wellington Street East and Salamanca Street to commemorate the victory over the French in the Spanish village of Salamanca in 1812, in which his son took part. Between Gray's Lane and Ravel Row there was a comb work, the only place of public employment in Parkhead except the Forge, which was then only a very small concern. Opposite the south end of Ravel Row was the 'Old School' pit, bounded on the east by the Pump Riggs, now Sorbie Street. Willox recollected the stone-built engine house of this pit and its massive cast iron beam protruding, working up and down like some gigantic pendulum moving the wrong way. Next came the 'black engine' pits, two in number, reached by the Back Causey. The nearby Colliers' Row was occupied by a colony of interrelated families, mostly Haddows, Baxters, Tennants and Winnings. Although in later years a great number of new weavers came into Parkhead, chiefly from Girvan and Maybole, and assimilated with the native weavers, the division between the colliers and the weavers always remained, leading to the occasional stone battle. Finally came Westmuir quarry, owned by Thomas Nisbet. This was where the soldiers from the barracks used to practise ball firing at cloth targets, and the local boys pursued the highly dangerous pastime of sailing on rafts made of pieces of wood.

East of the quarry stood the 'Caroline' pit, called after Queen Caroline. According to David Kirkwood, this was not so much in honour of the unattractive queen as in contempt of her royal husband. The 'Karleen' was perhaps the most important pit in the district, where the engines not only raised great quantities of coal and other material, but also had to pump immense quantities of water out of the underground workings. When Gray discovered that he was pumping water from seven other pits extending as far away as Airdrie, he asked the owners to share the cost. When they refused, he stopped pumping, and forced the other owners to install expensive pumping machinery of their own, but in so doing he sacrificed his own lucrative Caroline pit.

Willox now returns to the Sheddens and takes us along Great Eastern Road towards Tollcross. At the corner with Westmuir Street formerly stood one of Parkhead's best-known buildings, occupied by Gilbert Watson, who was both postmaster and master baker. Gibbie's bakery was on the ground floor and the post office above was reached by an outside stair on which the guards of the London and Edinburgh coaches received the mail bags. The opening of Gibbie's bakery was a great event and celebrated by a supper at the Black Bull, Parkhead's oldest pub, founded in 1760, and immortalised in a poem by the Parkhead poet, John Breckinridge:

> It's auld Ne'er-day, an! we're met i' the 'Bull',
> Wi' our hearts dancin' licht, an' a bowl flowing full,
> Let envy and spite throw aff a' disguise,
> And drink to young Gibbie that's gi'en us the pies.

After the gushet-house came Montgomerie's Opening, which led to the old Parkhead bowling green, familiarly known as the 'Old Bog Hole'. Also down Montgomerie's Opening was a building with a little hall where public meetings and dances were held. Montgomery's pub was the forerunner of the present Bowlers Tavern. A breakaway from the old bowling club formed the Belvidere Bowling Club in 1853 with their green down Elba Lane, on ground later occupied by Celtic Football Club and then by Barr's lemonade works.

At this point in the tour Willox takes us down Helenvale Street. This was formerly the main access to Belvidere Big House and was

Shinty Ha' was a long row of one-storey houses with attics above, which stood on the south side of the Great Eastern Road at a considerably higher level than the causey, fronted by a dyke with openings and steps up to every door. The houses were occupied by weavers. David Willox spent part of his boyhood there.

known as the 'Coach Road'. The grounds became the site of Belvidere Fever Hospital in 1870. In Willox's youth Helenvale was a short street and at one time there appears to have been a plan to make it the centre of a village called Helenvale, built at the 'head' of Belvidere 'park'. The name 'Parkhead' has not been traced back further than the Statistical Account of 1794. In Helenvale Street stood old Hay's farmhouse and steading with byres and barns, and McEwan's cottage, with a little flower plot in front. The McEwans owned a tobacconist's business in Glasgow. McEwan Street was known as 'Juck Street', taking its name from a game in which children threw and caught pebbles or 'jucks'. The sports ground at Helenvale Park was originally used by employees at the Corporation tram depot, now the bus depot.

Returning to the Great Eastern Road and continuing eastwards, we come on the south side of the street to the long row of one-storey weavers' cottages with attics above known as Shinty Ha', where Willox spent part of his boyhood. The houses stood at a much higher level than the causey, fronted by a dyke with openings and steps opposite every door, which made a fine playground for the children. When a stranger enquired the way to Shinty Ha' the children would chant:

Doon Salamanca Street
Alang the Ravel Ra'
Up the Pump Riggs
And intae 'Shinty Ha'.

A little further on, on the site of the present bus depot, was the Ree, where the Willox family had also lived after falling on hard times. The Ree consisted of two long collier rows, each house a 'but and ben' with earth floors and reeking with damp. When Willox lived there they were occupied by weavers, the one apartment serving as living room, where the family ate, slept and carried on all other domestic concerns. The other room served as a workshop for two looms, with a small bed, in some instances, squeezed into a corner. The tour ends at Tollcross United Presbyterian church manse, which stood a little off the road, opposite the Ree. In 1920 the manse was still standing, but broken up into small dwellings.

One of the village characters who stood out most clearly in Willox's memory was Bob Arbuckle, a big powerful fellow, who sometimes wove a little, but was more interested in ferrets, game cocks and fighting dogs. It was in Bob's house that Willox saw for the first time a ferret kill a rabbit. The arena was a large empty box, and

Stone decoration on tenements at Parkhead. Heads of the two members of the Watson family on the building at the corner of Duke Street and Westmuir Street.

Co-operative building, Westmuir Street.

Glasgow Savings Bank building, Parkhead Cross.

tears came into the boy's eyes to see the poor rabbit done to death by his ruthless enemy. Willox saw several cock-fights in Bob's house, and another repulsive sight was a real set dogfight between the family bitch, Gem, and another dog, whose teethmarks scarred her for life. The Cherries, a family who supplemented their income by snaring birds and selling them in cages at the bird market in Glasgow, are also mentioned.

Less repulsive sports were foot-racing, jumping and quoit playing, the latter chiefly among the colliers. Young children played 'louping oysters', 'table the duck', 'the wrong sow by the lug', 'hurley-burley' and 'smugglers'. The bowling green was patronised principally by the shop-keeping class, though an old weaver now and then tried his hand, and much time was devoted by all to gardening, in the hope of carrying off a prize for flowers, vegetables or pot plants at the annual show. The serious minded could attend the lectures of the Scientific Association, founded in 1838, and borrow some of the 896 books in the lending library.

Highlights of village life were the visits of the ballad singers, street criers and the candy man, who exchanged candy, marbles, jories, chuckies, chinas and reddies, bead buttons and windmills for 'rags, bones and old iron'. 'Penny reels' were held at the Black Bull, when each male dancer paid a penny and took his partner to the dance. Best of all were the walking weddings. The wedding party walked in procession, headed by a fiddler or two, to and from the minister, 'the best man cleeking the bride to have the knot tied, and the young guid man cleeking his young guid wife home'. The ceremony included the 'running of the braes', which involved two of the party running for a bottle of whisky, the winner returning and meeting the wedding party and giving them a refreshment by the way.

Parkhead forge: 'clouds of smoke and shafts of fire'

Parkhead forge was founded in 1837 on a small site of less than two acres to the west of Duke Street by John Reoch, an ironmaster from Cramond, who set up with his brother Andrew where they could use the abundant supplies of local coal to transform scrap-metal into forgings for machinery of all kinds, including steam-engines for land and marine use. The business was sold four years later to David Napier, who appointed William Rigby as manager. Much of the progress of the plant in the early years was due to Rigby, who improved the Nasmyth steam hammer and equipped Parkhead with Chromis, Cyclops, Tubal, Vulcan, Hector, Priam and Achilles – a series of hammers called after mythological figures – as well as a crane called Hercules. Rigby also introduced rolling mills to produce iron plates such as were used to clad HMS *Black Prince*, launched from Robert Napier's yard at Govan in 1861.

The same year marked the start of the association of the Beardmore family with Parkhead. William Beardmore took over control after Rigby's death two years later, and was joined in 1871 by his brother Isaac. After the premature death of William in 1877, the business was carried on by Isaac in partnership with William's son, William Beardmore junior, who took an active part in management after completing his studies in metallurgy and chemistry in 1879. William Beardmore became the sole partner in 1887 at the age of thirty-one, and remained at the head of the firm for forty years.

Young William Beardmore introduced new ideas by beginning steelmaking at Parkhead in 1879, setting up with Siemens-Martin

William Beardmore, Lord Invernairn. A sketch from the *Bailie*, 12 February 1902.

open hearth furnaces which used haematite pig-iron imported from Spain to make the acid steel plates preferred by shipbuilders. One of the great sights in the Parkhead of these days was the departure of a great forging on its journey to the shipyard. The plates, propellers or keels were placed on a 'monkey' – a chariot-like contrivance drawn by a team of a dozen or more horses. On the first part of the journey, from the forge up the steep incline to Parkhead Cross, the horses frequently got stuck, whereupon Isaac Beardmore would round up the workers standing at the corners and call on them to help the horses by hauling at a rope. Once the cargo was safely on its way along the Gallowgate, Beardmore and the men would adjourn to the corner public house, where 'all would engage in drinks at Isaac's expense'.

Isaac Beardmore seemed to provoke varied reactions in people. A 'brawny puddler' is quoted as saying, 'Beardmore's weel liket – he'll come oot and swear at ye as if he were nae better than yersel.' On the other hand, David Willox, who got on well with William Beardmore senior, dismissed Isaac with: 'He is a tyrant of the deepest die. There is as much difference betwixt him and his late brother as there is betwixt good and evil!'

The year 1881 saw the arrival of Samson, which was introduced to prepare the steel slabs for rolling into plates and make the latest forgings. 'When Samson let fall his 100 tons on the iron plates', wrote David Kirkwood, 'the whole district quivered as in an earthquake.' Dalrymple's distillery (the Home Brewery) was shaken to its foundations and in the walls of 'Rattray's Church' (Camlachie Parish) 'great gaps appeared'. However, Samson was soon outshone by the birth of Goliath, a monster with a 600 -ton fall. 'Once more Rattray's Church showed signs of cracking, though the firm had scarcely paid charges for the repairs of the last shaking. Dalrymple's distillery began to rock.' Another socialist, Tom Bell of the Scottish Labour Party, also wrote of his native Parkhead in his autobiography, *Pioneering Days*, describing how in the 1880s 'the smell of oil and smoke, the thud of the Sampson hammer and the glare of furnace fires were fast banishing the scents and sound and colours of the country'.

Beardmore's programme of expansion continued with the introduction of a cogging mill and a massive 12,000 -ton press, both designed to enable the plant to produce armour plate to Admiralty standards. By 1900 Beardmore had run out of credit and was forced into a merger with Vickers. With the company back on its feet again Beardmore purchased land at Dalmuir to lay out his own shipyard to consume the products of the Parkhead forge, and then bought Mossend steelworks to ensure supplies of materials. William Beardmore & Co. was now the largest single employer in the west of Scotland. The firm spent a quarter of a million pounds between 1884 and 1914 on new buildings at Parkhead, including fine offices in Renaissance style which stood until recent years on the north side of Shettleston Road. The gun quenching shop, 110 feet high and the highest building in Scotland when it was built in 1905, was a landmark in Parkhead and known locally as 'the Cathedral'.

At the outbreak of war Beardmore was called on to supply armaments ranging from shells and field guns to ships and aeroplanes, which he had begun to manufacture at Dalmuir the previous year. His chief shop steward was David Kirkwood, with whom he had an amicable relationship, until the militant Clyde Workers' Committee, of which Kirkwood was chairman, threatened to strike over dilution by unskilled workers and women. Lloyd George, then Minister of Munitions, agreed to meet shop stewards at Parkhead, but the meeting was acrimonious. In 1916 Kirkwood was deported to Edinburgh as a troublemaker but was later re-employed as manager of Beardmore's Mile-end shell factory, where his team broke all records for output. After the war Beardmore was dubbed 'Field Marshal of Industry' and was created Lord Invernairn in 1921. A year later Kirkwood entered parliament as ILP member for Dumbarton Burghs, and retained the seat until elevated to the House of Lords in 1951 as Baron Bearsden.

After the war, in anticipation of an upturn in trade, Beardmore began to produce pressed steel frames for motor cars and boilers and axles for the locomotives he was building at Dalmuir. The R34 was completed at Inchinnan, taxis were produced at Paisley and aero-engines at Dumfries. From 1919 to 1928 the firm built a few lorries and coaches at Van Street in Parkhead (called after Mrs Van, a draper). But Beardmore's optimism was misplaced and in 1927 the company was in serious financial trouble. Its reconstruction was entrusted to Montagu Norman, Governor of the Bank of England, and Invernairn was forced into retirement. He died in 1936 and is buried on his Highland estate at Flicherty near Inverness – his epitaph, 'a brain of steel, and a heart of gold'.

Beardsmore's workers were encouraged to take part in the many social activities organised by the firm: the forge amateur orchestra, the silver band, the dramatic club, which entertained patients in local hospitals, and the forge choir, which gave concerts in the St Andrew's

Halls in Glasgow. The choir met on Friday nights at 7.45 to enable men on night shift to go straight on duty. Lectures were arranged and it was a great disappointment when a talk by Major G. Herbert Scott, commander of the R34, about his recordbreaking double crossing of the Atlantic, had to be postponed because of a breakdown in the local train service. The forge had a swimming club, a cadet corps and four football teams, whose fortunes were reported in the house magazine, the *Beardmore News*, the stars being the Wheel and Axle Eleven, 'a very smart team, though to the light side'.

The company was steered through the 1930s and the 1940s by Sir James Lithgow, who retired shortly before nationalisation in 1949. After various changes of management William Beardmore & Co. ceased trading in 1975. A new shopping centre, known as 'the Forge' has been built on the site.

Directly opposite the new forge development are the premises of A.G. Barr, renowned as manufacturers of Scotland's other national drink, Irn-Bru, the drink 'made from girders'. The manufacture of aerated waters was begun in Parkhead in the nineteenth century by Andrew Stout, landlord of the Black Bull, who manufactured ginger beer, lemonade and, soda water in a small four-loom weaving shop. Tom Bell worked for the firm, first as a van-boy selling mineral waters to the ironworkers, who had a perpetual thirst, and then in the factory, where his most vivid memory was of the primitive bottling machine which reguarly exploded. 'There were not a few bottlers in those days with only one eye.' Bell began in the bottle washing department and. worked his way up to syruping and labelling.

In 1887 the business was taken over by R.F. Barr. The Barrs were a Falkirk family who had begun business as corkcutters and then set up as manufacturers of soft drinks in Falkirk in 1880. The Glasgow 'branch' became A.G. Barr & Co. in 1904. The firm sold Iron Brew and American soda water from carts drawn by Clydesdale horses, a day's round being twenty miles. The favourite horse was Carnera. When the company's new £2.5 million headquarters were opened in Parkhead in 1975, the chairman, Mr Robert Barr, and his wife arrived for the ceremony by horse and cart. For many years the firm advertised Irn Bru with a strip-cartoon chronicling the adventures of the turbanned Indian boy Ba Bru and his kilted pall Sandy. In the 1930s Barr's continued their flare for publicity by having the famous Irn Bru electric sign erected at the corner of Union and Gordon Streets, which was probably the first electric advertisement sign in Glasgow.

The company produce Irn Bru, Tizer and other popular brands, and remain one of Britain's largest soft drinks manufacturers.

Churches, schools and public buildings

The oldest surviving church building in Parkhead is the Congregational church built in Westmuir Street in 1879 for a congregation formed as a result of mission work undertaken by Elgin Place Church. In 1906 the third pastor, George Sharpe, left to found the first Church of the Nazarene in Scotland in Burgher Street, now known as the Sharpe Memorial Church of the Nazarene. Calton-Parkhead Church in Helenvale Street was opened in 1935 under the Church of Scotland extension scheme to provide a place of worship for the congregation of Calton Old, many of whom had been rehoused in the Newbank housing scheme, opened in 1924 by the then Minister of Health, Shettleston MP, John Wheatley. This congregation united in 1977 with the members of Parkhead Church, which had its roots partly in Camlachie Parish Church and partly in Parkhead UP Church in Westmuir Street.

St Michael's Roman Catholic church at Parkhead Cross was opened in May 1970 and replaces the former church in Nisbet Street. A statue of St Michael armed with a spear and standing over a dragon tops the steeple. St Michael's Primary School also occupies a new building in Springfield Road. The Salvation Army citadel is in Tollcross Road.

Three stone school buildings remain in Parkhead, but only one, Quarry Brae Primary School, is in use as a school. The former Parkhead Public School in Westmuir Street has the date 1878 and is now used as a resource centre. Newlands School in Springfield Road is used for local social services and the janitor's house is used for the GEAR Arts project.

Parkhead Cross is the best of Glasgow's remaining crosses. In the early twentieth century the 'Sheddens' was 'improved' when old cottages were replaced by tenements buildings. One old landmark which disappeared was Gibbie Watson's bakery and post office, later the premises of J. Wilson, which was replaced by the building subsequently occupied by the Bank of Scotland. The corner building erected in 1908 by the Savings Bank of Glasgow to the design of John Keppie was later occupied by Lloyds TSB. Both of these banks have relocated in the Forge shopping centre, but the Clydesdale Bank still occupies the handsome building erected in 1902 at the corner of Duke

Shops in Westmuir Street in 1905 with Messrs Watson's grocery on the corner of Gray Street. The shop was begun by 'Rab Watson' who sold all kinds of groceries and feeding stuffs for horses and cattle. The top flat where the family lived 'above the shop' had once been a school-room.

Street. The public library and the baths and washhouse in Tollcross Road were built in the same decade. Other notable buildings are the former premises of the Glasgow Eastern Cooperative Society on the south side of Westmuir Street. The eastmost building has a stone plaque commemorating the founding of the Parkhead & Westmuir Economical Society in 1831. This was one of the earliest cooperatives in Scotland, and amalgamated with the Eastern in 1901. The other building is decorated with the cooperative symbol of clasped hands and the date 1903. The houses on the upper floors of this tenement have been refurbished by WhatCo, which is a partnership formed between the Wholesale Coop Society and Whatlings, to provide flats for sale rather than for renting. Cooperation was vigorous in the East End of Glasgow and at the time David Willox was writing in the 1920s the society had a membership of over seventeen thousand.

Celtic Park

Celtic Football and Athletic Club began not in Parkhead but at a meeting held in St Mary's church hall, Bridgeton, on 6 November

1887. The chief enthusiasts for the formation of the club were Brother Walfrid, head of the Marist teaching order at Sacred Heart and several prominent laymen, notably the builder John Glass. The stated aim of the club was 'to supply the East End Conferences of the St Vincent Society with funds for the maintenance of the "Dinner Tables" of our needy children in the Missions of St Mary's, Sacred Heart and St Michael's'.

The first Celtic Park was a small stretch of ground to the east of Jeanfield Cemetery, on the site now occupied by A.G. Barr. The opening match was played on 8 May 1888 before a crowd of three thousand and was a Glasgow–Edinburgh derby – Cowlairs versus Hibernian ending in a goalless draw. On 20 May 1888 Celtic played their first game at Celtic Park, beating Rangers by five goals to two. The first Celtic team included experienced players from other clubs and in their first year they reached the final of the Scottish Cup. Three years later they won the trophy for the first time, by beating Queen's Park by five goals to one at Ibrox.

In the same year, 1892, the club moved to its present site on the south-west side of Jeanfield Cemetery. The new ground, when completed, was so far in advance of anything seen in Scotland that a pressman declared that it was 'like leaving the graveyard to enter Paradise, and Celtic supporters have known it by this name ever since. By the 1890s football had become 'a mammoth boom' and in 1898 Celtic Park was the venue for the Scotland–England International, watched by a crowd of fifty thousand, who caused a traffic jam with their 'limbering char-a-bancs, ancient buses, festive four-in-hands, decayed broughams, resurrected stays, natty hansoms and flag-bedizened brakes'.

It was the wish of the Church authorities that the new Celtic Park should have facilities for other sports, and two tracks were added for foot-running and cycling. Scotland hosted the world cycling championships at Celtic Park in 1898. The cycle track was later used for motor-racing. For many years the Celtic Sports were held on the second Saturday in August and attracted entrants from all over the world. Other events held at Celtic Park included a parade of home and colonial troops during the coronation celebrations in 1911; displays of trench warfare by wounded servicemen before they returned to action during the First World War; and baseball games between teams of American navy men stationed on the Clyde during the Second World War. When Celtic won the European Cup in 1967, beating Inter

The 'Lisbon Lions' show off the European Cup at Parkhead in 1967. *Back Row:* Auld, Gemmell, Wallace, Chalmers, Simpson, Craig, McNeill, Clark and Murdoch. *Front with trophy:* Johnstone and Lennox.

Milan 2–1 in the final at Lisbon, sixty thousand people were waiting at Celtic Park to give a heroes' welcome to the 'Lisbon Lions' and their manager, Jock Stein. Celtic celebrated their centenary year 1988 with a £2 million extension to their main stand, and by winning both the Scottish Premier League and the Scottish Cup. The club celebrated season 2000–01, the first of the new millenium, by again winning the Scottish Cup and the SPL Trophy and also the CIS Insurance Cup.

Camlachie: Easter and Wester

Debate continues as to whether Camlachie is the Camcachecheyn included in a list of the lands of the church of Glasgow drawn up at the request of Earl David (later David I) around 1124, but Camlachie must have been a place of some importance from its situation at Glasgow's eastern boundary, where travellers heading eastwards crossed over the Camlachie Burn and outwith the jurisdiction and protection of the town. In 1660 the 'maister of wark' was ordered to 'sight the calsey that gois to Camlachie, and to caus to mend the two meikle holes that is said to be brokin therein', and in 1665 a new brig at Camlachie cost the town £200. From Glasgow Cross to Camlachie Burn the road was called the Gallowgate and passed through the lands of Wester Camlachie. East of the burn the road was known as the Great Eastern Road and the lands as Easter Camlachie. These lands had separate histories until the nineteenth century, when both passed into the ownership of the Hoziers of Newlands and were developed for industry and housing. Today the Gallowgate extends to Parkhead Cross, and the road beyond is Tollcross Road. The name Camlachie is Celtic and signifies 'the muddy or miry bend of the burn'.

Easter Camlachie was originally part of the Tollcross estate and in 1751 the ground known as the 'Little Hill of Tolloross' – now the Eastern Necropolis – was feued to William Boutcher, a seedsman from Comely Gardens near Edinburgh, who set up a nursery intending to sell fruit and forest trees, evergreen and flowering shrubs to Glasgow gentlemen engaged in beautifying their estates. Mr Boutcher gave notice in the *Glasgow Courant* that all transactions would be for ready money only, 'as his principal servant is a stranger in the place, and so might give credit to improper persons'. The business failed three years later and was sold to another Edinburgh nurseryman, Patrick Tod, who met the same fate after two years.

The next proprietor of the Little Hill was not from Edinburgh, but was a well-to-do Glasgow eccentric, Robert McNair, who began business selling a basket of half-spoiled or oranges in the Trongate and finished up as a wealthy grocer and property-owner. His speciality was marmalade oranges, but he also supplied the citizens of Glasgow with new hops, English cheese, London soap, Tent, Lisbon and Zerrie wines, musk plums, almonds and carvie, barley sugar and orange peel, fine blue raisins of the sun, figs, citron and olives, all kinds of sugars, candie, syrops, treacle and sugar brandy, and free recipes for making a drink called English swats, which customers could brew at home from treacle, hops, bran and sowan seeds, all of which he advertised in verse:

> at my shop also may be had
> Good duble Rum strong and weel made
> Suger and limons to quench your Drouth
> will make good Drink to weat your mouth
> Call at my shop in the trone Street
> and if that thir we Do Not meat

go in the close and up one Stair
wher you will find ROBERT MCNAIR.

McNair decided to build a country retreat on the Little Hill and called it Jeanfield in honour of his wife and business partner, Jean Holmes. Mistress McNair drew up the house plans herself, only to find, after the local Camlachie mason was well on with the job, that they had forgotten to include an inside stair. The high, narrow house with irregular windows and stairs like a corkscrew was a landmark for coach travellers nearing Glasgow. In 1797 the house was bought and occupied for one year only by Mennons, the printer and editor of the *Glasgow Advertiser,* later the *Glasgow Herald.* The last two owners lost their fortunes trying to mine the Camlachie coal, and in 1847 Jeanfield was demolished and the grounds laid out for the Eastern Necropolis, locally known as Jeanfield Cemetery.

Camlachie Mansion was built in 1720 on the lands of Wester Camlachie by James Walkinshaw, whose grandfather had bought the

General James Wolfe was given the use of Camlachie Mansion, originally the home of the Walkinshaw family, when his regiment was stationed in Glasgow during 1749 and 1750. The house is now demolished. His name lived on in the nearby 'General Wolfe' public house until that too disappeared in 1986.

estate in 1669 as part of his marriage contract with Janet Anderson of Easter Craigs and Kenniehill, to make provision for 'the aires and bairns' of the marriage. When the family lost their estates of Barrowfield and Camlachie in 1723 as the result of their involvement with the Jacobites, Lady Barrowfield was allowed to keep Camlachie House for her own use. Although a modest residence compared with the manor place of Barrowfield, Camlachie Mansion was much superior to anything else in the district. It was a two-storey house with attics, had a slate roof, and stood on its own, a little back from the road, with a parterre in front. The connection of the Walkinshaws with the district came to an end in 1734 when Lady Barrowfield sold the house and ground to John Orr for £500.

In Camlachie the mansion is better remembered by its alternative name of General Wolfe's House. James Wolfe, then a lieutenant-colonel in command of Lord George Sackville's regiment, arrived in Glasgow in March 1749. As there were no barracks in the city, the soldiers were billeted on the townspeople, and as a leading citizen John Orr was expected to provide accommodation for Wolfe, who was given the use of Camlachie Mansion during 1749 and 1750. Wolfe's well-known comment on the women of Glasgow was written in this house: 'The Women here are coarse, cold, and cunning; for ever enquiring after Men's Circumstances: They make *that* the standard of their good breeding.' Wolfe was then twenty-two years old and died nine years later on the Heights of Abraham winning Canada for the British. It is the hero of Quebec who is remembered in Camlachie, while the Walkinshaw and Orr families have faded into obscurity.

In 1753 the house was occupied by a company manufacturing woollens – possibly the company who were paid £59 10s 6d for 'scarlett and bleu cloath' to make uniforms for the town officers and drummers of Glasgow. The lower floor was later converted into shops and a public house, and tenements were built on either side. After the house was demolished its name lived on in the nearby 'General Wolfe' pub until that too disappeared in 1986.

Camlachie began to change from a rural to an industrial community after forging and marine engineering were begun by Duncan McArthur, who, in 1815 and 1816, engined five of the earliest ships to be driven by steam in Scotland: the *Greenock*, the *Dumbarton Castle* and the *Rothesay Castle*, all built by Archibald McLauchlan of Dumbarton; the *Britannia*, built by John Hunter and the *Neptune*, built by John Wood, both of Port Glasgow. McArthur trained David

The nursery class of 1926 at Camlachie Primary School.

Napier, who then set up his own foundry beside the Camlachie Burn, where he built his first marine engine in 1816 for the *Marion*, which operated a passenger service between Glasgow and Rutherglen. In 1821 Napier moved to Anderston, which was more conveniently placed for fitting engines into wooden hulls built downriver, but other members of the Napier family remained in business at Vinegarhill as chemical manufacturers until the 1880s. Vinegarhill took its name from one of the several chemical and vinegar works which were set up in the neighbourhood.

    Camlachie distillery began production in 1834. By the time Alfred Barnard described it in his *Whisky Distilleries of the United Kingdom* in 1887, the name had been changed to Loch Katrine and 'the little old-fashioned, distillery on the banks of the stream' had given way to 'a handsome pile of buildings' covering almost six acres. The annual output of pure malt was three hundred thousand gallons, and the premises included a cooperage, an engineer's workshop, and a dessicated grain factory, where cattlefood was made from the draff. The firm had its own fire-brigade equipped with hydrants, fireplugs, reels and hose, extincteurs, water force pumps and hand grenades ready. to meet any emergency from fire or explosion. The distillery continued production until taken over by the Distillers

A Mo-Car built at Camlachie in 1901 by the Arrol-Johnston Company. This four-seat dog-cart is on display at the Glasgow Museum of Transport in the Kelvin Hall.

Company in 1920, after which the warehouses were used for storage until demolition.

The first all-Scottish car went into commercial production at Camlachie in 1896, when Sir William Arrol and others formed the Mo-Car Syndicate, later the Arrol-Johnston Company. The designer was George Johnston, the son of the minister of Springburn UP Church, who had trained as a locomotive engineer in the works of the Hyde Park Locomotive Company, and had designed a steam tramcar for Glasgow Corporation which had the misfortune to catch fire during a test run. George began to strip down imported car engines at the family home and soon had his own car on the roads of Glasgow, where he incurred further disfavour by driving at 17 mph – 13 mph over the permitted limit. The Mo-car was of dog-cart design and the bodies were made from solid oak or mahogany. In 1901 the premises at Camlachie were destroyed by fire and production moved to Paisley and then to Dumfries, where it survived into the 1920s. A dog-cart built at Camlachie is included in the collection of early vehicles in Glasgow's Museum of Transport.

Vinegarhill was also well-known as a showground after the shows,

which were traditionally held at the foot of the Saltmarket, were
moved out to Camlachie in 1870. In Victorian times 'douce citizens'
are reported as making their way out to Camlachie to see the 'gipsies,
dwarfs, giants and other sights of the vagabond world, and to return
home, duly thrilled, though not a little frightened'. Around 1913 the
fairground was acquired by George Green, the proprietor of Green's
Playhouse, the well-known Glasgow cinema, who increased the
rentals, whereupon several showmen set up their own switchback
railway and shows on the other side of Vinegarhill Street. In 1931
the fairground was turned into a children's playground with swings,
maypoles and seesaws with a small park alongside. Some of the area
was apparently still occupied by travelling showmen four years later,
for in May 1935 an entry in the log books of Camlachie Primary
School complains of the absence of thirty children – about ten per
cent of the total roll – 'from the Caravan dwellers' who were away on
a PSA trip. (These were 'Pleasant Saturday Afternoon' outings run by
the temperance movement, evidently inside school hours.)

Camlachie's two churches were the parish church opposite the
Necropolis and the Free Church at the west end of the village, of
which it was said, 'plain though the edifice may be, there is no
doubt that here the gospel will be preached as purely as in any of
the West-end Cathedrals, with their spires and towers, painted
windows, cushioned seats, and velvetfringed galleries'. Both have now
disappeared, along with the Camlachie Institute and police station,
which stood between Camlachie Street and the Gallowgate. In 1986
the last close in Camlachie disappeared as the remaining tenements,
including the 'General Wolfe', were demolished, relegating another
little bit of living tradition into the history books – and into folksong,
as immortalised by Rikki Fulton and Jack Milroy, otherwise known
as 'Francie and Josie'.

> Camlachie, Camlachie, I love you my ain
> I love every stick, every brokendown stane.
> An' the tenement close where I played as a wean
> Was the nicest wee close in Camlachie.
>
> We raked through the middens all covered in glaur
> An' caught baggie minnies to swim in a jaur
> An' sometimes we'd steal a wee hurl in a caur
> We were heroes all right in Camlachie.

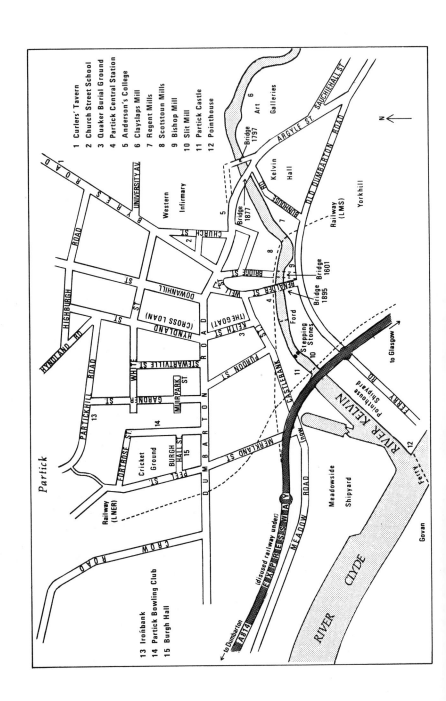

Partick

1 Curlers' Tavern
2 Church Street School
3 Quaker Burial Ground
4 Partick Central Station
5 Anderson's College
6 Clayslaps Mill
7 Regent Mills
8 Scotstoun Mills
9 Bishop Mill
10 Slit Mill
11 Partick Castle
12 Pointhouse

13 Ironbank
14 Partick Bowling Club
15 Burgh Hall

RIVER CLYDE

RIVER KELVIN

Art Galleries

Kelvin Hall

Yorkhill

Railway (LMS)

Western Infirmary

Meadowside Shipyard

Pointhouse Shipyard

Cricket Ground

BURGH HALL 15

Railway (LNER)

EXPRESS WAY
(disused railway under:)
to Dumbarton A814

MEADOW ROAD
MERKLAND ST
LOAN
CASTLEBANK
PURDON ST
STEWARTVILLE ST
MUIRPARK ST
GARDNER ST
WHITE ST
PEEL ST
PRIMROSE ST
DOWANHILL ST
KEITH ST (THE GOAT)
HYNDLAND RD (CROSS LOAN)
DUMBARTON ROAD
BRIDGE ST
WELL ST
BEARDEN ST
CHURCH ST
UNIVERSITY AV
BYRES ROAD
HIGHBURGH ROAD
HYNDLAND ROAD
PARTICKHILL ROAD
CROW ROAD

Bridge 1797
Bridge 1877
Bridge 1601
Bridge 1895
ARGYLE ST
SAUCHIEHALL ST
OLD DUMBARTON ROAD
DUMBARTON RD

Stepping Stones
Ford

to Glasgow
Govan Ferry
FERRY RD

N

6
PARTICK

The first known mention of Partick in written documents dates back to 1136, when King David I made a grant of part of his lands of 'Perdeyc' to the church of Glasgow on the great occasion of the dedication of the church to St Kentigern, more often referred to in Glasgow as St Mungo. This was a valuable gift, for it not only enabled the Church authorities to build a residence on the banks of the Clyde at Partick about three miles west of the cathedral, but it also gave them the opportunity of erecting a much needed new corn-mill beside the fast-flowing waters of the Kelvin, since by this time the Molendinar was no longer an adequate source of power for the town's mills.

Fifty years later Partick is mentioned in a manuscript life of St Kentigern written by a monk called Jocelyn, who was given the task of writing up the life and miracles of the saint. In Jocelyn's account 'Pertnech' figures as the royal residence of King Rederech of Strathclyde and his queen, Languoreth, the lady on whose behalf Kentigern performed the miracle of the salmon and the ring which forms part of Glasgow's coat of arms. The queen, it will be remembered, had foolishly given the king's ring to a knight, who had dropped it into the River Clyde. Kentigern had a salmon taken from the river, and the ring – miraculously found inside the fish – was restored to the lady's finger before Rederech even knew of the loss. However, Jocelyn, a monk of Furness in Lancashire, was writing from a distance about events that had taken place over five hundred years before, and so references to 'royal Partick' have to be taken with a certain amount of caution.

'Pertik' (local pronunciation), like other west coast names of Norse origin such as Brodick and Prestwick, indicates some kind of harbour, probably used in connection with the important early religious centre at Govan and affording easy access to Glasgow. A house of some importance certainly existed at Partick in 1277, when a grant of wood from the Lord of Luss for repairs to the church at Glasgow was drawn up at 'Perthec'. At the Reformation Archbishop James Beaton is supposed to have escaped to France from his house at Partick, concealing the relics and records of the cathedral in his meal mill nearby until it was safe to ship them to France.

The mills of Partick

Milling has been carried on at Partick for over eight hundred years. The first mill dates almost certainly from the twelfth century with three others built in the sixteenth and one in the eighteenth century.

The medieval monks were the experts of their day in making dams, water-courses and mill machinery and would certainly have selected the best site on the Kelvin for the Mill of Partick. This site, just below a natural weir, is now occupied by a nineteenth-century mill with distinctive stone wheatsheaves on the top of the gables, which has been converted into twenty apartments and renamed Bishop Mill. For centuries mills provided an important source of income for their owners. The farmers of a district were 'thirled to the mill', an arrangement which obliged them to bring their pease and bere to one particular mill to be ground into meal, paying over a proportion of the meal ground as multures.

At the Reformation the Mill of Partick became the property of the crown and in 1573 it was given by James VI to Thomas Crawford of Jordanhill as a reward for capturing Dumbarton Castle two years previously. Shortly after, Crawford made an annual grant to Glasgow University of sixteen bolls of 'good and sufficient oatmeal' to maintain a student during his 'philosophical course'. The Crawford or Bishop Bursary was converted to money in 1890 and now forms part of a general bursary fund. The mill passed into the ownership of the town of Glasgow in 1608. Straight away the authorities had to deal with complaints that James King the miller was stabling his horse in the mill and allowing his two servants to help themselves to more than the traditional 'lick of goodwill' from each sack of meal. After the abolition of thirlage in 1799, mills became less attractive as a source of income and the town sold the mill to the proprietors of the nearby Slit Mill. After a fire the present mill was rebuilt in 1839 for William Wilson, a miller and grain merchant. The original water-wheel was replaced by a turbine and latterly the mill was operated by electricity.

Scotstoun Mills stand on the west bank of the Kelvin on the site of the Waulk Mill of Partick, which was begin in 1507 for the preparation of woollen cloth. Around 1847 the mill came into the

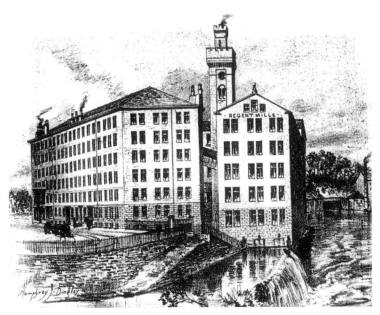

Regent Mills, named after Regent Moray, who granted the ground and the right to build a wheat mill to the millers of Glasgow as a reward for providing his army with bread at the time of the Battle of Langside. The mills produced 'Lofty Peak' flour for the SCWS until demolition in the 1970s.

possession of John White, who built the first parts of the present buildings for grain milling in 1877. A bottle placed in the wall when the building was extended in 1898 was recently recovered. It contained notes describing the firm as flour and grain millers, producing 3,000 sacks of flour and 3,000 sacks of feeding meals each week, the flour being sold principally in Scotland and some in the north of Ireland and in the north of England. John White was the second provost of Partick, holding office from 1857 to 1860 and his son John was provost from 1905 to 1908. The mill is now used by Rank Hovis, who mill white flour from wheat grown in Berwickshire, Yorkshire and as far south as Lincolnshire. About 1,200 tons of bread flour is produced per week and much of it goes in bulk to the company's Duke Street bakery, one of the biggest in Europe.

Under the Scotstoun Mills there was at one time another small mill, known as Wee Mill, driven by water collected in the Wee Dam just below the fall. The Waulk Mill was supplied with water from a pond into which the overflow water was allowed to run from the Bishop's Mill dam.

The Clayslaps Mill was known as the New Waulk Mill of Partick and dates back to at least 1517, when Donald Lyon was entered in the diocesan rental book as rentaller. In 1554 his son Archy obtained permission to convert the mill into a grain mill on condition that he ground all the wheat required for the archbishop's house. (Wheat bread was a prestige food, eaten only by the better-off until the end of the nineteenth century.) This mill was the highest of the mills of Partick and it was also situated beside a natural weir. However in 1569 Archy Lyon's mill was affected on account of the Bakers of Glasgow 'biggin' up ane dam to their mill newly biggit'. This was a reference to the building of the Regent Mills a little downstream, and a few years later Archy sold his mill to the town of Glasgow, which demolished it in 1874. The Art Galleries were built on the site in 1901.

The Regent Mills are traditionally believed to have been built by the bakers of Glasgow after they were given both the right and the land to build a wheat mill by Regent Moray as a reward for providing his army with bread at the time of the Battle of Langside in 1568. The mill was also known as the Bunhouse Mill from its proximity to the Bun and Yill House, a hostelry on Old Dumbarton Road. The mill had an artificial weir and a lade 320 yards in length The premises were destroyed by fire in 1886 and then rebuilt as flour mills by John Ure. The mills were bought by the SCWS in 1903 and produced 'Lofty Peak' flour until the 1970s. The site is now the car park for the Kelvin Hall.

The last mill to make use of the water power of the Kelvin at Partick was the Slit Mill, which was erected around 1734 by the Smithfield Iron Company for slitting imported iron bars to make into nails. This was the lowest mill on the Kelvin and around 1789 it was converted into a grain mill. It was demolished in 1862 to make way for boiler works.

Roads, bridges, railways and ferries

The earliest travellers from Glasgow to Partick made their way along the north bank of the Clyde to Pointhouse and crossed the Kelvin a short distance upstream by stepping stones or by a ford. On the Partick side of the ford two short roads were formed, the Horse Brae and the Kiln Brae (or Kilbrae), which led up to the Meadow

The Old Bridge, Partick, with the house known as the 'Ark' in the foreground and Bishop Mill just visible behind the bridge. From William Simpson's *Glasgow in the Forties*.

Road (now Castlebank Street), which was the principal east–west route through the village before Dumbarton Road was formed. At the top of the Kilbrae the traveller could cross the Meadow Road and continue northwards up the Goat, so named from the 'gott' or ditch which ran down the east side. This later became Kelvin Street and is now Keith Street. The route then continued uphill towards Hyndland as the Cross Loan (now Hyndland Street). The Quaker burial ground in Keith Street is an approximate landmark for the centre of the village.

In 1601 a stone bridge was built over the Kelvin just below Bishop Mill by Crawford of Jordanhill. The route from Glasgow was now along Old Dumbarton Road, across the bridge and into the village by Bridge Street, or alternatively by the Knowe Brae, which joined Castlebank Street a little east of Keith Street. Knowe Brae disappeared when Partick Central Station was built in 1897. When the railway company took down the bridge, two sculptured stones were revealed, both with the date 1601. One bore Crawford's coat of arms and the other the Lennox arms and the initials L.S.D.L. (Ludovic Stewart, Duke of Lennox).

Crawford's bridge made the journey between Glasgow and Partick easier, and in 1611 a leading Glasgow merchant, George Hutcheson, had a new house built at Partick, which became known as Partick Castle. The house was possibly built on the very site previously occupied by the bishops of Glasgow. This was followed by stone and thatched cottages in the village. An inn with the date 1619 was still standing in Castlebank Street when James Napier published his *Notes and Reminiscences of Partick* in 1873.

A picturesque inn called the Ark was built at the north-west end of the bridge and other hostelries of high repute were the Old Bridge Inn, managed by Mrs Craig, and the Bun and Yill House, managed by Mr McTyre. The Partick inns became very popular with visitors from Glasgow. Ducks came in droves to the Kelvin to feed on the grain from the mills and Glaswegians came in throngs on Saturdays to Partick to feed on roast duck and green peas washed down by bumpers of cold punch.

On the west of the village, near where the Thornwood roundabout now stands, there was another inn known as Granny Gibb's, kept by Elizabeth Gibb and her daughters, 'Mother Gibb' and 'Aunt Gibb'. This was the favourite howff of the drovers coming from the West Highlands to the Glasgow markets, who slept in the loft while the cattle and sheep grazed in the field now occupied by the Meadowside granary. Mr Inglis of Low Balshagray Farm also let out fields for this purpose. The market was held on Mondays and the drovers arrived at Yoker on Saturday afternoons and were eagerly awaited by the youths of Partick, who were allowed to help drive the animals along the road.

Another ancient route led from Partick to Glasgow Cathedral by way of Byres Road and a track later known as Dobbie's Loan and later still, at its western end, as University Avenue. Until 1839, when Great Western Road was formed, Byres Road only went as far north as the present Hillhead library, before veering westwards across Horslethill towards Kirklee. The small hamlet of the Byres of Partick, where the bishop is traditionally believed to have kept his cattle, was at the south end of Byres Road. Until the nineteenth century there was a farm in the triangle now occupied by Church Street School (and formerly by Partick Academy), complete with byre, stable, midden-stead, cart-shed and barn. This was occupied by Anthony Inglis, who also operated a contractor's business, transporting coals and stone from the many pits and quarries in the vicinity of Byres Road. The old name of the land around Byres village, including the site of the Western Infirmary, was the Brewlands, where presumably ale was brewed by the side of the Brewster Burn, which ran down the west side of Byres Road and across Well Street (later Cooperswell Street) to the Kelvin.

A new route into Partick was formed when New Dumbarton Road, now Argyle Street, was opened and a new bridge built around 1797. This bridge is the one which now stands inside the Kelvingrove and is fenced off. This led to the building of a number of small mansion-houses along the north side of Dumbarton Road. When tenements were built over these small estates, their names were perpetuated in Dowanhill Street, Stewartville Street and Muirpark Street. Muirpark House was occupied by the paper manufacturer Edward Collins before he built Kelvindale House at Maryhill.

The first public transport vehicles made their appearance in Partick in 1844, when Messrs Wylie and Lochhead began to run a stage-coach to Glasgow every two or three hours for a fare of fourpence. Their stable was at the south-west corner of Crow Road, then called Jordanhill Street, but it was moved to Whiteinch so that the tenements called Downie Place could be built on the site. The name was given in honour of two sisters, the Misses Downie, who became Mrs Wylie and Mrs Lochhead. Until recently the name could be seen on the building at first floor level. In 1847 a rival coach service was begun by James (Hookey) Walker, and in 1860 several Partick gentlemen formed the Glasgow and Partick Omnibus Company which had stables at Whiteinch Farm and an office at the south-west corner of Peel Street. Partick children loyally supported their own green-painted buses by chanting

> We'll not go into Hookie's 'bus
> Nor yet into Lochhead's,
> But we'll step into the Company's
> And run them off the streets.

All this hectic activity required yet another new bridge, and in 1877 New Dumbarton Road was realigned and the present Partick Bridge erected by the Trustees of the Glasgow & Yoker Turnpike Roads to cater for the ever-increasing traffic. The engineers were R.B. Bell and D. Miller and the contractor was Hugh Kennedy. The bridge was opened by Lord Provost William Collins in 1878. The outer sides of the bridge are decorated with iron representations of the coats of arms of Glasgow and Partick. The latter include a master galley with oars in action, a castle with two circular towers, a bishop's mitre, two millstones with a wheat sheaf, and the motto 'Industria Ditat' – Prosperity through Industry.

The first railway line to be built through Partick was the Stobcross line, built by the North British Railway Company, later the LNER, in the 1870s. This now forms part of the present Glasgow to Helensburgh line. The line approached Partick across the long viaduct which spans Ferry Road, the former Pointhouse shipbuilding yard, and the River Kelvin. Until the 1960s this bridge had an iron footbridge attached on the south side to maintain an ancient right-of-way over the Kelvin. The original right-of-way was across the stepping stones and its purpose was to enable villagers to pass freely to Pointhouse and from there by ferryboat to church at Govan. Partickhill Station on this line was moved from the north side of Dumbarton Road to the south side in 1958 and renamed Partick.

In 1895 the Caledonian Railway Company, later the LMS, demolished Crawford's 1601 bridge in order to construct the Partick section of the Lanarkshire and Dumbartonshire railway. The line came from Glasgow via a tunnel under Yorkhill, then crossed the Kelvin by a two-span iron bridge – which can still be seen just above Bishop Mill – before reaching Partick Central Station. The company then built a new road bridge over the river, the railway and the station platforms at Benalder Street. The booking office can still be seen beside the bridge at street level. Stairs led down to the platform below, and a concrete wall is still visible alongside the station, which was only twelve feet above the level of the Kelvin. The line is now closed and the part between Meadowside and Balloch has been used for the Glasgow to Loch Lomond cycleway.

From earliest times there has been a link across the Clyde between Pointhouse and Govan. The first ferries were open rowing-boats, but following an accident in 1861, when the Govan ferry capsized with the loss of seven lives, and another at Anderston in 1864 when nineteen lives were lost, a pier was built at Pointhouse and steam vessels introduced. In 1857 the Clyde Navigation Trust introduced a chain-operated vehicular ferry between Pointhouse and Govan which was replaced in 1912 by a variable-level boat of the type used at Finnieston. The vehicular ferry ceased in 1965 after the opening of the Clyde tunnel at Whiteinch and the last passenger ferry sailed on 22 January 1966.

Partick Castle

Partick Castle, as it became known locally, was built by George Hutcheson in 1611 on what may have been the site of the bishop's medieval residence, on slightly elevated ground on the right bank of the Kelvin. The site is now a scrapyard. George Hutcheson was a leading Glasgow citizen who, with his brother, Thomas, founded Hutchesons' Hospital and School for 'faderless and moderless bairnes or others poore and destitute of all support, because it were better to young anes to be unborne than unlernit in the mysteries of their salvation'. George and his wife Elspeth Craig lived in the Trongate above George's counting-house and were the owners of several other properties around Glasgow, including the mansion-house of Barrowfield, and land at Gairbraid, Carmyle and Yoker. Elspeth had a fine wardrobe of clothes which she bequeathed to her female relatives in her will. To her sister-in-law, Marion Stewart, wife of Thomas Hutcheson, 'she leives her best gowne, doublatt and skirt, in token of her guid will' and Elizabeth Pettigrew, her 'sister's dochter', was to receive 'her claith cloack'. Christian Herbertsone was left 'her gowne, doublat and skirt, quilk scho weirs on ye owik dayes', but even one of Elspeth's weekday gowns would be a garment of high quality. Elspeth's will also included 'insight plenishing', that is, furniture and

Partick Castle in 1828 from a drawing by Andrew McGeorge. An idyllic view of the house built by George Hutcheson in 1611 with the village and church of Govan in the distance.

household utensils, in the houses at Partick and Glasgow, and beir (barley) and mashlock oats (mixed grain), which had been grown on the orchard at Partick.

Partick Castle was a typical L-shaped Scottish tower-house of the early seventeenth century. The contract drawn up between Hutcheson and 'William Myllar masoune in Kilwinning' describes a house thirty-three feet high, with a hall on the first floor, a kitchen, cellars, pantry and girnal below, bedchambers above, and a turnpike stair nine or ten feet wide.

Little is known about subsequent owners of the castle, but according to James Napier, the house was inhabited around 1770 by 'common tradespeople', who let out the upper floor for dancing. Around this time the orchard and fields at Meadowside became a printfield and in 1844 became the site of the Meadowside shipyard. Stone from the castle was used in the early nineteenth century to build Merklands farmhouse, now also demolished.

Two businesses were then established on the site of the castle: the Partick foundry beside the river, and the Castlebank laundry

Castlebank Street was the main route through the village before Dumbarton Road was formed. The man with the barrow is standing outside the police office. The barrow was used to transport the drunk and incapables to the cells.

in a building with a tall chimney which stood in the middle of the scrapyard. The Castle Green, which lay between the stepping stones and the ford, became a commercial bleachfield, and large works were built over it in 1824. Behind the bleachworks, on Castlebank Street, there was a powerloom weaving mill, operated by the Lancefield Spinning Company, who employed a young man to sound a bugle through the village each morning at half past five in case their employees had missed the regular drumcall which went through the village at five o'clock. The bed-time drum was beat at nine o'clock. Bleachworks and weaving mill disappeared in the 1890s to make way for Partick Central Station.

The Quaker burial ground

When the roads were realigned in Partick in the 1960s in connection with the construction of the Clydeside Expressway, it was fortunate that the burial ground belonging to the Society of Friends, or Quakers, was completely preserved, for it is unique in Glasgow and one of the few in Scotland. It is a small rectangular plot of ground in Keith Street surrounded by a stone wall. A plate bearing an inscription has been transferred from the gate to the back wall and reads:

> Society of Friends. Burial Ground Gifted by John Purdon 1711. Last used 11.XII.1857.

The first meetings of Friends in Scotland are believed to have been held in the 1650s and by 1695 the membership had reached a thousand. The first person to be buried in the ground at Partick was 'Quaker Meg', the wife of the John Purdon, who gifted the ground. Quakers were not buried in Presbyterian ground and much superstition surrounded Meg's last resting place. Villagers believed that if they put their ear to Meg's grave at midnight and asked 'What did you get to your supper tonight, Meg', they would hear her say, 'Naething.' The Purdons were an old Partick family, and John Purdon's father was known as the 'riding beggar' because he rode about on an old horse, attending funerals and kirns – celebrations marking the end of the harvest – for the free handouts of meat and drink. Later Purdons resided beside the Old Bridge and became known as the lairds of the Brigend. The burial ground now belongs to Glasgow City Council and is cared for by some of the residents of Keith Court.

Shipyards and shipyard workers

In 1820 James Napier counted 247 families in Partick and estimated the population as 1,250. A great change came over the village in the 1840s when the Meadowside printfield became the site of Tod & McGregor's shipyard and Thomas B. Seath began shipbuilding on the opposite side of the Kelvin at Pointhouse. By 1851 Tod & McGregor were employing around 1,000 men and 150 boys in their yard, and between 1851 and 1861 the population of Partick more than doubled from 5,337 to 10,917. By 1884 the two yards between them had over 5,000 employees.

David Tod and John McGregor, both natives of Perthshire, began shipbuilding at Mavisbank, on the south bank of the Clyde opposite Anderston, in 1835. They were one of the first firms to combine iron shipbuilding with marine engineering, which both men had learned in the service of David Napier. When the Clyde Trustees needed the land at Mavisbank for harbour extensions in 1844, Tod & McGregor built a new yard downriver at Meadowside where there were better facilities for building ships for the competitive Atlantic trade. In 1850 the firm built the *City of Glasgow* for the Inman Line, which could steam at nine knots, using the screw as a propeller – faster than the Cunard Line paddle-steamers. Nineteen years later the *City of Paris* cut the Atlantic crossing to just under seven days. The *Lady Nyasa*, launched in 1861, was built at the request of David Livingstone to sail the Zambesi. Tod & McGregor also opened a graving dock in 1858. This was the first repair dock on the upper Clyde. The entrance can still be seen beside the wharf along the Kelvin which was used for berthing ships under repair.

In 1872 the yard and dock were purchased by Messrs Handyside & Henderson, who had founded the Anchor Line in 1859 The firm later became D. & W. Henderson, who built ships for the Anchor Line's North Atlantic and East Indian services, which, until the 1970s, departed from Yorkhill Quay. The firm also built many vessels for service nearer home. The *Lord of the Isles* was built for the Glasgow & Inveraray Company in 1877 to the high standard of comfort and finish required for the 180-mile daily return sailing from Glasgow to Inveraray. A second *Lord of the Isles* was launched in 1891. *Ivanhoe*, the 'teetotal boat', was built in 1880 for the Firth of Clyde Steam Packet Company to cater for those who wished to have a day out 'doon the watter' free of the drunken excesses encountered on other

The second *Lord of the Isles* arriving at Inveraray. The paddle-steamer was built in D. & W. Henderson's yard at Meadowside for the Glasgow & Inveraray Steamship Company in 1877.

vessels. Under the direction of Captain James Williamson and his smartly turned-out crew, she became a great favourite with genteel Glaswegians on the trip round the Kyles of Bute to Arran. Several famous racing yachts were also built in Henderson's yard at the end of last century to the design of G.L. Watson. The royal racing yacht *Britannia* was built at Meadowside for George V. In 1919 the yard was taken over by Harland & Wolff but became a casualty of the inter-war depression. During the Second World War landing craft which took part in the Normandy landings were built at Meadowside. The repair side of the business was carried on until the 1960s when the dry dock was filled in with masonry from the Grand Hotel at Charing Cross.

Pointhouse shipyard was founded by Thomas B. Seath in the early 1840s. When Seath moved his business to Rutherglen in 1862 the yard was taken over by Anthony and John Inglis, who already had an engineering shop in Anderston. The engines which they built there in 1851 for the Clyde Navigation Trust tender *Clyde*, to a design by Andrew Brown, can be seen on the quayside at Renfrew. The firm added a slip dock at Pointhouse in 1865, a few traces of which can still be seen on the east bank of the Kelvin, and also built boiler works which were not demolished until 1964.

The firm were general shipbuilders and engineers, building many vessels for the 'BI' – the British India Steam Navigation Company – a Glasgow shipping line in which Anthony Inglis held shares. The company was noted for their high-performance engines for short-distance, fast passenger ships and were regular builders of paddle-steamers in the 1890s for the North British Steam Packet Company. One of the finest, the *Waverley*, was launched on 29 May 1899. This elegant steamer with a single funnel, achieved the unusually high speed of 19.73 knots over the measured mile. Along with many other Clyde steamers, she served as a minesweeper in the 1914–18 war. She was sunk at Dunkirk on 29 May 1940 by German aircraft while evacuating troops from the beaches. The present paddle-steamer *Waverley* was also built at Pointhouse in 1946.

Anthony and John Inglis were Partick men, sons of John Inglis and Janet Morrison. John McGregor lived at Meadowside House, directly behind his yard, but the Tods went to live at the top of 'Tod's Brae' at Partickhill in a villa called Ironbank, from where they could keep an eye on progress down below in their own and surrounding shipyards. Tod took a keen interest in local affairs, becoming the first provost of Partick when the burgh was formed in 1852. The workforce came from all over Scotland. Tod & McGregor's manager, William McMillan, was a native of Ayr, and ship carpenters came from established shipbuilding areas as far afield as Kirkcudbright and Orkney. Many single men came from the West Highlands to work as labourers, usually lodging with a family from their own district – men like Donald Nicolson from Skye, Archibald McDonald from Moidart, Neil McVicar from Kilmartin, Donald McKenna from Benbecula, Archibald McLean from Tiree and Colin McDougal from Islay. The Highland girls went into service with middle-class families in Hyndland. The Irish worked everywhere as labourers. Peter McGowan from Sligo, for example, went down in a diving bell with a workmate to dig out boulders from the bed of the Clyde to deepen the channel for the large ships. The diving bell was a contraption six feet high, six feet long and four feet wide, with an open bottom into which air was pumped from the surface. Other Partick labourers, mostly Irish, worked an the punts which ferried the silt scraped up from the river bottom by the dredgers to the riverside. Mrs Rachel Hamilton or Johnston, 'Big Rachel' as she was known, worked as a labourer with Tod & McGregor. Over six feet tall and some seventeen stones in weight, she had come to Partick from Ireland at an early age, and with

Big Rachael, over six feet tall and seventeen stones in weight, worked as a labourer with Tod & McGregor, as a foreman navvy in the Jordanhill Brickworks, and was a special constable during the Partick Riots of the 1870s.

her 'cutty pipe' between her teeth, was a well-known local character. She was later employed as a foreman navvy in the Jordanhill brickworks, and a worker on an Anniesland farm. Big Rachel acted as a special constable during the Partick riots in the 1870s and died in 1899 at the age of seventy.

Churches and schools

Partick was originally part of Govan parish, and parishioners on the north side of the Clyde had to cross the river by ferryboat to attend services, baptisms and burials. In 1769 a petition was presented by the people of Partick asking for a church on the north side of the river, pointing out that the last people to get into the boat to go over to Govan 'find the service almost over before thay can get up to it, and at the dismissal of the congregation where is always such a hurry and throng about the boat, that very often the strong thrust the weak into the water to their great hurt and the spoiling of their clothes'. The petition was refused and it was 1834 before the Established Church built a chapel of ease, in Partick on ground gifted by Archibald Bogle of Gilmorehill. Partick was disjoined from Govan in 1869 and a parish church was built in Church Street ten years later. One of the most interesting memorials in Govan churchyard was erected by Robert Rait, a Partick chemist, in honour of his grandmother, Janet Brown, wife of George Craig. The inscription reads:

> In 1832 cholera broke out in Partick and the panic-stricken natives would have shunned the afflicted and fled had not Janet Brown Craig named above heroically led them on to nurse and succour the sick and dying and bury the dead.

Two churches were built in 1824 in Partick which until that date had none at all. Two Dissenting congregations, both of which had previously attended churches in Anderston, opened churches within two months of each other – the Secession in May and the Relief in July. The Relief was the first to secure a minister, James Ewing, an unfortunate young man who incurred much criticism for sliding on the ice on the Slit Mill dam on a Saturday during a curling bonspiel, and who died of fever in 1837, aged only thirty-three. He was followed by John Skinner, who left for America two years later, then by the Rev. Thomas Lawrie, who remained with his flock for forty-eight years. The congregation of Partick South are the successors of the Relief congregation and the church which was dedicated in 1988 is the third on that site in Dumbarton Road. The congregation has been known successively as the Relief, Partick West, Newton Place and Partick South.

The first Secession church, along with its school, stood on the west side of Byres Road, between Partick Cross and Torness Street. In 1865 the congregation left for a splendid new church at Dowanhill and the building in Byres Road was sold to their mission church. This congregation took the name of Partick East and built a new church in Lawrence Street. The two congregations were reunited in 1986. After a further union with Old Partick Parish Church, the three congregations now worship together in Lawrence Street in Partick Trinity Parish Church. Dowanhill Church, the first major work by the Glasgow architect William Leiper, has been converted to the Cottier Theatre, taking its name from Daniel Cottier, whose hand-painted and stencilled interior and stained glass windows have been painstakingly restored. The parish church became a furniture warehouse, but some of the fine stained glass by Steven Adam, David Gauld, Robert Anning Bell and Gordon Webster was saved. Also saved was the magnificent rose window by Gordon Webster in St Mary's Church, which stood at the corner of Peel Street and Burgh Hall Street until 1987.

There were 494 Gaelic speakers in Partick in 1881 and by 1891 there were 1,208, about three per cent of the population. The congregation of Gardner Street Church of Scotland was formed from a mission begun around 1875 for the Gaelic-speaking people of the district. The present church was built in 1905 and services are held every Sunday evening in Gaelic. Partick Highland Free Church at the corner of Dowanhill Street and Chancellor Street has a weekly Gaelic prayer meeting. Other Partick churches are the Free church and the Baptist church in Crow Road, the United Free church at Thornwood, the Methodist church in Dumbarton Road and the Congregational church in Stewartville Street, where the Rev. Vera Kenmure, the first woman minister in Scotland, began her ministry.

St Peter's Roman Catholic church and presbytery were built in Bridge Street in 1858 and a school was added on the south side of the church in 1864. The first priest was Daniel Gallagher, who came from Ireland as a boy to Blantyre, where he became friendly with David Livingstone. The congregation moved to a new red sandstone church in Hyndland Street in 1903, designed by Peter Paul Pugin of London. The congregation included many Irish as well as Italian families, who had cafés and chip shops in the district, such as the Arcari, Crolla, da Prato, Demarco, Massari, Saroli, Santangeli, Simioni and Zambardi families. The church in Bridge Street is now known as St Simon's and mass in Italian is held once a month. St Simon's is also used by the Polish community in Glasgow, and in 1979 St Simon's Black Madonna was taken on pilgrimage to be blessed in Warsaw by Cardinal Wyszynski.

It is not known when the first school was set up in Partick, but in 1652 the attention of Govan kirk session was drawn to the fact that 'ye bairnes in particke are verie much given to swearing and prophainis

Originally St Peter's Roman Catholic church and presbytery, this is now the Church of St Simon and is used for worship by the Polish and Italian communities in Glasgow.

the lord's day by playing in tyme of sermone on ye lord's day'. How long this behaviour was tolerated is uncertain, but in 1715 the session gave sixteen pounds Scots towards building a schoolhouse. This may have been the one reported as existing around 1750 on common ground on the east side of the Goat, with a playground stretching northwards to Dumbarton Road. The school and schoolhouse were rebuilt by subscription from eighty inhabitants of Partick in 1790. Several private schools also operated in the village at this time, the best known being Barr's school in a thatched cottage in Well Street and Dr Neil's school in Castlebank Street. All these schools declined after the churches opened their own schools. Partick Academy was built in 1850 in Church Street to supply higher education for the children of better-off Partick parents. The curriculum covered such diverse subjects as Latin and Greek, drawing and painting, bookkeeping, fencing and gymnastics. In 1878 the building was sold to Govan School Board and a new Partick Academy was erected in Peel Street, but the venture was unsuccessful and the academy closed in 1885. The school at Church Street was replaced by a new building in 1904, which is now used by the Social Work department.

The Anderson College of Medicine was the last building designed by James Sellars and it was completed in 1889 by John Keppie. The college originated as part of the Anderson Institution, founded in 1796 with money left by John Anderson, professor of natural philosophy at Glasgow University. Anderson's special interest was to provide practical training in applied science for mechanics and artisans as opposed to the theoretical instruction given at Glasgow University. Professor Anderson's fondness for scientific experiment, coupled with his fiery temper, earned him the nickname of 'Jolly Jack Phosphorus'. All the departments of the Anderson Institution, including the medical school, were in George Street in the city centre until 1886, when it became the Glasgow and West of Scotland Technical College, then, eventually, the University of Strathclyde in 1963. The building in Partick is now part of Glasgow University and houses the departments of dermatology and microbiology. David Livingstone attended the college when it was in George Street, and in the Hunterian Museum there is a section of a branch from the punda tree in Livingstonia, Northern Rhodesia (Zimbabwe), under or near which the heart of David Livingstone was buried by his servants and followers.

Business, politics and peisure activities

At a public meeting on 14 July 1852 it was agreed that Partick should be constituted a police burgh, and at the first council meeting David Tod was elected senior magistrate. He later became the first provost of the burgh. The handsome burgh buildings were designed by William Leiper and erected in 1872. The usual services were set up, including a police force and fire-brigade, but Partick was ahead of the times in having an officer of health who doubled as Surgeon of Police. One of the duties of the police was to quell the riots which broke out in Partick on 5 August 1875, when a procession to celebrate the centenary of the Irish patriot Daniel O'Connell was attacked by onlookers. The disturbance was brought under control but the rioting began again next day. The riot act was read, and although there were no fatalities several people were seriously injured and extensive damage caused to property.

There was again unrest in Partick during the 1915 Glasgow Rent Strikes, which were part of the attack on 'profiteering' that took place

The Steamie at Purdon Street. Old prams were used for bringing the clothes which the women washed on scrubbing boards or in a machine at extra cost, while exchanging all the gossip of the village. Luxury flats have been built on the site – 'From Steamie to Status'.

during the war years. In Partick the immediate cause was a sense of outrage and indignation at the attempts by landlords – seen as unscrupulous and unpatriotic – to exploit a shortage of housing by increasing the rents of soldiers' dependants and of the shipbuilding and munitions workers brought into the area to boost the war effort. The women were the front line troops, and the immediate enemy was the factor, who was regularly pelted with bags of peasemeal and chased down the street by women who 'upbraided him vociferously'.

Matters came to a head in November 1915 when one large Partick factor, Daniel Nicholson, applied for warrants of eviction against eighteen tenants after they refused a rental increase. The Glasgow

The 'Battle of Partick' as seen by the *Bailie* cartoonist in 1915.

Women's Housing Association organised a large demonstration on Saturday 13 November, four days before the tenants were due to appear in the small debt court. Women, men and children mustered in Victoria Drive South. Headed by a band, the procession then proceeded by Dumbarton Road to Partick, turned up Gardner Street, passing the factor's office, and continued to Thornwood Hill, where a platform had been erected overlooking the shipyards. The principal speaker was Mrs Crawford of the Women's Housing Association. Helen Crawford, the wife of a Glasgow minister, was a suffragette and ILP activist, and one of the most brilliant campaigners and feminist orators of the period. She dominated the meeting with her powerful rhetoric, telling supporters that 'the fight is essentially a woman's fight . . .' She respected all laws that were just and fair, but she did not ask them to 'respect the law which allowed increases in rents to be enforced at the present juncture'. Four days later a large crowd accompanied the Partick strikers to court, and at least five major shipyards and one armaments works struck work in their support. It was agreed to drop the cases and the dispute speedily moved from local to national level, forcing the Government to pass the Rent Restriction Act of 1915.

When Partick was annexed to Glasgow in 1912 the needs of its 60,000 population were catered for by local shops and family businesses such as Birss's household store, John Gardner's butcher's shop and Walter Hubbard's bakeries. The brothers William and John Thomlinson both set up in business in 1895, William as a leather manufacturer and John as a printer. Other Partick men founded very large firms: George Duckett was the owner of Bayne and Duckett, one of Scotland's largest shoemaking businesses and William Euing made a fortune in marine insurance. So fond was Euing of music that with friends he formed a glee and madrigal club called 'The Glasgow Larks', which met for practice at six o'clock in the morning. Euing left his valuable collection of music books to Anderson's College and the remainder of his library to Glasgow University. These ranged from classics printed by Foulis and a collection of English bibles to old chapbooks and broadsides. He also left over a hundred pictures to the city, mostly by Dutch and Flemish artists. The city's collections also include a valuable bequest of seventy paintings from the widow of John Graham-Gilbert of Yorkhill, including Rembrandt's 'Man in Armour', and several sketches of Clyde shipyards by the Partick-born artist, Muirhead Bone, who became an official war artist in the Great War.

Outlook unpredictable

'A quantum leap in the image, infrastructure and amenity of Clydeside on a scale not seen since the industrial revolution' is how Clydeport's chief executive described to the *Herald* in March 2001 the £500m Glasgow Harbour Regeneration Project for a two-kilometre stretch of the north bank of the Clyde between the SECC and the Clyde Tunnel. This ambitious scheme will not restore the shipyards and warehouses of the past, but is intended to replace them by hotels, entertainment and leisure centres, retail outlets and open parkland. If the development goes ahead, it is to include pontoons

Tenements in Crawford Street during the dustmen's strike of 1974, when decorated gable-ends were the fashion.

Tiny Partick Cross adds a footnote to the gable-end opposite: 'Painter put your brush away uzz Tiny Partick are here to stay.'

and slipways for visiting boats to encourage as much leisure use of the river as possible.

A different project, which has already been successfully established in Partick, is the Glasgow Gaelic Centre in Mansfield Street, one of only three in Scotland – the others are in Stornoway and Inverness – which aims to develop and promote the culture of the Highlands and Islands, the Gaelic language and the culture of the wider Celtic world. Almost half of Scotland's Gaelic speakers live in the central belt, 6,000 of them in Glasgow alone, and around 3,500 live in Partick and the West End, the largest concentration in any one location outwith the Western Isles. The centre has links with Strathclyde University Gaelic department and with Glasgow University Celtic department. Scotland's first dedicated Gaelic-medium primary school and nursery has now opened in nearby Woodlands as part of the ongoing renaissance of the Gaelic language.

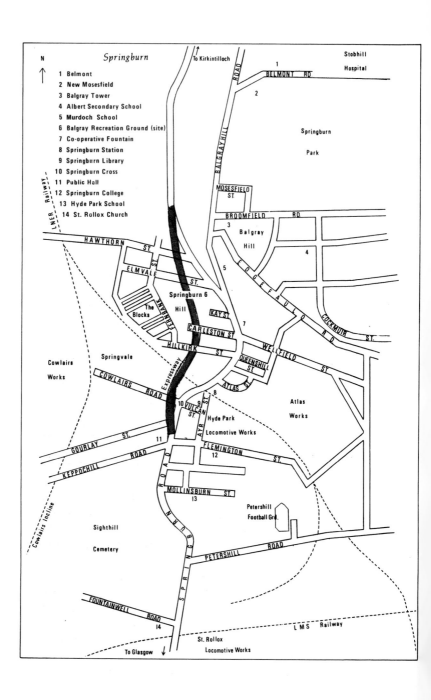

N

Springburn

To Kirkintilloch

Stobhill
Hospital

1 Belmont
2 New Mosesfield
3 Balgray Tower
4 Albert Secondary School
5 Murdoch School
6 Balgray Recreation Ground (site)
7 Co-operative Fountain
8 Springburn Station
9 Springburn Library
10 Springburn Cross
11 Public Hall
12 Springburn College
13 Hyde Park School
14 St. Rollox Church

BELMONT RD

1

2

Springburn

Park

BALGRAY HILL

MOSESFIELD
ST.

BROOMFIELD   RD.

3

Balgray

Hill

4

5

EDGEFAULD

COCKMUIR

ST.

LNER Railway

HAWTHORN   ST.

ST.

ELMVALE

ST.

The
Blocks

Springburn 6
Hill

FENNANT

KAY ST.

CARLESTON ST.

7

HILLKIRK   ST.

WELLFIELD

ST.

Cowlairs

Works

Springvale

COWLAIRS   ROAD

Expressway

QUEENSHILL
ST.

ATLAS   S.

8

Atlas

Works

9

VULCAN
ST.

AYR ST.

10

Hyde Park
Locomotive Works

GOURLAY   ST.

11

ROAD

FLEMINGTON   ST.

12

KEPPOCHILL   ROAD

MOLLINSBURN   ST.

13

Petershill
Football Grd.

Cowlairs Incline

Sighthill

Cemetery

SPRINGBURN

PETERSHILL   ROAD

FOUNTAINWELL   ROAD

14

LMS   Railway

To Glasgow

St. Rollox
Locomotive Works

7
SPRINGBURN

In the early nineteenth century Springburn was little more than a few cottages stretching along the Kirkintilloch Road, as Springburn Road was then called, about a mile and a half north of Glasgow, where the road threads its way between Springburn Hill and Balgray Hill, two of the small hills, or drumlins, that are a feature of the north of the city. Another line of cottages straggled up Centre Street, now Carleston Street, on the steep slope of Springburn Hill, and along the curve of Balgray Hill there was a line of villas, several built by Glasgow business men. Of these, the only survivor today is Balgray Tower, built around 1820 by David Hamilton for Moses McCulloch, a dealer in sedan chairs. The tower was also known as 'Duncan's Tower' or 'Breeze's Tower', after later owners. The other villas, Old Mosesfield, Edgefauld and Wellfield, are remembered only in street-names.

The 'spring' from which the village took its name arose on Balgray Hill, and the overflow from this spring formed a burn which flowed westwards across the fields along the line of what is now Hawthorn Street and eventually lost itself in Possil marsh. Until 1891 this line formed the northern boundary of Glasgow. Springburn has therefore always been part of Glasgow, unlike most of the other villages of Glasgow, which were taken into the city in the nineteenth and twentieth centuries.

A little to the south of Springburn was Springvale, another small village whose inhabitants were employed in Joseph Findlay's cotton spinning mill or as agricultural workers, quarriers and masons. To the west of Springvale stood the fine new mansion of Cowlairs, built by John Gourlay, a distiller, on the site of an earlier house built by Alexander Williamson, a Glasgow merchant, who had also built Petershill House. The only houses on the main road between Springvale and the Townhead of Glasgow were Flemington Farm, the tollhouse at Sighthill and an inn at the corner of Fountainwell Road with the curious name of Lodge my Loons, which was supposed to be the place selected by Rob Roy to lodge his followers while on their way to Glasgow to call on his kinsman, Bailie Nicol Jarvie. Near here

Opening of the Garnkirk & Glasgow Railway. View at St Rollox, looking south-east. Taken from *Views of the Opening of the Glasgow and Garnkirk Railway* by D.O. Hill. This was Glasgow's first railway, opened in September 1831. A goods train drawn by the *George Stephenson* has just arrived, and a passenger train drawn by the *St Rollox* is ready to leave. The smoke belching over Glasgow is coming from the chimneys of Tennant's chemical works and other factories.

stood Charles Tennant's St Rollox works, which by the 1930s were considered to be the largest heavy chemical plant in Europe.

In 1831 an event of great importance took place at St Rollox, This was the opening of Glasgow's first locomotive-worked railway, the Garnkirk & Glasgow, which was built mainly to bring coal direct into the city from the Monklands coalfield. Amidst great excitement two trains set off on the 27 September travelling in either direction along the ten-mile route. The eastbound passenger train was drawn by an engine called the *St Rollox*. The westbound train was pulled by the *George Stephenson*, named after its builder, and may even have been driven by the great man himself. This train hauled thirty-three wagonloads of coal, freestone and minerals. The momentous journeys were watched by crowds lining the route, and the day was rounded off with a grand dinner at the Black Bull in Argyle Street.

How many of the people lining the route that day in 1831 imagined the extent to which the railway mania that swept the country in the 1840s would transform Springburn from a rural community into the largest locomotive building centre in Europe? In 1842 the Edinburgh & Glasgow Railway Company brought a line through Springburn, followed four years later by the Caledonian, who incorporated the Garnkirk & Glasgow railway in their network. Both companies set up railway workshops. In 1861 'wee Walter' Neilson moved his Hyde Park works from Anderston to Springburn and immediately started building locomotives for a world market. By the end of the nineteenth century almost every family in Springburn was dependent, directly or indirectly, on the railways for its livelihood and Springburn had become, in the words of John Thomas, the railway historian and author of *The Springburn Story*, 'the Scottish Railway Metropolis'. Trains from Edinburgh still pass through Springburn before entering the tunnel which takes them down into Queen Street station in Glasgow, but a century and a half of locomotive building and repair finally came to an end at Springburn with the closure of the St Rollox works in 1987.

The Railway companies

The Edinburgh and Glasgow line was constructed by the firm of Grainger & Miller, who followed the route taken by the Union and Forth & Clyde canals via Linlithgow and Falkirk. This route is level all the way from Edinburgh to Cowlairs, a mile and a half from Glasgow city centre and 150 feet above the terminus at Queen Street. The railway then passes beneath the Forth & Clyde canal as the line makes its way down the famous Cowlairs Incline, a descent with a gradient of 1 in 46, mostly through a tunnel which took five hundred men working continuous shifts two and a half years to complete.

The engineers also had to devise a means of bringing the trains safely up and down the perilous incline, often over wet and greasy rails. This was done by a system of rope haulage. A winding machine was erected in an engine house at the top of the slope by the firm of Kerry Neilson & Co. of Stobcross, and this fed out an endless rope held in place just above the track. Trains were linked to the rope by a connecting chain called the 'messenger' and hauled up the incline. Trains did not go down the incline on the rope, but were attached to special brake wagons. The descent took eight minutes and was considered by some passengers to be worse than going down a deep colliery. The brake wagons were also attached up to trains in case the rope failed – as indeed it did, at the worst possible moment, just when a trainload of Edinburgh dignitaries had almost reached the top of the slope on their way back home after the ceremonial banquet held in Queen Street station after the grand opening of the railway on 18 February 1842. The brake wagons did their job and prevented a disastrous return downhill. The haulage system continued until 1908, when banking engines were introduced.

The Edinburgh & Glasgow Railway Company set up workshops on the west side of the lines at Cowlairs, where they could build and repair locomotives, carriages and wagons. This was one of the first railway workshops in Britain. The first employees settled in Springvale village among the cotton spinners and masons. The main street of the village was to become Cowlairs Road, and Cowlairs station was built at its western end. To provide more accommodation for their employees, the railway company built a row of thirty cottages along the east side of the line just north of Springvale village. These cottages were occupied by drivers and firemen and also several coachbuilders, coach painters and a coach spring maker from the Portobello and Musselburgh areas, who had probably worked before then at the company's St Margaret workshops in the east of Edinburgh.

By the 1860s still more accommodation was needed for the railway workers, and the company held a competition for a design for a model village to be built on the steep western slope of Springburn Hill. This was won by Andrew Heiton of Perth, who designed several terraces of houses in the Scottish baronial style with turreted staircases and crow-stepped gables. Unfortunately the scheme was too ambitious, and the intended schoolhouse, recreation grounds and library were never built. The 'Blocks' as they were known locally, were one of the sights on the Edinburgh to Glasgow route until demolition in 1967. Much of the increased business on the line came from the opening of Lenzie station. The railway company gave Glasgow businessmen free first-class tickets for five years if they built a house in the new township. The company made its profits from the sale of tickets at normal prices to the men's families and on the carriage of freight.

The North British Railway Company took over the Edinburgh & Glasgow in 1865 and made Cowlairs its principal workshop under the management of Superintendent Thomas Wheatley, who stepped up production of the company's famous green-liveries locomotives from six to forty engines per year. One of Wheatley's most famous, or infamous engines, was the 4-4-0 No. 224. This was the engine that went down with the Tay Bridge on 27 December 1879. It was recovered, returned to Cowlairs, refurbished and remained in service for some thirty years. It became known as 'the Diver' and was used as the emblem for the Cowlairs Co-operative Society.

Between 1842 and 1924 Cowlairs built around 850 locomotives, as well as maintaining and repairing the stock of the extensive North British railway. Locomotive construction finished when the company became part of the LNER in 1923 and the works became a modernised repair shop. When the railways were nationalised in 1948 Cowlairs continued to repair steam locomotives and carriages, but British Rail stopped using steam locomotives in 1968 and Cowlairs was closed. The site is now used as an industrial estate.

Railway development on a large scale at St Rollox began in 1846, when the Caledonian Railway Company took over the Garnkirk & Glasgow railway and began to run trains direct from Carlisle to Glasgow (previously passengers had to make the last part of the journey from Beattock by stage-coach). The terminus at Townhead was replaced by a new station at Buchanan Street, which was reached by a tunnel which passed under the Monkland canal and over the existing Cowlairs tunnel. Services from Buchanan Street ceased in 1966.

The Caledonian already had workshops at Greenock, but moved their 350 employees to new premises at St Rollox in 1856 to form the nucleus of a second centre of locomotive building not far from the rival establishment at Cowlairs. One of the best-known series of locomotives built at St Rollox were the Dunalastairs, named after the chairman of the Caledonian Company, James C. Bunten of Dunalastair, near Loch Tummel in Perthshire. When the fourth annual excursion for employees of the St Rollox works took place on Saturday 9 September 1899 – an event which has gone down in Springburn history as 'the great Caley trip' – fourteen Dunalastairs, each hauling a trainload of railwaymen and their families, steamed in procession at ten-minute intervals over Beattock summit and over the border to Carlisle. The splendid souvenir programmes issued for the occasion had covers printed in Caledonian blue with a border of rose and primrose – rose because the trip was going to England, and primrose because at Carlisle the 15,000 excursionists were given a speech of welcome by no less a person than the former Liberal prime minister Archibald Philip Primrose, 5th Earl of Rosebery, who reminded his fellow Scots that they had arrived on English soil on the anniversary of Flodden. However, this was not a day for remembering old feuds. The programme quoted a line from an old ballad, 'The sun shines fair on Carlisle Wall', and the citizens of the English town had put out banners proclaiming 'Welcome to the St Rollox visitors'. The hosts had brought entertainers from Scarborough and laid on two organ recitals of classical music for the Springburn visitors, who in turn brought with them the band of the Glasgow Highlanders and the Glasgow Male Choir to entertain the people of Carlisle in the public park. The first excursionists left Springburn at 5.10 a.m. and the last train arrived back home at one o'clock on Sunday morning. The outing made a nice break from routine, long hours and low wages – over seventy hours a week for around forty shillings for drivers and twenty-seven shillings for firemen.

Between 1856 and 1923 around a thousand locomotives were built at St Rollox, plus carriages and wagons. The Caledonian became part of the LMS in 1923, and, as at Cowlairs, locomotive building ceased in the 1920s. In 1987 repair work also ceased at St Rollox, marking the demise of a once great industry in Springburn.

The locomotive builders

For twenty years all locomotive building in Springburn was carried on in the workshops of the two railway companies at Cowlairs and St Rollox. In 1861 however, Neilson & Co. transferred their locomotive building business from Hydepark Street in Anderston to a more spacious site on level ground in the centre of Springburn so as to be near the lines of the railway companies for whom they had been building locomotives. Walter Neilson, the head of the firm, was the son of J.B. Neilson of hot-blast fame. Queenshill Street is named after the Neilson family estate in Dumfriesshire. At the International Exhibition in London the following year, Neilson displayed a splendid 2-2-2 locomotive with two 8ft. 2 ins. driving wheels, which caught the attention of Said Pasha, Viceroy of Egypt, who bought it there and then and ordered two more. Neilson also displayed a model of the *Rurik*, a locomotive fitted with runners which the firm had built the previous year to pull a three-coach passenger train over the ice between St Petersburg and Kronstadt.

Two of the employees who accompanied Neilson to Springburn were Henry Dubs and James Reid. Dubs left shortly after to found his own firm, the Glasgow Locomotive Works, at Polmadie. James Reid became the manager of Neilson & Co. in 1863 and gained

One of the 32 locomotives built for the Egyptian State Railways in 1947–48 leaves Hyde Park Works on its way through the streets of Glasgow to the docks. Note the police motor-cycle escort.

control of the firm in 1876 in circumstances which have never been fully explained. The ousted Walter Neilson then set up a second locomotive workshop on the opposite side of Springburn station, a stone's throw from his old premises at Hyde Park. He named his new works the Clyde Locomotive Works, but the business did not prosper and in 1888 it was taken over by Sharp Stewart & Co. of Manchester who changed the name to the Atlas Works.

In 1903 three firms, Neilson, Reid & Co. (now managed by James Reid's eldest son, Hugh), Sharp Stewart & Co., and Dubs & Co., amalgamated to form the North British Locomotive Company, always referred to in Springburn as 'the Combine'. The company was formed to meet American competition and became the largest railway manufacturing firm in Europe, with 8,000 employees, and exporting to over sixty countries. It was a regular sight in Springburn to see 80-ton locomotives pulled out of the works by horses or by steam engines into Vulcan Street and then down Springburn Road on their way to the docks at Finnieston. Unfortunately the company failed to make the transition from steam to diesel and closed in 1962. All that remains of the works is the handsome administrative building, opened by Lord Rosebery in 1909, which is now the home of Springburn College. Among its features are the sculpture of an 'Atlantic' locomotive on the tympanum over the entrance; the beautiful war memorial which depicts the fallen of the Great War bearing the crests of the regiments in which they served; and a window showing women workers in the Second World War, when they helped to produce howitzer carriages, torpedo tubes and tanks. The works were visited by King George VI and Queen Elizabeth in 1942. It is related that when the queen asked one of the apprentices what he was making, the youth replied, 'Time-and-a-hauf, mum!'

James Reid was an Ayrshire man who became not only a major employer in Springburn but also its leading citizen. Amongst his public offices was that of chairman of Springburn School Board whose meetings were frequently held in Reid's office at Hyde Park and which he attended conscientiously. New Mosesfield House and most of Springburn Park were the gift of the Reid family to the community. The house was formerly used as a museum and old men's club and is now used by the parks department. The family also provided funds for the winter gardens and a bandstand. The ornamental column in the park was originally part of a fountain which stood in the small Balgray recreation ground, another gift, which was destroyed to make way for the Springburn Expressway. The public hall in the centre of Springburn was a major gift in 1905. The statue of a Greek goddess can be made out on the façade, holding in her hands a locomotive.

James Reid lived for some time at Wellfield House on Balgray Hill, only a short step from his works. In 1875 he moved his home to 10 Woodside Terrace in Glasgow's West End, and also purchased a country estate and mansion-house at Auchterarder, which is now a hotel. In the last years of his life Reid's interests began to extend beyond Springburn. From 1882 to 1884 he was president of the Institution of Engineers and Shipbuilders in Scotland, and at the time of his death he was both Dean of Guild and President of the Royal Glasgow Institute of Fine Arts. His end came suddenly. As the centenary brochure of the North British Locomotive Works puts it, 'He dropped dead on St Andrews golf course on the 23rd June 1894, after a valiant but vain attempt to play his ball from a difficult lie in a bunker.' His statue, one and a half times life size, stands on top of the hill in Springburn Park, clutching a locomotive drawing in his left hand.

During his lifetime Reid formed an outstanding collection of paintings. After his death, his sons presented ten of the most valuable to the city of Glasgow, including oils by Constable and Turner and

James Reid of Auchterarder and the Hyde Park Locomotive Works surveys Springburn from his pedestal in Springburn Park. Auchterarder House was Reid's country residence.

important works by the French artists Corot, Troyon and Jacque. Reid's son Hugh inherited his father's good taste. His residence, Belmont, was built on one of the finest sites in Glasgow and was made of the very best of materials and workmanship. Hugh Reid left the house to Stobhill Hospital to be used as the Marion Reid Home for Children in memory of his wife. The house was used latterly for administrative purposes and was demolished in 1986.

Sighthill cemetery

In 1840 twelve acres of land at Sighthill were laid out as a cemetery and the area was later extended to forty-six acres. The cemetery occupies a sloping position and rises to a height of nearly 300 feet above sea level and affords views from Tinto to the hills of Perthshire. Several of the finest tombstones were erected by the firm of J.& G. Mossman, who also sculpted many of the statues in George Square and Cathedral Square. The firm is still in business in High Street and many of the early members of the Mossman family are interred in the cemetery.

The best-known monument is the obelisk erected to two weavers, John Baird and Andrew Hardie, the leaders of the 'Radical Rising' of 1820. This was erected by public subscription and was cleaned and restored in 1986. The events leading up to the death of the two men began when notices were posted in Glasgow calling for a general strike and support for a provisional government. On the night of 3 April, Hardie led some seventy men armed with pikes, swords and muskets towards Falkirk, where they believed English radicals were on the point of seizing Carron works. They were joined at Condorrat by a small band of weavers led by John Baird. Most of the men returned home when they discovered that no English radicals had appeared, but a group of some thirty men camped at Bonnymuir and defied orders from the 7th Hussars to disperse. Eighteen of the men were charged with high treason and Hardie and Baird were convicted, hanged and beheaded at Stirling. The other convicted men were transported though pardoned fifteen years later. James Wilson, a Strathaven weaver who led about a hundred men to join the others, but finding no evidence of support for the rising, returned home, was nevertheless publicly hanged and beheaded in Glasgow's Jail Square as a ringleader, before a crowd of 20,000. The bodies of Baird and Hardie were reinterred in Sighthill cemetery in 1847. Wilson is buried in Strathaven, but his name was added to the memorial.

A tall granite column marks the resting place of Bailie James Moir, 'the Gallowgate Slasher'. Bailie Moir was a great fighter for parliamentary reform. He left his collection of books to the city and the James Moir Hall in the Mitchell Library is names after him. Bailie Moir lived in Partick. He was a tea merchant in the East End, where he sold his wares at low prices, hence his nickname.

Driver Alexander Deuchar was a Springburn man of outstanding bravery who died following an accident on the footplate of his engine – the 8 p.m. express from Edinburgh to Glasgow – on Saturday tile 27 May 1922, when the boiler burst near Manuel junction. Deuchar pushed his fireman out of danger and groped through the steam himself to apply the brakes. He died the following Wednesday

The Martyrs' Memorial at Sighthill Cemetery. John Baird and Andrew Hardie were hanged at Stirling for their part in the Radical Rising of 1820 and reinterred at Sighthill in 1847. The high flats are built on the site of Tennant's chemical works.

from burns and scalds and was buried close to the Cowlairs incline, not far from his home at 4 Alford Street. Footplatemen contributed to a memorial to commemorate his bravery. The stone bears the inscription:

> He gave his richest gift, his life,
> On the altar of honour.

A simple white granite tombstone in the shape of an Iona Cross marks the grave of Mackenzie Murdoch, fiddler. The inscription on this monument reads:

> Homage to the memory of W. Mackenzie Murdoch, violinist and musical composer, born at Glasgow, 28th July 1870, died 28th April 1923. The most

renowned interpreter of the Soul of Scotland's music in his day. Erected by admirers whom he charmed by the magic of his bow. Unveiled by Sir Harry Lauder, 25th September 1924.

Mackenzie Murdoch was the composer of the song 'Hame o' Mine' and was already a well-known fiddler when Harry Lauder joined him in taking a concert party on tour round Scotland. Harry Lauder, then just beginning his career, was not only the comic, but also posted the bills and took the money at the door.

Other stones commemorate Robert Curle, shipbuilder, James Hedderwick, founder of the *Glasgow Evening Citizen*, William Leiper, architect, and Dr William Dougan, a general practitioner in Springburn, another victim of golf, said to have died 'from the effects of a severe drenching whilst playing the Great Game at Turnberry'.

Churches and schools

The first church in Springburn was built in 1842, the same year that the Edinburgh to Glasgow railway line was opened. It was built on a commanding site in Hill Street (now Hillkirk Street), conveniently placed for both the villagers of Springburn and the railway communities growing up at Springvale and Cowlairs. It was known as Springburn Hill Church and became the parish church when the extensive new parish of Springburn was formed in 1854 from parts of both St Mungo's (the cathedral) and the Barony parishes.

By the end of the nineteenth century about a dozen churches had been built in Springburn, but no churches were built in the inter-war years. After the Second World War many Springburn people were moved to Cumbernauld, Bishopbriggs and Kirkintilloch under an 'over-spill' scheme. In the 1960s more people were moved from the centre of Springburn to new tower blocks, and the resulting loss of population led to the union of congregations and the closure of church buildings. Between 1965 and 1985 nine Springburn churches were closed and demolished either because of vandalism or to make way for new roads which formed part of the comprehensive development plan. A new parish church was built in 1978 on a central site at the corner of Atlas Street and Springburn Road for the united congregations of Springburn Hill, Springburn North, Sighthill, Cowlairs-Somerville, Johnston Memorial and Wellfield. The Church of Scotland built Balornock North Parish Church and Barmulloch Church in the areas of new housing in the 1950s.

The ladies and gentlemen of Springburn Parish Church choir photographed. by William Graham, a railwayman who turned professional photographer in 1893 after being suspended during a strike.

St Rollox Church is also a new building which was erected in 1084 in Fountainwell Road to replace an 1894 building which was destroyed by fire. The name St Rollox is a corruption of St Roch's Loch. It is believed that there was once in the area a chapel dedicated to St Roch, who cared for those suffering from the plague and that victims of the plague in Glasgow were buried in this area.

The oldest church building in Springburn is now St Aloysius Roman Catholic Church, which was built in Hill Street in 1882 and incorporates part of an earlier church of 1856. The first priest was Father Dugald McDonald, a native of Moidart. Above the door is a sculpture of St Aloysius, the patron of youth and protector of students. A school which was attached to the church entered the state system in 1918. The present St Aloysius Primary School in Carron Crescent was opened in 1967.

Two well-known figures in Springburn were the evangelists Seth and Bessie Sykes. Seth Sykes was a tram conductor with Glasgow Corporation who gave up his work in 1929. From that date Seth and Bessie travelled to mission churches throughout Britain with a barrel organ, singing, preaching the gospel and retelling Bible stories by means of lantern slides. The Sykes are remembered as far away as the United States, where some of their songs have been adopted by evangelical Churches. Many Glaswegians first learned the choruses sitting on the sand at seaside missions at Clyde Coast resorts, accompanying the songs with the appropriate hand movements. Among the favourites were:

> Wide, wide as the ocean, high as the heavens above,
> Deep, deep as the deepest sea, is my Saviour's love

and

> Running over, running over, my heart's full and running over,
> Since the Lord saved me, I'm as happy as can be,
> My heart's full and running over.

Another Springburn personality who gave pleasure to thousands through music was Father Sydney MacEwan, the world famous tenor, who was born in 1908 in Keppochhill Road. The family lived at 248 Gourlay Street before moving to Knightswood. Father MacEwan served as parish priest at St Margaret's in Lochgilphead and at Kingussie and he has told the story of his boyhood in Springburn and his tours to New Zealand and Canada in his biography *On the High C's*, which he wrote after he stopped making recordings in 1973.

Two schools are known to have existed in Springburn in the 1840s. Murdoch's School was an old-established school built and maintained out of funds left by a Mr Murdoch, who supported four schools in Glasgow. This school was situated at Balgrayhill on the same site as the present Albert Primary School. The second school was set up by subscription and was situated in Centre Street in a converted six-loom weaver's shop with a coalyard alongside and stabling for the coalman's donkey on the ground floor. In spite of the surroundings the curriculum included book-keeping, Latin and mathematics as well as the usual reading, writing and arithmetic. When Springburn School Board was formed in 1873, the children from the subscription school were transferred to a new Springburn public school in Gourlay Street. In 1883 this school (presently Springburn Nursery School) became the infant's department when Murdoch's School was purchased by the school board and became the main school. The infants were under the supervision of Miss Kate Robb, with Miss Maggie Hughes as assistant. Attendances in the first weeks were low because of the bitter weather and an outbreak of measles and scarlet fever. On 19 January

Springburn was a prosperous place in the 1900s, but the wealth was not evenly spread, and the poor physical condition of children such as those here in Hawthorn Street gave much concern to school teachers and to medical officers of health.

1883 the log book records: 'One little boy, Thomas Gilfillan, died this morning after three days Illness of Scarlet Fever.' By March there was an outbreak of whooping cough, and mumps were also reported from time to time. Frequently children had to be sent home suffering from infectious diseases. Over-crowding and shortages were problems then as ever: 'Find very great difficulty in making satisfactory work, as we have neither seats, slates, nor teachers for such numbers – at the writing and drawing hour there were 96 children without slates.' In 1887 the infant school assumed the name Victoria School in honour of the queen's jubilee, and two years later it was decided that the main school should be called the Albert School. The name Victoria disappeared, but Springburn children today attend Albert Primary School in a modern building on the same site at Balgray Hill as Murdoch's School.

Albert Secondary School, built nearby in 1930 has now been renamed Springburn Academy. As part of the on-going modernisation of Glasgow's twenty-nine secondary schools, a completely new school is being built on an adjacent site, designed to hold 950 pupils. Another new school for up to 1,100 pupils will replace the present All Saints Secondary at Barmulloch, and St Roch's Secondary will be comprehensively refurbished. Every pupil will have access to the latest classroom technology. Classrooms will be wired up and pupils will have their own e-mail address and access to a computer and a bank of computerised learning programmes.

A record of the past and the present

Charles Forsyth, the headmaster of Springburn School, delivered his entertaining 'Reminiscences of Springburn 40–50 years ago' in Springburn Hall in 1940. The lecture was later printed and gives an interesting account of the Petershill area. A farmhouse known as Petershill House stood on the top of the hill until 1931. Petershill football ground now occupies the site. Hyde Park School was built on the site of a clay quarry which made the area unsafe for housing, and much of the Petershill area was used for recreation and entertainment. At one time no fewer than seven football pitches lay within half a mile of the Hyde Park Works. In the days described by Charles Forsyth the local team was the Northern Football Club, whose great rivals, Cowlairs, played on the other side of Springburn at Springvale Park. A favourite little pleasure ground at Petershill was 'Paddy Orr's Park' and over at Flemington Road there was another recreation ground where, in the dark on autumn evenings, crowds of five to six hundred used to gather to await the arrival of Sequah who, dressed as an Indian chief, would arrive to the sound of music on a four-horse charabanc. By the light of flares Sequah would offer the crowd various remedies for coughs and colds and dispense 'prairie cream', a cure for rheumatism, and then perform 'painless' extractions of teeth. Another entertainment was the 'geggie' or travelling theatre. The audience sat on planks and the show lasted for three hours with an hourly change of programme. The audience paid 2d at 7 p.m., 2d at 8 p.m., and 2d at 9 p.m.

   Several authors have left reminiscences of their Springburn childhood. Tom Weir, whose article 'A Springburn Boy Looks Back' was printed by Springburn Museum, recalls how as a boy he used to race up to Springburn Park on clear mornings to see his beloved mountain peaks. His sister, the actress Molly Weir, evokes her

J.M. Millen's grocery at 734 Springburn Road, photographed by William Graham in 1906. Note the Bilsland's loaves, Marshall's Semolina and Gray & Dunn biscuits.

Springburn childhood with much charm in *Shoes Were for Sunday*, relating her adventures in Paddy Oak's Park behind Hyde Park School; hunting for 'baggies' which died as soon as they were fished from the pond; taking bottles of water and jeely pieces up to the public park for a picnic; eating sherbet bads and sugarally straps and 'chittering bites', after a visit to the baths in Kay Street, and indulging in orgies with a cinammon stick 'sitting round a fire in the dark smoking this scented tube'.

A good photographic record of Springburn exists for the period 1893 to 1914 thanks to the work of William Graham, an engine driver with the NB Railway Company who took up photography professionally after being suspended in 1893 following a railway strike.

His fine collection of glass plate negatives, covering the whole of Glasgow and beyond, is now in the care of the Mitchell Library. John Thomas wrote articles on railway topics from the age of fourteen and left such masterpieces of railway history as *The West Highland Railway* and *The Springburn Story*.

Speaking at the time of the closure of St Rollox in 1987, Michael Martin, the local MP and now Speaker of the House of Commons, recalled his first memories of Springburn as a boy of fifteen. The streets were black, absolutely covered with workers making their way home, and from the top of a tram all to be seen was a sea of heads. The length of Springburn was unbroken with shops – gents outfitters, cleaners, restaurants, hairdressers, jewellers – you name it! And now, in the whole of his Springburn constituency there was not a single Co-op left.

The Cowlairs Co-op was the pride of Springburn and its demise marked the passing of an era. An early co-operative society existed in Springburn village, but in 1881 a group of railway workers founded their own co-operative society. Local traders appealed to the works' owners to sack the railwaymen, but the Cowlairs Co-op quickly became the largest retail organisation in the area, with thousands of members, all house-wives claiming a dividend, or 'divvy'. A granite fountain which was presented to the community by Cowlairs Co-op on their twenty-first anniversary in 1902 was moved from its original site in Vulcan Street to the new Springburn shopping centre opened by the lord provost, Dr Michael Kelly, in 1981. The inscription symbolises the qualities of co-operation and self-help which were the features of the Springburn community – 'Each for All and All for Each'.

In less than one generation Springburn saw the demise of its once great railway industry and the dispersal of much of its population to outlying areas. The final blow was the comprehensive development approved in 1973 which saw the centre of Springburn reduced to a short traffic-free stretch of Old Springburn Road and its character utterly changed by the building of an expressway and link roads. About seventy per cent of the nineteenth-century buildings were lost, along with many public amenities. The public hall, an A-listed building, has been spared, but now stands neglected and forlorn. The fire station has been refurbished for housing. The baths in Kay Street have gone, but they have been replaced by a new sports centre. In front is a 'larger than life' statue in fibreglass of an athlete, sculpted

The Boundary Bar, on the corner of Springburn Road and Hawthorn Street, at the northern limits of the old village, was designed in the Art Deco style of the 1930s, with transport themes etched on the windows. Now demolished.

by Andrew Scott and entitled 'The Bringer'. The young people sit around on the steps and eat their burgers and pizzas. No cinemas remain and the small downstairs room in Quin's Bar, that well-known Springburn landmark at the foot of Balgrayhill, is now no more than a verse in a song:

Doon in the wee room, underneath the sterr,
Everybody's happy, everybody's therr.

Not far away, at the northern limits of the old village on the corner of Hawthorn Street, was The Boundary bar. The bar was designed in 1937 by James Weddell and William Beresford Inglis, the architects of Glasgow's Art Deco hotel, the Beresford, in Sauchiehall Street. Transport themes were etched on the windows and several of these depicted Stephenson's *Rocket*. The counter of Clark's Bar at the corner of Petershill Road and Springburn Road survived to become the counter of the Reformed Dram Shop in the People's Palace, where tea, coffee and strictly non-alcoholic drinks were served to visitors.

After a series of moves to set up a museum, the reading room of the public library was refurbished and Springburn Museum opened in 1986. It acquired an impressive amount of memorabilia and photographs, and mounted exhibitions which attracted support from far beyond Springburn. Regrettably, lack of funding forced the museum to close on 30 March 2001. Facing the library and on the site of the Hyde Park Works, new houses have been built round a grassed over area, now known as Atlas Square, as part of the regeneration of Springburn. A plaque on the wall of the library reads:

ATLAS SQUARE
built
in the year
of the
GLASGOW GARDEN FESTIVAL
named by
Margaret Welsh age 10
David McKay age 10
Louise Rae age 11
Springburn children
opened
on June 6th 1988 by
Tom Weir MBE
local born
broadcaster & writer
1988

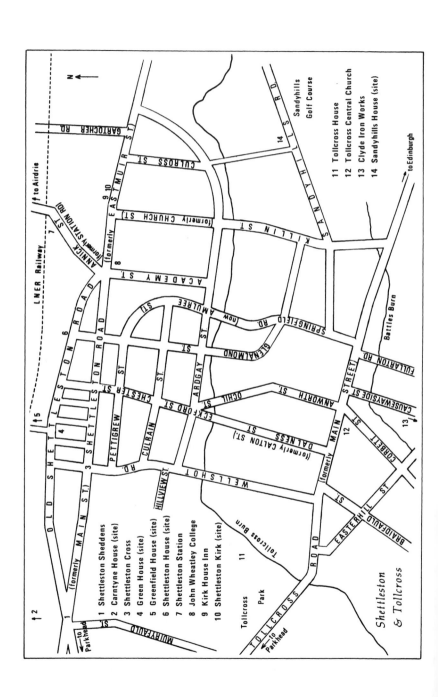

N

to Airdrie

LNER Railway

to Parkhead

to Parkhead

GARTOCHER RD.

ANNICK ST. (formerly STATION RD)

OLD SHETTLESTON ROAD (formerly MAIN ST.)

SHETTLESTON ROAD

EASTMUIR ST.

CULROSS ST.

(formerly CHURCH ST.)

ACADEMY ST.

now AMULREE ST.

KILLIN ST.

GLENALMOND ST.

SPRINGFIELD RD.

ARDGAY ST.

ECKFORD ST.

OCHIL ST.

DALNESS ST.

(formerly CALTON ST.)

AMWORTH ST.

MAIN (formerly STREET

CAUSEWAYSIDE ST.

FULLARTON RD.

Battles Burn

CORBETT ST.

PETTIGREW ST.

CHESTER ST.

CULRAIN RD.

HILLVIEW ST.

WELLSHOT RD.

Tollcross Burn

BRAIDFAULD ST.

EASTERHILL ST.

TOLLCROSS ROAD

to Parkhead

Tollcross Park

SANDY THORN RD.

Sandyhills Golf Course

to Edinburgh

MUIRYFAULD ST.

1 Shettleston Sheddens
2 Carntyne House (site)
3 Shettleston Cross
4 Green House (site)
5 Greenfield House (site)
6 Shettleston House (site)
7 Shettleston Station
8 John Wheatley College
9 Kirk House Inn
10 Shettleston Kirk (site)

11 Tollcross House
12 Tollcross Central Church
13 Clyde Iron Works
14 Sandyhills House (site)

Shettleston & Tollcross

8

SHETTLESTON and TOLLCROSS

The villages of Shettleston and Tollcross lie about a mile distant from each other near the eastern boundary of Glasgow. Although the green fields which separated the two until the 1920s are now covered with houses, the two villages have kept their own identity, with Shettleston claiming the territory north of the Tollcross Burn and Tollcross the land to the south. Nevertheless the two names are closely bound historically, for by a charter granted by Alexander II to the Bishop of Glasgow in 1226, the provost and officers of Rutherglen were forbidden from taking toll or custom within Glasgow, but were authorised to collect legal dues 'ad crucem de Schedenestun' – to take 'toll' at the 'cross' of Shettleston. 'Sheddens' denotes a parting of the ways, and a cross may have marked the spot where a branch road led down to a ford across the Clyde, but the location of any such junction remains unknown.

Nearly fifty different spellings of 'Shettleston' are recorded before modern times, so it is not surprising that other explanations of the name have been given. If Shettleston is the 'villam filie Sedin' referred to in a papal bull dated 1179 addressed to the Bishop of Glasgow, then Shettleston may have been the place where a son or daughter of some person of importance called Sedin may have had a residence over eight hundred years ago. In Ross's map of Lanarkshire of 1773 the spelling is 'Shuttleston', and five communion vessels owned by the parish church are each inscribed 'Shuttlestoun Kirk – 1783'. It may be that at a time when weaving had become all-important as a means of livelihood, the villagers themselves transformed the name.

Shettleston takes shape

By the sixteenth century the 'villam filie Sedan' had grown into a fair-sized community complete with its own tradesmen. In 1597 Matthew Fischer and his spouse, Janet Cuik, transferred a 6s 8d land to John Cuik, a shoemaker, and his spouse Jonet Winzet, and the transaction was witnessed by John Hucheson in Scheddilstoun, John Meik, a skinner in Middle quarter, John Selkrig in Badhill and

Old cottages with outside stairs at the corner of Old Shettleston Road and Fernan Street about 1898.

Malcolm Robeson in Middle Quarter. The old name Badhill lives on in Budhill Avenue north of Shettleston station. An agricultural return of the middle of the seventeenth century lists a 'West quarter of Schettilstoune' and a 'Middle quarter of Schettilstoune', as well as the lands of Sandihillis and Glenduffhill, Over Carntyne and Nether Carntyne. This return shows the district well suited for the growing of oats, bere [barley] and peas. Most people worked on the land, but mining was also carried out, for a record of 1564 describes a John Gray as a *carbonario*, or collier.

Around 1703 John Pettigrew built Green House on a piece of land on the south side of Old Shettleston Road between what is now Kenmore Street and Vesalius Street. Green House was a substantial two-storyed dwelling-house with crow-stepped gables which was not demolished until 1929. The house can be seen on General Roy's map of 1755 in the centre of Shettleston – shown as a sizeable village extending from what is now Shettleston Sheddens to Annick Street, where the road takes a sharp turn northwards in the direction of Airdrie. Shettleston Kirk is also shown on a minor road leading to the villages of Sandyhills and Hole. Greenfield and Tollcross estates are shown as enclosed, and a main road (now Wellshot Road) leads southwards to Tollcross from the centre of Shettleston.

The Statistical Account of 1794 gives the combined population of Shettleston and Middle Quarter as 766, and the population of Sandyhills &c. as 341. The lay-out of Shettleston was radically altered during the first part of the nineteenth century after a new road, called Main Street, was opened through the village parallel to, and a few hundred yards south of, the Old Shettleston Road. This new road continued eastwards past Shettleston Kirk in the direction of Baillieston, and the villages of Eastmuir and Sandyhills were now added to Shettleston's eastern flank. Shettleston and Tollcross became part of Glasgow in 1912, and the development of Shettleston was completed with the building of houses on the Carntyne, Greenfield and Sandyhills estates to the north and south of the village.

The Muirdibs, Auld Prickie and other Shettleston pits

Coal was mined in the Shettleston area at least as far back as the sixteenth century. The Grays of Carntyne and the McNairs of Greenfield were the principal coalmasters over several generations. The extensive coalfield at Mount Vernon was operated by the Buchanan family. Coals were mined at first for smithy work, but during the seventeenth century there was an increasing demand for supplies of coal for the brewing, pottery, glass, soap and other manufacturing industries which were growing up in Glasgow. Coal was also needed for the burning of limestone in kilns for use as a fertiliser on the land as improved methods of agriculture became better known.

The first coals were won by the simple process of digging them out from an outcrop, the miners following the seam underground. These workings were called ingaun 'e'en' (ingoing eyes). Where the seam was underground, but near the surface, the method was to sink a short vertical shaft to the coal. The shaft bottom was then widened out to form a 'bell-pit', and the coal extracted. The coal was hewed by the colliers, then carried up ladders and out of the pit by bearers, who were generally the women and children of the family. Until 1799 miners were bound to a particular colliery for life, living in a virtual state of serfdom. In 1842 the employment of females and boys under ten was forbidden by law, although this seems to have died out in the Shettleston area before then. By that time bearers had been largely replaced by hutches hauled to pit shafts by ponies, but sometimes also by men or boys.

Shettleston Cross, looking eastwards along Main Street, now Shettleston Road, about 1906. The shop on the corner of Main Street and Wellshot Road was one of the numerous branches of Andrew Cochrane Ltd, Tea and Provision Merchants.

The largest problem affecting the mining industry was drainage. Various methods were used to pump or raise water from pits by manual, horse, water and wind power, but it was not until the early eighteenth century, when Newcomen's steam-engine was adapted for use in collieries, that any real progress was made. After James Watt made improvements to Newcomen's engine it was possible to work deeper seams of coal.

John Gray is reported as using a windmill pump from 1737 until 1740, when it was blown to pieces in a great storm long remembered by local people as 'the windy Saturday'. Gray also installed the first steam engine in a mine in the Glasgow area at Carntyne in 1768. The improvements in drainage and the sinking of deeper pits coincided with a period of increased demand for fuel. This came on the one hand from the domestic needs of the inhabitants of the expanding Glasgow conurbation and on the other hand from the rapid expansion of the iron industry after the invention of the 'hot-blast' process by S.B. Neilson at the Clyde ironworks in 1828. However, the problems of drainage in the Carntyne or, as they were usually known, the

Westmuir, pits, was never properly overcome and coal working was finally abandoned by the Gray family in 1875.

The Westmuir colliery extended from Parkhead to Eastmuir. The Wester, Old School, Black Engine and Caroline pits are described in the chapter on Parkhead. In Shettleston, travelling from west to east, the first pit was the Sheddens, then a small pit at the top of Hillview Street, near Tollcross Park. The Muirdibs was a larger pit beside Carntyne Old Church at Shettleston Cross. The Muirdibs was so shallow that the workers could hear the mail coaches thundering along the road overhead. The Wellshot pit was somewhere in the vicinity of Shettleston bowling green. The Dog Pit near the Salvation Army Hall was 'merely a large opening in the ground which was fenced round and was so called from the fact that someone had dropped an unwanted dog into its depth'. The Pricklismuir pit was at Budhill, just north of Shettleston railway station. 'Auld Prickie' was on McNair's Greenfield colliery and was abandoned and used as a basin for the water coming from the other workings on the same property. To keep the water out of their own Westmuir colliery the Grays had to install a pump in Auld Prickie in order to conduct the water to the Camlachie Burn by an underground course. At Eastmuir there was the Kirk pit on the site of the original Shettleston Kirk and the Eastbank pit in the vicinity of the present parish church in Killin Street. The Palace pit opposite Culross Street was on the Mount Vernon Colliery, wrought by the Buchanan family.

The Gray family seem to have owned the lands of Carntyne for more than two hundred years before Robert Gray built Carntyne House in 1802, at the same time converting a farmhouse which stood on the site into offices. It is probable that the Grays resided earlier at Carntyne Hall, a house on the north of the estate. Like many other old Glasgow families, the Grays had their share of characters. One of the first lairds sheltered 'outed' ministers in Covenanting times. His grandson ended up in prison when his wife told the authorities that he intended joining the 45 Rising. When St Andrew's-on-the-Green Episcopal church was being built – the first church in Scotland after the Reformation to have an organ – an elderly aunt of the family made off with the mason's mallet concealed in her muff, advising others to do the same so that 'the House of Baal would not be biggit for twelve months to come'. The last Gray of Carntyne was a clergyman who resided in England but who was buried in 1867 alongside his ancestors in the crypt of Glasgow Cathedral. Carntyne

House stood in the middle of the inter-war housing scheme of South Carntyne.

The lands and mansion-house of Greenfield came into the ownership of the McNair family in 1759. The McNairs owned other properties in the area, including Shettleston House, which stood on the north side of Old Shettleston Road opposite McNair Street. In the early years of the twentieth century Greenfield estate became a golf course. It was also used for housing between the wars. Part of the estate is preserved as Greenfield Park.

Churches and schools

Shettleston Kirk was built on ground gifted by James and George Reston, the proprietors of Budhill, who in return were granted a pew in the church and a lair in the churchyard. Although the old church is now demolished, the churchyard is still intact. The stone structures on either side of the gate were used by watchmen guarding the churchyard against body-snatchers. Just to the west is the Kirkhouse, the modern successor of an eighteenth-century hostelry, which

Shettleston Parish Church in Eastmuir Street, now Shettleston Road in 1898. Note the weather-vane surmounted by a three-crested ship in full sail, the crest of the Bogle family, who subscribed generously towards building the church.

claims a foundation date of 1771. Horses and vehicles were put up at the Kirk House on Sundays while their owners were at worship. The Bogle family were among the subscribers who gave money to build the kirk, and their crest, a three-masted ship in full rig, was erected on the spire as a weather-vane. A replica can be seen on the roof of the church hall, built in Killin Street in 1953.

Shettleston Kirk was built for the convenience of the inhabitants of the east end of the Barony parish, who found the four-mile journey into Glasgow particularly arduous in winter, and also for the people of the west end of Old Monklands parish. Barony kirk session received two-thirds of the collections at the church door and Old Monklands one third. It was intended that the building should be paid for from subscriptions from the heritors, or landed proprietors, of both parishes, but in 1760, 'tho' the outmost care was taken by the managers to have everything done in the most frugall manner yet they found themselves considerably in debt'. A petition was subsequently presented by Colin Dunlop of Carmyle and the managers to Glasgow Town Council, pointing out that a considerable number of Glasgow feuars resident in the lordship of Provan also used the church, and requesting financial assistance. The council agreed and gave the sum of £25 sterling to clear off the debt incurred in building the church.

Shettleston parish was disjoined from Barony in 1847. During the ministry of the Rev. John White it was decided to build a new church in Church Street, now Killin Street, but this time it required legal action to force some of the 'absentee' landowners to pay their share. The new church was opened for worship in 1903. John White later became minister of the Barony Church. At the reunion of the Free Church and the Established Church in 1929, the church became known as Shettleston Old Parish Church.

Other Church of Scotland congregations worship at Sandyhills, Carntyne Old and Eastbank churches. Sandyhills Church began when John Thomson, the minister of the parish church and part of his congregation 'came out' at the Disruption. The present church, built in 1975, is the third on the site. Carntyne Old, at Shettleston Cross, was opened in 1893 for another Free Church congregation formed around 1884, and is now linked with Eastbank Church, which was built for a United Presbyterian congregation in 1896. Other places of worship are Shettleston Free Church of Scotland, St Serf's Episcopal Church, Shettleston Baptist Church and Shettleston Methodist

Church. The Salvation Army now operate from their Goodwill Centre in Etive Street.

The Church of St Paul at Eastmuir is a striking modern building, designed by the architect Jack Coia. Its main architectural feature is a hanging copper Calvary within a tall arch at the front of the building. The church was erected to celebrate the centenary of the building of the first church of St Paul in 1857. Before that time there was no Catholic church between St Mary's, Abercromby Street and St Patrick's, Coatbridge, except a small wooden building with a school nearby. The first parish priest, Father Patrick McLaughlin, served in a territory reaching from the far side of the Monkland Canal in the north to the banks of the Clyde in the south. Father McLaughlin went to prison for contempt of court rather than give the name of a thief who had handed over stolen money in the confessional.

In 1905, St Mark's Church, Carntyne, was formed as a daughter church of St Paul's. The building contained a chapel on the upper floor and a school below, and a presbytery was built alongside. A separate church was built in 1927, but this building was destroyed by fire and replaced by the new St Mark's in Muiryfauld Drive in 1980. Between 1912 and 1945 St Paul's and St Mark's were administered as joint parishes, but were separated again following the death of Father James Kearney, a much-loved priest who had served the parishes for twenty-three years. A new church, St Barnabus, was opened in 1962 in Darleith Street as a place of Catholic worship in the centre of Shettleston.

Four schools were in existence in Barony parish in 1795, and probably earlier, supported by the heritors who also paid the teachers' salaries. These schools were at Anderston, Maryhill, Shettleston and Ruchazie. Even after Shettleston became a separate parish the costs of the school continued to be paid by the heritors of the whole Barony parish, and the masters appointed by the Barony church. An arrangement existed whereby, if any of the schools was without a teacher, the other teachers would share the salary given to the whole four, but it not known whether this unusual arrangement ever took effect.

In 1873 the parish school at Shettleston was transferred to the Shettleston school board, who built a new school at the corner of Gartocher Road and Eastmuir Street. Shettleston Public School was always known in its early years as 'McHaffie's School', after headmaster James McHaffie, but it later became Eastmuir Primary

The infant girls' class of 1896 at Eastbank Academy, resplendent in lace collars and Sunday best.

School. Eastbank Academy, on the other hand, was always referred to as 'Scott's Folly', not after the headmaster, but after the chairman of the board, whose idea it was to transfer the pupils of the school at Eastmuir to splendid new premises opposite Station Road. The new school which was opened in 1894 with the more fashionable name of 'Eastbank Academy' was an intermediate school with a three-year secondary course. Beyond that stage pupils had to attend Hamilton Academy. Changes were introduced after Shettleston became part of Glasgow in 1912. A separate primary school building was erected on the west side of Academy Street, and by 1917 Eastbank Academy had attained full secondary status and was teaching to sixth-year level. In the years that followed the school acquired a reputation for educational excellence, together with an impressive variety of other activities, such as its many musical productions.

To accommodate an ever increasing school population, the academy was transferred to a new, larger school building in 1986 on the west of Academy Street. The old building was then refurbished and is now an adult education college known as John Wheatley College. A major extension and refurbishment of Eastbank Academy is now underway to provide modern accommodation for up to 1,400 secondary pupils. Similar refurbishment will take place at Bannerman High. St Andrew's Secondary at Carntyne will be a new school designed for 1,700 pupils, the largest in the project to modernise all of Glasgow's twenty-nine secondary schools.

Shettleston expands

The first manufactured goods in Shettleston were for agricultural purposes. In the middle of the nineteenth century John Anderson was making tiles and Robert Law was producing not only wooden agricultural implements but also iron ploughs, harrows, threshing machines, shovels and spades. This business later became Law, Duncan & Co., who described themselves as engineers, boiler and agricultural implement makers, railway waggon and iron house builders.

The opening of the North British railway line through Shettleston in 1871 encouraged the growth of industry in the north of the village. The Shettleston Ironworks were built around 1874; the Glasgow Rope Works around 1877 in a long shed which extended behind the houses on the north side of Eastmuir Street (now the site of Annick Street Industrial Estate); Carntyne Dyewood Mills around 1883; and the North British Bottle Works in 1904. On the south side of the village the Wellshot Laundry began around 1904 in Glenalmond Street and Shettleston Co-operative Society built stores, a creamery and offices in Pettigrew Street in 1910. Large numbers of workers, shopkeepers and tradesmen moved into Shettleston in the 1890s. The same decade saw the founding of Shettleston Football and Athletic Club, Shettleston Harriers, the Shettleston Bowling Club and the Sandyhills Golf Club. Many photographs of Shettlestonians during their working and leisure hours have been published by Sandyhills East Community Council in *Shettleston from Old and New Photographs* and *Shettleston Past and Present,* each with an informative commentary by Thomas M. Waugh.

Eight-pound cottages and other housing

John Wheatley, the MP for Shettleston who became Minister for Health in the Labour Government of 1924, was born in Bonmahon, Co. Waterford, in 1869 and at the age of nine came with his family to Bargeddie, now part of Blackhill in the north-east of Glasgow, where his father found employment in the local pit. Between the ages of

The Master Builder – Mr John Wheatley. 'Well, if the Wheatley cement mixture won't work, what will?' How the *Bailie* cartoonist viewed John Wheatley's Grand Housing Scheme on 11 June 1924, the day after the passing of the 'Wheatley Act' which subsidised public-sector housing.

eleven to twenty-four he also worked in the pit. During this time the family of thirteen lived in a single apartment house in cramped and primitive conditions. After leaving the mines he ran a small grocery business with his brother Patrick, which did not prosper, but both later set up successful publishing businesses.

As a young man Wheatley was a supporter of the United Irish League, and in 1906 founded a Catholic Socialist Society, with the aim of persuading Catholics that voting Labour was compatible with their religious beliefs. After being elected to Glasgow Town Council he began his campaign for good quality, subsidised public-sector housing in place of city slums with the publication of a pamphlet entitled 'Eight-Pound Cottages for Glasgow Citizens', and campaigned under the slogan 'Homes not Hutches'. In 1922 Wheatley was elected to Parliament as ILP member for Shettleston. As Minister of Health two years later in Ramsay MacDonald's cabinet he saw his ideas come to fruition with the passing of the 'Wheatley Act', which enabled local authorities to build houses for let at a price the average working-class family could afford to pay. Wheatley's view became increasingly left-wing and he was not offered office in the Labour government of 1929. He died at Shettleston in 1930.

During the progress of the bill through Parliament, the parliamentary correspondent of the *Glasgow Eastern Standard* kept its readers in touch with events in London. Tuesday 10 June 1924 had been a 'great day' in the House and the vote of hundreds of millions of pounds for houses went through without a division. 'Mr Asquith and Mr Lloyd-George did the Minister the honour of coming in to hear what he had to say,' wrote the correspondent, 'while Mr Baldwin lolled on the front Opposition bench!' A fortnight later the *Standard* was reporting local reaction under the heading 'Grown – in a night – the suburb of Sandyhills':

> Even yet the people of Shettleston and Tollcross have to rub their eyes to take a second look when they pass the Glasgow Corporation village at Sandyhills. The growth of the new community has been too like that of those Mushroom Cities of the prairies, or of the Wembley British Empire . . . Only a few weeks ago it seems Eastbank children were taking a short-cut over the meadow where the houses now stand.

Another distinguished member of the Wheatley family was John Wheatley, who was Lord Justice Clerk from 1972 until his retirement in 1985 and who was created a life peer in 1970, taking the title of Baron Wheatley of Shettleston. Lord Wheatley, who died in 1988, was the son of Patrick Wheatley and the nephew of John Wheatley MP. His autobiography, *One Man's Judgment*, tells of his boyhood in Main Street, Shettleston and after 1923 in a semi-detached house in Sandyhills. He is best remembered for the 'Wheatley Report' of 1973, which reorganised local government in Scotland on a regional basis.

All roads lead to Tollcross

Authorities have not been able to agree on the exact location of the historic cross of Shettleston, where the royal burgh of Rutherglen was allowed to collect tolls, but it is possible that the cross stood near the west end of the present village of Tollcross, from where early travellers may have been able to follow the Tollcross Burn southwards to the Clyde and cross over to Rutherglen.

Although Tollcross did not develop as a village until the late eighteenth century, the name 'Towcorse', 'Towcors' or 'Towcross' – 'towl' being a common Scots form of 'toll' – appears throughout the medieval period and increasingly in connection with road improvements as Glasgow's commerce began to expand. In 1717 John Bowman, provost of Glasgow, attended a meeting of the Commissioners of Supply for Lanarkshire, the body responsible for the upkeep of the roads at the time, and spoke of 'the great inconvenience to the leidges for want of a bridge over the burn near to Towcorse, betwixt Hamilton and Glasgow', and the dangers of crossing in time of flood 'when neither coaches, carts nor passengers can pass to Glasgow'. The shire granted Glasgow 500 merks towards building a bridge and ordered the inhabitants of adjacent parishes to give their labour by bringing stones, lime and other necessary materials. Two masons, James Rae and Robert Wodrop, each received 100 merks in 1720 for work carried out on the bridge.

A new system for financing the roads was introduced in 1753, when an act was obtained which gave the landed proprietors of the district, including the provost and magistrates of Glasgow, the powers to keep roads in good order and erect turnpikes and tollhouses and levy duties to meet expenditure. The route followed by the turnpike road from Edinburgh to Glasgow at this time makes interesting reading and it is easy to see why the journey took two days:

> through the counties of Linlithgow and Lanark, leading from the east end of Livingstoun to Polkemmet, in the county of Linlithgow; and from thence by the Shotts Hills, Kirk of Shotts, and Muriehall, in the Parish of Shotts; and from thence by Hollowtoun and Bells Hill, in the parish of Bothwell; and from thence by Boghall and Towcross to the city of Glasgow.

The London to Glasgow mail coach service was established in 1755 and shortly after a daring attempt was made one winter's morning to rob the coach, which had just set off from Glasgow, as it passed through a small wood of fir-trees a little way east of Tollcross. The highwaymen tied a strong rope from one tree to another across the road at the height of the positions usually occupied by the coachman and the guard, but the plot was foiled when the rope caught a waggon of hay lumbering up the road towards Glasgow instead.

Sixty years later it must have been a fine sight for the people of Tollcross when the coach bringing the news of Wellington's victory at Waterloo thundered past, a red flag floating on the roof of the coach, the horses decorated with laurels and the guard resplendent in his best scarlet coat and gold ornamented hat jubilantly sounding his bugle.

Tollcross village, church and estate

Tollcross is typical of many villages which grew up towards the end of the eighteenth century, with weavers' and tradesmen's cottages built along either side of a main street. Pigot's Directory of 1825–26 lists in the village a slater, nailer, wright, two blacksmiths, a boot and shoe-maker, three tailors, two grocers who also sold spirits, seven spirit dealers and two publicans, John McAlpine and Walter Wilson. The first cottages, described as 'neat and thatched' were built at the east end of the village in the vicinity of Springfield Road (now Amulree Street) and were known as 'High Dennistoun' and 'Low Dennistoun'. From here a road led uphill to a bleachfield at the side of the Tollcross Burn at Springfield Farm. Northward expansion of the village was hindered by a large sand-pit occupying all the ground between Springfield Road and Upper Dunlop Street (now Anwoth Street). Calton Street (now Dalness Street), at the west end of the village, was originally a separate little community, described in the 1860s as 'occupied by that class who generally live in the Caltons of larger towns', presumably the low-paid, unskilled workers. Mutton Pit is shown on the OS map of 1897 in the Calton in the area of the present Altyre Street. Calton Street led uphill to Wellshot Cottage, beyond which was the farm of Egypt, so named by a farmer who had once served in that country with the British army. Some original eighteenth-century cottages with outside stairs and strips of land to the rear survive in the vicinity of Tollcross Central Church.

There was a great influx of population into the Tollcross area at the end of the eighteenth century with the opening of the bleachfield, the expansion of the weaving trade, the extension of coal mining and the establishment of the Clyde Iron Works at Fullarton by Thomas Edington and William Cadell in 1786. For this increased population there was only one church – the chapel of ease at Shettleston, which was overcrowded. The Reformed Presbyterians, who had built a

Tollcross Filling Station at 1217 Tollcross Road, on the north side of the road just before the city boundary at Amulree Street. The driver sits in the car while a boy fills up his tank at the pump. The car is a 1926 Austin 12.

meeting house at Sandyhills and held their open-air communions on the 'preaching braes' there in summer, had moved to Glasgow.

The Relief Church agreed to build a church in Tollcross and this building, latterly known as Tollcross Central, was built in 1806, with 1,231 sittings, in the middle of the village. Many of the congregation had previously attended East Campbell Street Church in Glasgow, which had an elder's district in Tollcross and Carmyle. In 1834 a steeple with four clockfaces and a bell was added to the building – unusual features for a Relief church. An acre of land was donated by Mr Cadell of the ironworks on which to build the church and lay out a burying-ground, on condition that he should have 'free of all charges, one front pew with another immediately behind it in the gallery'. Cadell was commemorated with a stained glass window in the church.

Tollcross Central Church was damaged in a fire in 1990 and is now demolished, but the churchyard is still intact. The poet William Miller is buried there in an unmarked family grave. A monument in the Necropolis beside Glasgow Cathedral commemorates him as 'The Laureate of the Nursery'. Miller, who spent most of his boyhood in

Tollcross Central Church was the oldest church in the village until it was damaged in a fire in 1990 and demolished. It was built in 1805 and the distinctive square clock-tower added some years later., The poet William Miller, who wrote 'Wee Willie Winkie', is buried in the churchyard.

the village of Parkhead and was a wood-turner to trade, published a collection of charming children's poems in 1863 under the title of *Scottish Nursery Songs and Poems*. The best known is the old favourite, *Wee Willie Winkie*:

Wee Willie Winkie runs through the toon,
Upstairs and downstairs in his nicht-gown,
Tirlin' at the window, crying at the lock,
Are the weans in their bed, for it's now ten o'clock.

Hey Willie Winkie – the wean's in a creel,
Wamblin' aff a bodie's knee like a varra eel,
Ruggin' at the cat's lug and revelin' a' her thrums,
Hey, Willie Winkie – see, there he comes!

The Tollcross estate belonged to the Corbett family for hundreds of years and was very extensive, once stretching as far west as the 'Little Hill of Tollcross' at Camlachie. The part of the estate containing Tollcross House was sold to James Dunlop of Garnkirk in 1792 and passed to his son Colin in 1816 and then to Colin's nephew, James Dunlop, in 1837, along with the extensive Clyde ironworks, which had come into the ownership of the family around 1812. James Dunlop belonged to the Edinburgh branch of the family and was not considered to match his Glasgow predecessors in business acumen, but he did have an eye for a good architect. He commissioned David Bryce, who enjoyed a fine reputation as a builder of country houses, to build a new mansion at Tollcross in 1848 in the Baronial style. The estate became a Glasgow park in 1897 and until 1972 the mansion-house was used as a children's museum. One of the most popular exhibits was a glass case depicting the nursery rhyme 'Who killed Cock Robin', which is now in Kelvingrove Museum. After the museum was closed a proposal to convert the mansion to luxury flats was rejected in the face of local opposition and it is now a sheltered housing complex for the elderly. James Dunlop, who built the house, was particularly interested in woodland, and the beautiful arrangement of trees in the glen and the fine lime tree avenue leading to the house was his personal selection. Tollcross has again become one of the city's most

A pencil sketch of the first mansion-house of Tollcross. A new mansion-house was built on the site in 1848 to a design by David Bryce.

attractive parks. An international rose trial garden has been planted in recent years on the lawns west of the house and the conservatory has been rebuilt and upgraded. The new swimming pool and leisure complex at the east end of the park is particularly popular with local families and visitors.

There was once a deer park in the grounds and the last deer, Bobby, was preserved by a taxidermist and given a home in Kelvingrove Museum. Across Shettleston Road, facing the site of the deer park, is a long row of tenements which originally went by the name of Rock Dove Gardens. During the course of construction the builder paid a flying visit to Ireland and happened to attend a race meeting where he was persuaded to put some money on a horse called Rock Dove. The horse won and made him so much money that the name was bestowed on the property.

Auchenshuggle

An OS map of 1859 shows the small village of Auchenshuggle laid out in a series of rows round the junction of Easterhill Street and Dunlop Street (now Corbett Street), behind the burial ground of Tollcross Church and close to the Battles Burn, which formed the boundary with Old Monkland parish. At the time there were about 260 people in 56 households living in Auchenshuggle. Half of the men were miners, and others were employed as weavers or tradesmen, labourers and carters. The majority of women worked as bleachers or weavers of cotton, two older women were embroiderers, and there was a dressmaker, a bonnetmaker and a shirtmaker. Other women were employed as servants or as dairymaids. Most people lived in houses with one or two rooms, but eight families enjoyed a three-roomed house. One of these was the schoolmaster, John Kinniburgh, whose mother, now in her ninetieth year, lived with the family. A school first mentioned in 1826 was held in the Session House of Tollcross Church until Tollcross Public School was built after the passing of the 1872 Education Act. This school was under the patronage of James Dunlop with no support from the parish, the salary of the teacher being derived from the pupils.

The name Auchenshuggle is Gaelic and denotes 'a field of' rye. The name is best known to Glaswegians as the name of a tramcar terminus, and it frequently features in pantomimes at the Metropole Theatre when the audience was invited to join in such choruses as:

Fares please, fares please, you can hear me sing.
As I collect the coppers and the punching bell I ring.
I'm in the Corporation, you can tell me by my dress,
I'm Jeanie McDougall frae Auchenshuggle
The caur conductoress.

Alternative last lines were:

Mary Ross from Govan Cross
Jessie McGhee frae Polmadie
Lizzie Todd frae London Road.

The last tramcar in service in Glasgow ran on the Auchenshuggle to
Dalmuir route on 4 September 1962. The next day rain-soaked crowds,

A trip on Coronation Tram no. 1297 to Auchenshuggle via Shettleston X
makes it 'a day out of this world' for young visitors to the Glasgow Garden
Festival in May 1988.

estimated at 200,000, nearly one quarter of Glasgow's population, turned out to cheer a procession of twenty trams from Dalmarnock Depot to Coplawhill. Every tenement window along the three-mile route was occupied by 'hingers-oot'. In London Road the eighth car had a breakdown, and in true tramway fashion, all those behind were held up for ten minutes.

Thousands of people had a nostalgic ride on an Auchenshuggle 'caur' during the Glasgow Garden Festival of summer 1988 on Coronation Tram number 1297, and two hundred former Glasgow conductors and 'clippies' turned up for a special reunion on the site.

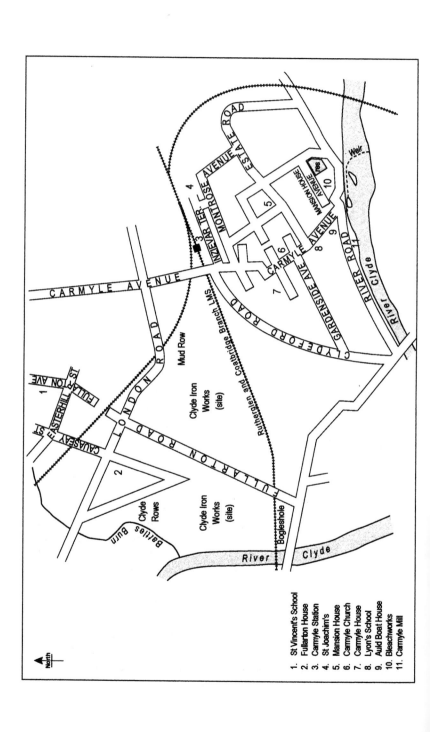

North

1. St Vincent's School
2. Fullarton House
3. Carmyle Station
4. St Joachim's
5. Mansion House
6. Carmyle Church
7. Carmyle House
8. Lyon's School
9. Auld Boat House
10. Bleachworks
11. Carmyle Mill

CARMYLE AVENUE

LONDON ROAD

FULLARTON ROAD

FULLARTON AVE

EASTERHILL ST

CAUSEAY ST

FULTON AVE

Clyde Rows

Clyde Iron Works (site)

Clyde Iron Works (site)

Mud Row

Bogleshole

Baillies Burn

River Clyde

River Clyde

Rutherglen and Coatbridge Branch LMS

CLYDEFORD ROAD

GARDENSIDE AVE

CARMYLE AVENUE

INZEVAR TER.

MONTROSE AVENUE

ESTATE ROAD

MANSION HOUSE

RIVER ROAD

Weir

Dog

9

CARMYLE

The village of Carmyle is situated on the north bank of the Clyde on the eastern boundary of Glasgow, about five miles from the city centre. It was taken into the city, with the neighbouring districts of Fullarton and Kenmuir, as recently as 1975. Before that date the area formed part of Old Monkland parish, in the county of Lanark.

For many centuries Carmyle formed part of the extensive bishopric of Glasgow, and the name appears many times in medieval charters and church records. Around 1150 Bishop Herbert gifted the lands of Kermyle to the Cistercian Abbey of Newbattle, with the waters and fisheries pertaining to it. In 1268 Bishop Cheyam bought back the lands and erected a meal mill. A mill was still working at Carmyle last century.

Some of the early residents of the district make their appearance in the rental book of the archbishop in the time of Mary, Queen of Scots: Jhone Gwne and Jonat Legait in Westyr Carmyll, Thomas and Andro Tennand and Marion Lwk in Vuer Carmyld, and Wilzam, James, Jhone and Robert Bogyll in Neddyr Carmyle. Thomas and Gilbert Durandis, Wilzam Mathy and Jhone Cors are recorded as rentallers of 'Clyddis Myls'. In the seventeenth century the Bogles and Corbets became prominent families in the area as they rose from being rentallers or tenants of the bishop to become landowners and wealthy merchants in Glasgow.

In olden times the east end of Glasgow was known as 'the granary of Glasgow', and in his account of Old Monkland parish in 1793, the Rev. John Bower speaks of the fertility of the parish. Along the river banks grow luxurious crops of every grain, especially wheat, and oats and potatoes are produced as well. The reason for such a high degree of cultivation is that 'when a merchant has been successful, he purchases a piece of land, builds an elegant villa, and improves his property at the dearest rate'. Considerable quantities of flax are also grown. This is ready for pulling about the first of August and nine women, at 10d, will pull an acre in a day. In the parish there are two lint mills at which flax is skutched and dressed, and 400 weavers who all work for the manufacturers of Glasgow.

Cross Roads Carmyle, looking north up Carmyle Avenue towards Tollcross at the junction with London Road. Now a busy junction with access to and from the M 74 extension.

Although the area was largely agricultural till the eighteenth century, some industrial activity was already in progress two centuries earlier. In 1546, Jhon Govan, 'burges of Glasgow', took over from his deceased father the 'tuenty s land of Carmyle, alias Fullerton'. This is one of the earliest known appearances of the name Fullarton, and suggests that a separate community of 'fullers', whose task it was to felt cloth by wetting and beating it, had already been established to process cloth. 'Westyr Carmyll' was an alternative name for 'Fullartown', and the work may well have taken place along the Battles Burn, which was the western boundary of the Monklands. The burn, now culverted, passes through Fullarton near Tollcross Road.

The long-established cloth industry was revived on a more commercial scale in 1741 with the erection by a Mr McKenzie of a bleachfield at Carmyle. There is no indication that Carmyle was laid out as a planned industrial village, but the arrival of this new venture, the changes in agriculture, and the technical progress made in the equally long-established coal-mining business in the area encouraged people to move from small 'ferm-touns' into the village which was beginning to take shape on either side of Carmyle Avenue, the main road leading down to the river. By the end of the eighteenth century the population of the village had risen to over five hundred and a bequest had been made for a school in the expanding village, but Carmyle did not have its own church until a century later.

The Bleachfield, Fullarton and the ironworks

By the 1790s the bleachfield begun by Mr McKenzie employed around fifty people and processed light muslins on a ten-acre site, drawing water from a well six feet deep, which took twelve hours to fill. This was replaced at the end of the nineteenth century by a reservoir. In 1861 Alexander Millar, the owner of the business was employing 30 men, 20 boys and 110 women. Millar lived in the old mansion-house of Carmyle, and the Park family occupied the house for much of last century. James Park & Co. described themselves as bleachers and finishers, finishing by machine fine cottons and linens from Nottingham and Manchester. The factory closed in 1961 and was then used for some years by William Morris, the furniture makers. The Ardargie private housing estate was built over the site in the 1970s.

The development of Fullarton as a community of coal and iron workers began when James Dunlop began to mine coal extensively on the Carmyle estate, which he had inherited in 1777 from his father, Colin Dunlop, a leading Glasgow tobacco merchant, who thirty years previously had the foresite to invest his fortune in an estate rich in mineral deposits. Between 1777 and 1793 James Dunlop invested £10,000 in the Fullarton coalmine, the largest on the estate. The improvements included the installation of a steam engine which drained a field of 800 acres and machinery which replaced a horse-gin for carrying the coals out of the pit. In 1793 the number of people employed at Fullarton pit was 150, of whom 75 were colliers earning from 2s 6d to 3s 6d per day. The parish minister commented on the difference emancipation had made for the colliers: 'Instead of being considered as inferior beings, which was formerly the case, they now behave and dress like their fellow citizens.' An old man, called Moss Nook, once told Colin Dunlop, son of James Dunlop, how he had come to Fullarton:

> Do you not know that your father brought me here long ago from Mr McNair's of the Green? Your father used to have merry meetings with Mr McNair, and one day he saw me and took a liking to me. At the same time Mr McNair had taken a fancy to a very nice pony belonging to your

father, so they agreed on the subject, and I was niffered awa' for the pony. That's the way I came here.

James Dunlop's coalmining activities at Fullarton and elsewhere in the west of Scotland enabled him to survive bankruptcy when the family tobacco firm foundered in 1793, and by 1810 he was able to take over the Clyde ironworks, which had been started in 1786 by Thomas Edington and William Cadell on a site about a mile south of Fullarton village, in order to make use of the excellent Fullarton coal and the abundant supplies of local ironstone. In 1793 about three hundred men were reported as employed at the iron works, smelting ore in two blast furnaces and producing a variety of cast-iron goods, such as pots, pans and boilers. Expansion was taking place so that pig iron could be converted to bar iron which works such as Carron were anxious to procure at a cheaper price than had to be paid for the imported sort.

Colin Dunlop succeeded his father as owner of the Clyde Iron Works in 1816 and was persuaded by J.B. Neilson, a native of Shettleston, to allow him to experiment at the works with a process of using hot instead of cold air in the blasting furnace. The success of the hot-blast process in 1828 led to a major reduction in costs in the production of iron and quickly transformed the Monklands into the ironmaking centre of Scotland. Improved methods of production did not necessarily lead to better conditions of employment, for the ironworkers continued to work twelve-hour shifts, from six to six, and because they were paid monthly the men, or their wives, had frequently to apply for advances of wages from the company. These were granted on condition that a percentage of the money, sometimes up to seventy per cent was spent in the company's 'store', where prices were high and the goods were of inferior quality. A favourite trick was not to give back the odd farthings in change. Sugar was described as 'enough to scunner a taed' [toad] and the butter as 'only fit to oil cart wheels'. A tied store, known as the Clyde Store, operated in Causewayside Street, the main street of Fullarton village. One of the colliers, Thomas Kerr, was the 'colliers' justice man'. His duty was to see that each man in the 'gang' got his proper share of the wages.

The colliers at Fullarton village lived in 'rows' and 'lands': Store Row, Cuddy Row, School Row, Dunlop's Land, Scott's Land, Dunn's Land and others. There were also miners' rows at Carmyle. The Pit Row was at the end of Inzievar Terrace, where St Joachim's Church now stands, and the Carmyle Rows were opposite the bleachfield on the river side. The Dunlops built a separate village on their Fullarton estate on the south side of London Road for the colliers, blast furnacemen, labourers and other workers in the Clyde ironworks. The 'Clyde Raws' as they were known, stood on the north-west of the estate and in the 1860s they were occupied by about 120 families living in the two-room houses in the long Rail Row, or in the one-room houses in the short Bank Row, Brick Row, Kiln Row and part of Dandy Row. The four houses in Clydeside Row all had five rooms and were occupied by a blacksmith, a carpenter, an engineer and the blast furnace overseer. John Baird, the works cashier, occupied the nine-room Clyde Cottage. About fifty colliers' families lived in the two-room houses at Mud Row, which stood on its own on the east side of Fullarton Road. The company also erected and supported a school in Fullarton Hall. James Dunlop told an enquiry in 1842 that many of the boys had free time during working hours to attend the works' school, each child paying 10d a month. He was in favour of children being obliged to go to school till twelve years old, as had previously been the rule. John Kinniburgh, the schoolmaster, was well thought of in the village, for visiting the stricken during a cholera outbreak, and for taking a leading role in winning the famous case against Thomas Harvey, the landowner who tried to close the ancient right-of-way along the river from the city to Carmyle.

Nothing now remains of the two mansion-houses of the Dunlops of Carmyle. The Mansion House at Carmyle was described in 1860 as 'an old house in good repair, built about 200 years ago', and it was latterly occupied by successive owners of the bleachfield. The modern street names, Estate Road and Mansionhouse Road, Avenue and Drive indicate the site of the house on the hill on the east of Carmyle Avenue.

Fullarton House is remembered in a rather special way, by the establishment of Glasgow's first community nature park in part of the grounds. The aim of the project is to encourage a wide range of flora and fauna, especially to replace native species of trees and flowers, and to this end nearly nine hundred native trees were planted during National Tree Week in 1982, including oak, ash, hazel, rowan, gean, alder, willow and birch. A variety of wild flowers have been planted and of special interest is the high concentration of orchids. The park has been named Auchenshuggle Wood, because, we are told, it was near the no. 9 tram terminus.

In 1930 the Clyde ironworks became part of the Colville's group and were a landmark just beyond the city boundary until, as part of the British Steel Corporation, they closed in the 1970s. The workshops were converted into small business premises as part of a special project set up by the British Steel Corporation within the Cambuslang Investment Park.

Carmyle in the nineteenth century: 'a straggling, rural appearance'

In 1822 a school-house was erected in Carmyle village on the area now occupied by the sheltered housing complex of Orchard Court, and a teacher's house was built on the opposite side of Carmyle Avenue. An inscription on the front of the building recorded that the school was endowed with £1,000 by William Lyon Esq. of Savanna la Mar in Jamaica on 29 April 1799. In 1882 the funds of the school were transferred to the school board of Old Monkland parish, who sold the property in 1889 to the Misses Jane and Lillias Buchanan. The school was used by the residents of Carmyle as a Sunday school, for political meetings and other functions. An application from Gavin Paterson, of Mud Row, Clyde Iron Works, for the use of the school for a wedding party in October 1886, for example, was granted by the board, 'with the usual conditions'.

The money from the bequest was then used to provide scholarships entitling the holders to free education with books and stationery at Mount Vernon Public School, and bursaries ranging in value from £5 to £7 10s. For the year beginning January 1887 seven scholarships were awarded – five to children of miners, two boys and three girls, to the daughter of a labourer at Carmyle, and to the son of an engine-fitter at Carmyle. Five boys were awarded bursaries, the top mark in the competition being gained by the son of the coachman at Wester Daldowie. The recipients were all aged between ten and thirteen.

The village continued to expand during the century. In 1837 Pigot's Directory lists several Carmyle residents: Thos. Smith, schoolmaster; Wm. Rodger, bleacher; Eliz. Brechin and Wm. Hamilton, spirit dealers; John Sligo, esq; Laurence Drew, miller and farmer. John Sligo, listed under the heading of 'gentry', married a niece of Colin Dunlop and had a house designed in the 'cottage house' style of the 1830s by William Burns. The original name, Carmyle Cottage, was later changed to Carmyle House. The house is now occupied by the Verona Fathers, a group of missionary priests. Laurence and Peter

The Auld Boat Hoose in River Road. This public house was established in 1825 at the point where a ferry crossed the Clyde to Cambuslang.

Drew were millers and farmers at Clydes Mill and John and Andrew Drew farmed at Bogleshole. There were Drews at 'Ower Carmylye' in the sixteenth century. Seven hundred years of meal and flour milling at Carmyle came to an end in 1926, when the mill was converted into a sawdust mill. The site has now been landscaped and is used as a car park.

The Auld Boat Hoose in River Road, opposite the spot where a boat ferried people over to Cambuslang, and the Auld Hoose or 'top shop' round the corner, a few yards up Carmyle Avenue, are the successors of two older inns. Thomas Hamilton and his wife, Ann Calderwood, kept the ferryboat, while her grandfather and father were among those who kept the Boat House, which also had the ferry rights. Ann's daily duty was to row the miners across, either going to or returning from the pits. When 'Boat Ann' died in 1912, aged ninety-seven, her obituary was printed in the *Herald*: 'Mrs Hamilton was an active and powerful woman, and when some of the colliers lads became obstreperous she was in the habit of dipping them in the Clyde.'

Although the village had grown in size by the end of the nineteenth century it remained unspoiled, and in 1882 Carmyle was described as presenting 'a straggling rural appearance, with intermixture of garden-plots and trees', with a station on the railway, and old-fashioned meal-mills, with foaming dams, and a population of 536.

Expansion in the twentieth century

The opening of Carmyle station on the Rutherglen and Coatbridge branch of the Caledonian Railway encouraged development at the north end of the village. Among the villas built there were the manses of both Victoria Tollcross and Tollcross Central Churches. There were no churches in Carmyle until an iron church was erected in 1902 for a United Free congregation, formed as the result of mission work from Victoria Tollcross. The present Carmyle Church of Scotland was opened five years later. Carmyle Church was linked with Kenmuir Mount Vernon Church in London Road in 1978. For the Roman Catholics in the Carmyle area a new parish of St Joachim's was founded in 1954 from St Joseph's in Tollcross. Mass was said in a temporary church converted from a farmhouse in River Road until the new Church of St Joachim was opened in 1957 in Inzievar Terrace.

St Vincent's Home for Blind, Deaf and Dumb Children in Fullarton Avenue was founded by the Daughters of Charity of St Vincent de Paul, who came to the area in 1911 and had their convent in Fullarton. Both the original school and the convent have now gone. The present St Vincent's Special Needs School was built on a new site in 1966. Until the 1960s primary children in Carmyle attended Mount Vernon Primary or St Joseph's Primary at Tollcross. The children now attend Carmyle Primary in Hillcrest Road or St Joachim's Primary in Montrose Avenue.

More industry came into the area last century with the arrival at Fullarton in 1913 of the Clydeside Tube Co. Ltd, part of the recently formed Stewarts & Lloyds. Andrew Stewart began his firm in Glasgow in 1861 to take advantage of the booming urban market in gas and water pipes and tubes and moved to Monklands to be nearer a supply of raw materials. He provided the funds to found the Adam Smith chair of Political Economy at Glasgow University in 1896. The merger with Lloyd & Lloyd took place two years after his death in 1901. A large part of the site of the works is now a grassed-over area with the remainder used for housing. Another new industry was the Clyde's Mill power station on the south bank of the river, which provided

A grand bazaar which lasted three days in March 1906, was held in the Trades Hall in Glasgow to raise funds to help build Carmyle Parish Church, the first church in the village. The Mount Vernon Amateur Dramatic Club provided the Saturday night entertainment – a comedy sketch *A Pair of Lunatics* and a farce in one act, *Ici on parle Francais*.

employment for local workers. This was both a coal-fired and a hydro-electric station, using the Clyde waters.

In the last half century Carmyle has grown considerably in size, with several areas of new housing, but it still remains a compact village. Two new roads have been built: the Clydeford Road, opened in 1974, which branches off from Carmyle Avenue and leads to Cambuslang and Hamilton and the extension of Gardenside Avenue on to Clydeford Road. The M74 extension passes through the north of Carmyle at London Road.

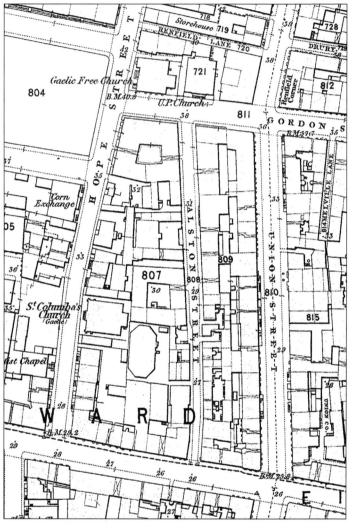

The village of Grahamston, 1858, from Ordance Survey map of Lanarkshire, reproduced by permission of the Trustees of the National Library of Scotland. Alston Street is the main street of the village.

10

GRAHAMSTON

The village that disappeared

The village of Grahamston took its name from John Graham of Dougalston, who, in 1709, feued about seven acres of the lands of Blythswoodholm, part of the estate of Colin Campbell of Blythswood. The feu-duty was six bolls of good and sufficient farm bear, the equivalent of £4 6s 6d sterling.

The area between Grahamston and Buchanan Street was then still green fields, and to the west were kitchen gardens let out to gardeners, who grew vegetables to supply the city markets. The village eventually extended from the west side of Union Street to the west side of Hope Street. It consisted of one street, named Montrose Street by the Grahams and later renamed Alston Street, which ran from the north side of Argyle Street up to and above the line of Gordon Street. After the Caledonian Railway Company began the development of a new terminal on the north side of the Clyde in the 1870s, Grahamston was buried, almost without trace, under Glasgow Central Station.

It is not known why Dougalston feued this land, and there is no detailed account in any of the Glasgow histories of the lands or the village of Grahamston, which lay outside the royalty boundaries. Glimpses of Grahamston in the eighteenth century emerge from the Glasgow burgh records: in 1739 payment of 8s 6²/3d sterling to John and Thomas McFies 'for mending and caswaying the "sink" [a sunken stretch of road] at Grahamston', and to James Cross, 'masson', 8s 6²/3d 'for lighting and laying a syer there'.

Brewing was an early industry in the village. According to the New Statistical Account of 1835, soon after the Union, Mr Crawford of Milton erected an extensive brewery at Grahamston, afterwards the property of Mr Cowan. Disputes were ongoing between Crawford and the town council 'anent the arrears of impost charged on him and his company, partners in a brewarie at Grahamestoun, on the two pennies on the pint of ale, and what deductions and allowances he ought to have'. One dispute in 1762 was referred to the lord advocate. A notice of the sale of the St Enoch's factory at Grahamston in the

Journal of 1 August 1757 indicates that weavers were also among the first inhabitants of the village. The property, belonging to Alexander Gordon, consisted of working shops, looms and utensils, as well as a large dwelling house, garden, stables and a pump well in the court, the whole with a large entry from the street.

The lands remained with the Grahams till 1754, when they were sold by John Graham's grandson to John Miller of Westerton, maltman in Glasgow, who was a tenant of one of the breweries in Grahamston. Miller owned much property in the city, and around 1770 he feued out Miller Street, which was for long a fashionable locality. He was

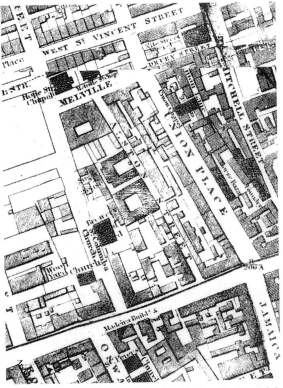

Part of the *Plan of the City of Glasgow and its Environs* by David Smith and James Collie, 1839. This shows the village of Grahamston, which extended from Melville (now Gordon) Street down to Argyle Street, and from the west side of Hope Street to the west side of Union Place (now Union Street). Alston Street was the main street of Grahamston village.

succeeded at Grahamston in 1790 by his grandson, John Alston, a merchant, who proceeded to feu off the ground in lots, advertising the situation of the grounds as agreeable 'as they lie without the Royalty' and because persons settling there 'will enjoy all the advantages of the city, while they are exempted from all burghal taxes . . . which must be a considerable inducement to purchasers'.

For nearly one hundred years Grahamston was a separate and isolated village. It had been quite a busy place with its market gardens, weaving factory, breweries and theatre, and by 1791 the population of the village had risen to 896. The first of many granaries were erected there after completion of the Glasgow branch of the Forth & Clyde Canal to Port Dundas in 1790. With the opening of the canal Grahamston changed from a rural village to a bustling centre of manufacture, distribution and storage.

The Glasgow Directory of 1790 lists what was probably the last of the gardeners, A. and J. McAulay and the Scotts, father and son. The occupations of the inhabitants in 1801 include a grain dealer and five corn factors. Other new businesses include R. Muirhead & Co, timber merchants, and a ropeworks, saddler, saddle-tree-maker, shoe shop, watch-maker and five grocers. By 1806 John Wotherspoon, a partner in the Grahamston Bakery Company, was manufacturing bread in the village and selling it in Glasgow, sparking off more disputes over duties, and a sugar-house was erected in 1808. Union Street was laid out in 1802 and a further encroachment on the open land west of Grahamston was made with the extension of Hope Street, originally Copenhagen Street, down into Argyle Street.

Robert Lindsay's Grahamston: 'a pleasing account'

In 1893, Robert Lindsay, who had spent a happy childhood in Grahamston, wrote his memoirs, a valuable record of the village around the 1820s, and entitled them *Quiet old Glasgow; its Latter Days before Railways, with Many other interesting matters, giving a Pleasing Account of the village of Grahamston, which was situate on that part of Argyle Street then known as Anderston Walk, by a Burgess of Glasgow.*

Lindsay begins his tour on the west side of Union Street at the corner of Argyle Street where stood the mile-stone-like pillar which marked the then boundary of the city. The buildings fronting Union Street, and along the north side of Argyle Street, were all included in the village. On the west side of Alston Street, looking into Argyle

Street, was the residence of Mr Marshall, the village schoolmaster, whose class-room, or school-house, was on the opposite side of Alston Street, in Dallas Court. Nearly all the villagers, and many from other places, attended his school. Mr Marshall was a very painstaking teacher, with a peculiar method of punishment. When he saw anything wrong going on, he calmly threw the tawse over to the offender, ordering him to bring it up. Then he placed an old wig on the head of the culprit, who had to march foolishly through the schoolroom with his right forefinger in his ear and the left one in his mouth. Lindsay considered that for a very sensitive youth, especially if he had a sweetheart among the girls, 'this was a very trying mode of punishment'.

Between Union Street and the back of the houses in Grahamston there was a piece of neutral ground where the schoolboys could settle their quarrels by fighting, having stone battles, or playing games with boys from Brownfield village to the west or from the small community at Drury Lane to the east. One or two tenements of first-class housing had been erected at the upper end of Union Street, but the housewives in Alston Street still managed to find enough space for bleaching their clothes by coming in and out by their back windows, about two feet from the ground. Above these tenements stood the stores of the Hurlet and Campsie Alum Company. This was a large brick building, extending from the line of Union Street nearly back to the houses in Grahamston. A branch of the Forth & Clyde Canal had been opened up near the village of Campsie, and the produce and manufactures of that part of the country were now brought into Port Dundas and the merchandise brought into the city by Port Dundas Road. The goods were stored in Grahamston and then taken by carrier to the various towns and villages where they were required.

To the west of the stores of the alum company, and fronting on to Alston Street were two large old granaries, and above these the starch works of Mr Lockhart. These were the first grain stores in or around the city and had been placed in this out-of-the-way village as being the nearest point to Port Dundas Road, and immediately beyond the boundary of the city. Beyond this point there was a large extent of vacant ground, from Grahamston up to and beyond what became Melville Street, which was later renamed Gordon Street. Local families used to climb the steep slope to the top of Blythswood Hill for picnics. From here they could enjoy the view, looking down on the river with its scanty shipping then turning round and viewing the extensive shipping at Port Dundas, and wondering how the ships got there, as there was no water to be seen from this point.

Lindsay now takes us across to the west side of Alston Street, where the sugar-house, or sugar refinery, stood almost opposite the old granaries. A little west from this, where the Corn Exchange later stood in Hope Street, there was a small piece of marshy land and at the edge of this willow bushes had been planted for making creels and baskets used by the market gardeners. The rubbish heaps of the sugar-house was where the boys went to get 'sugar-mug' – pieces of broken sugar moulds saturated with sugar. The sugar-house was six stories high and very narrow in proportion to its great height. This was the scene of a great calamity in 1848 when, without any warning, the building fell, or rather crumbled down, killing twelve of the eighteen men employed at the works. Workmen from the timber yards and workshops at Blythswood hurried down to the scene but little could be done. It took four days to recover the bodies. Four hundred pounds was raised for the families of the bereaved in eight days. The cause was probably vibrating machinery which had weakened the walls.

We now continue down to the brewery which stood about midway down the east side of Alston Street. When this brewery was offered for sale in 1780 it was advertised in the *Mercury* as 'that large and commodious brewerie at Grahamstone, which consists of steeps, maltbarn, kill, loft, cellars, vaults &c, sufficient for carrying on an extensive business in brewing strong ale, small beer, two penny and whisky, with proper utensils for the same'. The small beer was very much used by the working classes as a beverage at meals. Butter milk was then very scarce, and only to be had at certain times of the year. The beer was used chiefly at breakfast, taken with porridge, and formed an excellent and agreeable substitute for milk. Included in the sale was a good dwelling house in the same square with servants' houses, stable, hay loft etc., with a large garden behind the brewery and an excellent well in the close, remarkable good water for brewing.

Grahamston was also known for its manufacture of 'luggies'. These were small wooden bowls with one or two handles formed from projecting staves, used for serving milk with porridge. There was a cooper's shop which made luggies with peas in them – dried peas between two buttons – so that they rattled melodiously and encouraged the children to hurry through with their porridge so that they could then listen to the music.

The best-known building in Grahamston, the theatre, stood further

This sketch shows the buildings along part of the north side of Argyle Street in 1793. The buildings formed part of the village of Grahamston which disappeared when the Central Station was built over it in the 1870s.

down Alston Street on the east side. This was believed to be the first regular theatre in Scotland – with the exception of one established in Edinburgh about eighteen years earlier – and was built around 1764, at a time when there was strong feeling against theatres in Scotland. When a group of Glasgow gentlemen agreed to erect a theatre at their own expense, they had to go outside the city to purchase a piece of ground at Grahamston from a Mr Miller. The erection of the building caused a great sensation among the people in the city and in the village, and before the opening night it was set on fire. It was said that the attempt to destroy the theatre was instigated by a preacher who told his hearers that the previous night in his dreams he was in the infernal regions at a great entertainment attended by all the devils in hell, at which Lucifer gave a toast to honour Mr Miller, who had sold him ground for a house. The fire damage was repaired and the theatre was opened by Mrs Bellamy, then a popular actress in London, who had lost, in the fire, a wardrobe and jewels which she valued at £900. But through the kindness of the ladies of Glasgow she received 'above forty gowns on the night of her appearance, with under garments and presents of all kinds'. The theatre remained open till 1780 when it was burned to the ground, amidst the shouts of the excited crowd and cries of 'Save the ither folk's houses an' let the deil's house burn.'

Next to the ruin of the theatre stood two tenements of dwelling houses with other buildings and houses behind. All these houses, and others on the east side of the street, were chiefly occupied by market gardeners, granarymen and carters employed in carting grain from Port Dundas. On either side of the street at this point the buildings were set back about forty feet, leaving a large open space on which the carts stood when work was over, and behind these were stables and dungpits. Lindsay considered that these carters and granarymen were rather a superior class. They were often seen on summer evenings seated on their carts, at times discussing the movements of the Radicals and the possiblity of a general rising and overthrow of the Government. And on quiet Sabbath evenings, when all was still, for there was no thoroughfare, small family groups might be seen engaged in reading or in serious conversation, while enjoying the pure fresh air of the street.

Gordon Street and Hope Street

On the north of the village, Melville Street (later Gordon Street) was laid out through the vacant ground which separated Grahamston from the new town of Blythswood on the hill above. Three churches were built here and Lindsay particularly remembered the United Secession Church directly opposite the top of Alston Street. The church was opened in 1823 with seating for 1,600 and was always filled by members and adherents drawn by the eloquence of the Rev. Alexander Beattie, 'an earnest, powerful preacher and not a man to express himself on any subject with bated breath'. During his thirty-year ministry Mr Beattie found time to attend medical classes at the University of Glasgow and take the degree of MD and then receive a DD from Oxford College, Ohio. Although strict about the 'Sanctity of the Sabbath', Dr Beattie took no notice of those who used their own or hired carriages for conveyance to church on the Sabbath. This gave great offence to his people, who considered that it was being done through fear of, or in deference to, one of his members. This was the architect Mr James Smith, father of the notorious Madeleine, whose trial for the murder of her lover caused a sensation in 1857. Because of the great increase in the value of property in Gordon Street, the congregation decided to sell their church and build another on a new site in St Vincent Street to plans by Messrs A. & G. Thomson, Architects, Glasgow. On the morning of 16 March 1858, after invoking the blessing of God on the work about to be begun, Dr Beattie lifted the first sod from the foundation of St Vincent Street UP Church. Sadly, Dr Beattie died before the completion of Alexander Thomson's 'splendid and unique specimen of classical architecture', which continues to draw admiration today.

The first Gaelic chapel in Glasgow was built in Ingram Street at the corner of Queen Street in 1767 with funds contributed within the

The architect James Smith with his wife and seven children. The family attended the United Secession Church in Melville Street directly opposite the top of Alston Street. The tallest girl is the infamous Madeleine, whose trial trial for the murder of her lover caused a sensation in the city.

synod of Argyll. In 1837 the property was sold to the British Linen Bank for £12,000, 'a fabulous sum', and two years later a new Gaelic chapel, to be known as St Columba's Church, was opened on the east side of Hope Street, extending back to Alston Street, where the church officer had his dwelling. This move was made during the ministry of the Rev. Norman Macleod, who worked to make a wide range of Gaelic writing accessible to the new literate public created by the Gaelic Schools Movement. His works were published posthumously with the title *Caraid nan Gaidheal* 'Friend of the Gaels', by which name he was known. The congregation then moved to the Waterloo Rooms, later the site of the Alhambra Theatre, until the present St Columba's Church at the west end of St Vincent Street was opened in 1904. His son, also Norman Macleod, became the minister of the Barony and chaplain to Queen Victoria, and his statue stands in Cathedral Square.

Lindsay's tour ends as he takes up down Hope Street. The buildings on the west side of the street were on, and formed the boundary of Grahamston. For a few years, after the opening of this street, the lower end on both sides was entirely covered with workshops of various trades, large and small. Among those on the west side was a large horse-shoeing and veterinary establishment. As a boy, Lindsay noticed numbers of well-dressed people, and others of less respectable appearance, apparently engaged in looking after the horses, going out and in about these premises. But it was not publicly known that parties met in the back premises to engage in the brutal practice of cock-fighting. The new pit which Glasgow got in 1835 in Hope Street seated about 280 with suitable accommodation for the judges, handlers and feeders. This cruel sport had formerly been very prevalent, even by schoolboys, and despite increasing public disapproval, commented Lindsay, it had never disappeared.

A more prestigious building was erected at the south corner of Hope Street and Waterloo Street in 1840. This was the Corn Exchange, built for the convenience of the numerous corn dealers of the district, who until then had transacted their business in front of the Tontine at Glasgow Cross. But by this time Grahamston had been overtaken by Anderston as a centre of warehousing as goods were increasingly shipped into the Broomielaw. All the market gardeners had left, the neat, well-kept gardens were no longer to be seen, their places in the village having been taken by pastry bakers, a lock-maker, a piano tuner, a bedding manufacturer, an upholsterer's furnisher and others. The churches made way for business premises, which gradually covered what had been the playground and battlefields of groups and young children and lads, until all that was once connected with Grahamston was swept away, and the once pleasant, quiet, rural village was also blotted out, and buried under the station.

Central Station is built on three levels: high level, where the site was built up to the level of the incoming rail tracks; street level; and underground, where lies, waiting to be rediscovered, according to the persistent Glasgow myth, under the railway tracks, an entire buried street, complete with shops and houses. One certain reminder of Grahamston does remain. As you walk up Union Street, notice that the angle of the street does not conform to the surrounding grid street pattern, because it was laid out in line with Alston Street. And spare a thought for the village that disappeared.

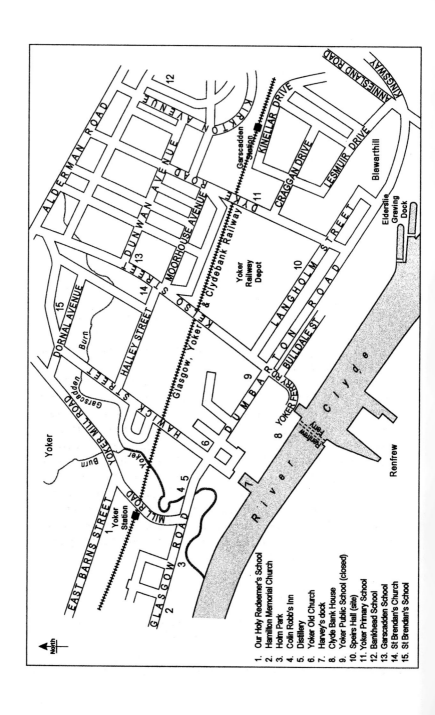

North

River Clyde

Renfrew

Yoker

Yoker Station

Yoker Railway Depot

Garscadden Station

Blawarthill

Elderslie Graving Dock

Passenger Ferry

Yoker Ferry

Glasgow, Yoker & Clydebank Railway

EAST BARNS STREET

ALDERMAN ROAD

DORNAL AVENUE

DUNWAN AVENUE

MOORHOUSE AVENUE

KIRTON AVENUE

ANNIESLAND ROAD

KINGSWAY

KINELLAR DRIVE

CRAGGAN DRIVE

LESMUIR DRIVE

LANGHOLM STREET

DUMBARTON ROAD

BUILDALE ST.

HALLEY STREET

HAWICK STREET

GLASGOW ROAD

YOKER MILL ROAD

MILL ROAD

Garscadden Road

Burn

Yoker Burn

1. Our Holy Redeemer's School
2. Hamilton Memorial Church
3. Holm Park
4. Colin Robb's Inn
5. Distillery
6. Yoker Old Church
7. Harvey's dock
8. Clyde Bank House
9. Yoker Public School (closed)
10. Speirs Hall (site)
11. Yoker Primary School
12. Bankhead School
13. Garscadden School
14. St Brendan's Church
15. St Brendan's School

11
YOKER

Yoker lies on the north bank of the Clyde, six miles downriver from the centre of Glasgow. It is only partly within the city boundary. That part of *The Yoker*, as it is locally known, which does not belong to Glasgow, east of the Yoker Burn, was not annexed from Renfrewshire until 1926. The part of Yoker west of the burn remains in Dunbartonshire.

Although Yoker did not develop as a village until the eighteenth century, the name appears in charters and exchequer rolls in the early sixteenth century and the lands of 'Yochyrr' were sufficiently well known to appear an Blaeu's map of Clydesdale, surveyed by Timothy Pont in the 1590s. On General Roy's Military Map, prepared between 1747 and 1755, 'Yoker Briggs' is marked on the road from Dumbarton to Glasgow and 'Thirdpart' is shown surrounded by cultivated land, important information for the quick movement and provision of troops.

Until the deepening of the Clyde in the eighteenth century, Yoker occupied an important site at the highest point of navigation for ships of any size. In the reign of David I it stood opposite the High Steward's castle and town of Renfrew. Norse raids were made as far up as Yoker but ceased after Somerled, Lord of the Isles, was defeated and killed at the battle of Renfrew in 1164. The Steward was rewarded with a charter for the founding of Paisley Abbey, after which the district round Yoker on the north of the Clyde was taken into the jurisdiction of the Abbot of Paisley. The present boundary between Glasgow and Dunbartonshire at the Yoker Burn is the same age-old boundary which separated the lands of the new Stewart dynasty from the ancient kingdom of Strathclyde.

The little village of Yoker remarkable only for its large distillery

Until the middle of the nineteenth century Yoker was a community of farmers and millers and it was a farmer, John Harvey, who brought the first industry to the district around 1740 when he established a distillery on the Yoker Burn, one of a number along the Clyde making use of the plentiful local barley and the abundant pure water from the burns rising in the Kilpatrick Hills to distill whisky on a commercial scale. The business prospered and remained in the family till around 1900, after which Yoker Distillery was sold and finally ceased production in the 1930s. The warehouses continued in use but were badly damaged during the Clydebank Blitz. The Harvey family also owned Dundashill and Ardentinny Distilleries and established Bruichladdich on Islay.

When Alfred Barnard wrote about Yoker in his *Whisky Distilleries of the United Kingdom* in 1887 he reported that the whisky was grain with an admixture of malt, the annual output 600,000 gallons, with between fifty and sixty employees and six excise officers. Mr Barnett Harvey resided on the property, in a quaint and picturesque house, whilst on one side of the old-fashioned garden was a large bowling green kept up for the use of the men in the distillery and in the village. Barnard particularly noted the private wharf feued by Harvey where barley and maize was landed by lighters direct from the ships at Glasgow, free of all duties and charges. The firm also had the right to draw water from the Clyde, and had a circular reservoir for filtering purposes. Several wells of spring water were on the property, but for distilling purposes Loch Katrine water was used. 'Harvey's Dock' was in fact the terminus for a wooden waggonway from Knightswood Colliery, built in the late eighteenth century by John & William Dixon of the famous 'Dixon's Blazes' family. The line existed to supply coal to the great Dumbarton Glass Works, another Dixon enterprise. The small dock can be reached a short distance downstream from the ferry at Yoker.

The distillery was built on the east side of the Yoker Burn, to the north of the main road from Glasgow to Dumbarton, for below that point the Clyde was regularly in flood. The highway was impassable in winter to carriages but underwent improvement around 1770 when the duke of Argyll provided a much needed bridge to replace the ford over the burn. A toll-house was built an the south side of the bridge on the Dumbarton side, and with the great increase in traffic the outlay proved profitable. On the west side of the burn was a road which led northwards up the brae to Third Part corn mill and the mill owner's house where there was also a grinding mill. This was the route used by the drovers coming down from Stirling or Loch Lomondside. Near the foot of the road was the Lochinvar, a very ancient inn, popular with drovers and the local farmers who drove

Yoker Distillery, said to have been founded by Thomas Harvey around 1740 on the east bank of the Yoker Burn, remained in production till the 1920s. From Alfred Barnard's *Whisky Distilleries of the United Kingdom.*

down in their pony traps. Another hostelry popular with the drovers was Colin Robb's public house. The Lovat Arms stands today on the same site. A map of 1734 shows a village beginning to develop here with houses on both sides of the burn. More houses were built by Harvey for his workers on three sides of a square which lay behind the site of the Lovat Arms.

After the establishment of the distillery Yoker continued as a rural community undisturbed for a further hundred years. A survey of 1818 says 'that part of Renfrew lying north of the Clyde has a deep and fertile soil', and the Statistical Account of Dunbartonshire in 1836 remarks that seen from the river, at the village of Yoker, the country is 'flat and well cultivated, having all the appearance of land that will repay the skill and toil of the husbandman'. One such husbandman was Farmer Hamilton, who at that time farmed the land stretching westwards from Yoker Burn, the area appearing on Pont's map as 'Barnes'. Hamilton was renowned for his skilful management of his East Barnes farmlands, where he had introduced new crops and was using the new methods of cultivation such as crop rotation. Two small farms which may at one time have been part of East Barnes, were Stevenson's Farm and Yoker Holm Farm. Rothesay Dock was built over much of these two farms in 1907, but part of Yoker Holm, survived as Holm Park, the ground of Yoker Athletic FC. Third Part was another very old farm, shown to the east of the burn on Pont's

Colin Robb stands in front of his premises on the north side of Glasgow Road, Yoker. The inn stood on the site presently occupied by the Lovat Arms, and was a popular haunt of cattle drovers in its earliest days.

map as 'Threapyaira'. This was at one time a vast expanse, slowly eroded by the sale of parts round the fringes. It was farmed latterly by the Paterson family and finished as a pig farm. Third Part is the only remaining farm on a map of the area published in 1938.

Yoker Mains was one of the largest farms in the area and is mentioned in a directory entry of 1820 which dismisses Yoker in one curt sentence: 'Yoker has a distillery and a farm called Yoker Mains.' It is described in 1860 as having 'an excellent farm house and offices, belonging to Mr Speirs of Elderslie and occupied by Mr Fleming'. The last farmer was Walter Pollock, whose name was given to Walter (later Langholm) Street and Pollock (later Kelso) Street. Much of Knightswood was built over Yoker Mains and the neighbouring Bankhead Farm, which became a golf course before being used for housing. Drew's Dairy belonged to a family who lived in a house adjoining Yoker School and kept cows and horses on ground which later became the school playground. Most of the farms were dairy farms, supplying milk and butter to the ever growing city of Glasgow. In 1923 there was an outbreak of foot-and-mouth disease at Third Part Farm, which infected two other farms. The disease reappeared three years later when Dickie the local blacksmith lost his herd of over forty dairy cows. In 1938 a further outbreak wiped out the last traces of local farming.

The Clyde made Yoker

Although no industrial development took place at Yoker during the century after the establishment of the distillery, much was happening on the river Clyde, and this was eventually to transform the village from a rural to an industrial community. In 1781 John Golborne, who had begun work ten years earlier to improve the navigation on the river, was asked to advise again on obtaining greater depths to improve the channel up to the Broomielaw. At his suggestion the deepening was done in two stages, concentrating first on obtaining a ten-foot depth up to Yoker, so that large coastal vessels could load coal directly from the quay there, and so generate more revenue for the second stage from Yoker to the Broomielaw. The day-to-day management of the Clyde was put into the hands of a river superintendent and the house built for him at Yoker, later known as Clyde Bank House, can be seen on Richardson's map of 1795 with the name of the first superintendent, Mr Bennet, alongside. John Bennet was followed in 1798 by James Spreull, under whose supervision the whole character of the Clyde was completely changed as the river became a canal.

This stage of the work required the replacement of the ford at Blawarthill Sand by a ferry. This was the best ford in the Yoker district and a small community already existed close to the river side. The first ferry was rowed across the river by two men with heavy oars, between Blawarthill and the King's Inch on the Renfrew side at Braehead. The ferry was later moved downriver to its present site, and a new boat, built to transport carriages, put into service. In 1868 a new chain-hauled steam-driven vehicular ferry was introduced. Two modern vessels, the *Renfrew Rose* and the *Yoker Swan* now make the 400-yard crossing. This is a passenger-only service with space for an ambulance and bicycles, and is the only remaining ferry on the river.

After the transfer of the ferry to the present site, a ferry house was erected to provide accommodation for tile ferrymen and their families and the Ferry Inn was built. This was described in 1860 as 'a respectable hotel with stabling attached and occupied by Mr Norrie'. Further down the river, just west of Harvey's Dock, was Yoker Lodge, at one time the country residence of James Lumsden, Lord Provost of

The steam-driven chain-hauled ferry in this picture was built in 1897. Its predecessor, which operated from 1868, can be seen lying on the Yoker shore. From the Stromier & Vogt collection, Glasgow City Archives.

Glasgow from 1844 to 1848. The house was later occupied by William Simons, who had begun the Jordanvale Shipyard at Whiteinch in 1853. Seven years later Wm. Simons & Co. moved across the river to Renfrew. One of the most unusual vessels they built there was the elevating vehicular ferry *Finnieston*, which was fitted with a deck which could be raised or lowered to align with the quay. The firm later specialised in building dredgers. The ship's carpenters and riveters, who lived at Ferry Road Head, almost certainly formed part of Simons' workforce. Until about 1850 this little community at the junction of Ferry Road and Glasgow Road consisted mostly of agricultural labourers, but later a variety of occupations were represented. Arthur Graham, for example, a native of Argyll, was the policeman there around 1870.

Shipbuilding began at Yoker in 1877 when Messrs Napier Shanks and Bell moved downriver from Cessnock to a more spacious and convenient site just west of the Yoker Burn, where they built both steam and sailing vessels, including the paddle-steamers *Neptune* and *Mercury* in 1892, which were the first two steamers to be designed for the Glasgow & South Western Railway Company. The firm was again displaced to Old Kilpatrick in 1906 by the building of Rothesay Dock. Many of the shipyard workers occupied the tenements which had now been built along Glasgow Road in the part of Yoker west of the burn. Another group of men here worked at James White's chemical works to the north of the village. At one time this factory manufactured more than half the iodine used in Britain from seaweed brought from the Western Isles.

At the end of the nineteenth century the speed of growth of heavy industry in Yoker was breathtaking, particularly along the river bank. Among the first arrivals was Bull's Metal and Marine Ltd. The company, founded by John Bull, specialised in the manufacture of ship propellers. They were followed by Drysdale & Co, who became a leading manufacturer of pumps for shipbuilding, dock pumping and a wide range of other uses. Yoker Electric Power Station, Rothesay Dock and Elderslie Dock were built, and Yarrows opened a shipyard on the eastern fringe of Yoker. All this took place in the space of ten years between 1897 and 1907 along a stretch of some two miles of the north bank of the Clyde. G. & J. Thomson had already moved their yard from Cessnock to West Barns O'Clyde in 1872, where it was taken over in 1899 by John Brown & Co. Further back from the river George Halley built a factory on part of Third Part Farm where his company, Halley Industrial Motors, specialised in the production of fire engines. Several of these companies had come from Bridgeton or Anderston and brought their skilled workforce with them. Others came from further afield. John Bull, for example, was a Norwegian, George Halley a Dane, Alfred Yarrow began shipbuilding on the Thames and John Brown was a steel maker in Sheffield. The Napiers, the Thomsons and Drysdales were Scots. The site of Bull's works in Bulldale Street is now occupied by Walker Macleod Fabrications, a leading sheet metal work producer, but other industry at Yoker is now mainly located in two industrial estates at Halley Street and behind Langholm Street on old railway sidings, and at the Scotrail and Railtrack Yoker Depot at Dyke Road.

Churches and schools

At the beginning of the twentieth century there was a pressing need in Yoker for housing for the new workforce, for public buildings and for the supply of services. The first of many red-sandstone tenements, some of which remain a feature of Yoker, were erected about 1906 at Yoker Perry Road and at Greenlaw Street. The terraced, semi-detached and self-contained houses in the Coldingham Avenue area were built

Shops on the south side of Dumbarton Road, just east of Yoker Ferry Road. Note the Art Deco glass in the windows of Peacock the baker, and the tempting display of cakes.

for management and supervisory staff. Yoker's first church, opened in 1855, was the Free Church on the boundary between Yoker and Clydebank, built on ground gifted by Miss Hamilton, the owner of the Barns and Cochno Estates, herself an Episcopalian, and this became later the Hamilton Memorial Church. Yoker Old, which became the parish church in 1906, was erected in 1897 as a chapel of ease from St James' Church in Clydebank. The site was purchased for a nominal sum from Mr Alexander Archibald Hagart Speirs. For the many Roman Catholics now coming to work in the area a chapel-school was founded in 1889 at the foot of Kilbowie Road in Clydebank and placed under the care of Father Evans, who travelled daily over to Yoker from St James' Church, which was located near the landing stage at Renfrew. In 1902 the present Our Holy Redeemer's Church was erected in Glasgow Road. St Paul's at Whiteinch was opened the same year and Catholic children could attend school at either Clydebank or Whiteinch until St Brendan's School was opened in Yoker in 1945.

In 1873 the newly formed Renfrew School Board resolved to erect a school in Yoker village and the Old Kilpatrick board agreed to pay their share of the cost of education for those children of the village resident in their parish. When no action had been taken by the following year, 118 Yoker householders signed a petition 'praying that an elementary school, jointly or separately, be erected for the children at Yoker'. Building work finally got underway and in 1877 Mr Archibald Walker took up his post as headmaster of Yoker Public School. The school was extended in 1902 and a gymnasium added. The extra accommodation was desperately needed, for the population of the Scotstoun–Yoker portion of Renfrewshire rose by one hundred and fifty per cent between 1901 and 1911. The situation was also relieved by the opening of Elgin Street School by the Old Kilpatrick School Board in 1897 for Yoker children living west of the burn.

Annexation

Although the population of Yoker now consisted mainly of incomers, there was a remarkably strong sense of community and in 1911 a public hall was gifted to the people of Yoker by Mr A. A. Hagart Speirs, whose father had bought up all the land on the north side of the Clyde from Blawarthill to the Yoker Burn. This lay across the river from the family estate of Elderslie, formed by Archibald Speirs, the outstandingly successful Glasgow 'tobacco lord'. Mr Hagart Speirs was a keen sportsman and his other gifts included ground for a bowling green and a curling pond in Harvey (later Hawick) Street, and tennis courts in front of the Speirs Hall in Langholm Street. Lady Anne Street and Bouverie Street are named after his mother. The Speirs Hall has been replaced by Yoker Sports Centre and Langholm Street has been renamed Speirshall. Terrace. The Clydeside Walkway and Cycleway passes along the back of the sports centre on the old Lanarkshire and Dunbartonshire Railway line. The war memorial to the men of Yoker who fell in the Great War was erected in the recreation ground opposite the hall in 1921. It was Mr Hagart Speirs who led the successful fight in 1912 to prevent Yoker from being annexed to Glasgow, when the city boundary was moved west to Westland Drive taking in Partick, Whiteinch and part of Scotstoun. In 1926, however, the remainder of Renfrewshire north of the Clyde became part of Glasgow, and the city boundary is now the Yoker Burn.

The land annexed by Glasgow included a large part of the then undeveloped land between Knightswood and Yoker, on much of which the Knightswood housing estate was subsequently built. The

The memorial to the men who fell in the First World War was erected in the recreation ground in front of the Speirs Hall in 1921, The hall has been demolished and replaced by the new Sports Centre. The street behind, Langholm Street, has been renamed Speirshall Terrace.

first of the new primary schools to be built was Garscadden in 1931, followed by Bankhead two years later and by St Brendan's in 1945. The modern Yoker Primary School was opened in Craggan Drive in 1975 and the old building in Dumbarton Road is now used for social work. Our Holy Redeemer was opened in 1980 in East Barns Street.

In the dark days of the Second World War, Bankhead School was partly demolished early in the war in a 'hit and run' raid, and six people were killed when four high explosive bombs fell on a, building at the east end of Langholm Street. During the Blitz of March 1941 Yoker suffered lightly in contrast to its near neighbour Clydebank, but considerable damage was done from incendiary bombs and the number of Yoker fatalities is put at about forty. The toll-house, the smiddy beside the burn, Colin Robb's Inn and a number of houses were completely destroyed, many others seriously damaged and only a minority remained unscathed. Although a number of red sandstone tenements survive along Dumbarton Road, new blocks of flats have filled up the empty sites, and it is left to names like Clydeholm Court, Newshot Court and the Cooperage to keep alive the memory of the village which grew up 'both sides of the burn'.

FURTHER READING

General and Reference

Fisher. J., *The Glasgow Encyclopedia*, 1994

Richardson, T., Map of the town of Glasgow and country seven
miles round, 1795

Ainslie, J., Map of the County of Renfrew, 1796

Crawfurd, G., *General Description of the Shire of Renfrew, 1710*,
continued by Semple, J., 1782, and by Robertson, G., 1810

MacGibbon, D. and Ross. D., *Castellated and Domestic Architecture of
Scotland*, 1887

Senex (Robert Reid), *Glasgow Past and Present*, 1884

Gibb. A., *Glasgow – The Making of a City*, 1983

Worsdall, F., *The Tenement, A Way of Life*, 1979

Handley, J.E., *The Irish in Scotland*, 1945

Hume, J.R., *The Industrial Archaeology of Glasgow*, 1974

Slaven, A., *The Development of the West of Scotland, 1750–1960*, 1975

Macdonald. H., *Rambles round Glasgow*, 1854

Cardonald

Innes, J.A., *Old Cardonald Had a Farm*, 1993

Lindsay. J., *The Canals of Scotland*, 1968

Kempsell. A., *The Golden Thumb: History of Washington Mills*, 1964

Forsyth, J.B., *Cardonald Parish Church, The First 100 Years*, 1989

Lochhead, A., *The First Sixty Years; 30th Glasgow (Cardonald) Scout
Troop, 1909–1969*, 1969

Cathcart

Gartshore, A., *Cathcart Memories*, 1938

Marshall, J., *Cathcart and its Environs*, 1990

Reader, W.J., *The Weir Group: Centenary History*, 1971
Kernaham, J., *The Cathcart Circle*, 1980

Gorbals

Ord, J., *The Story of the Barony of Gorbals*, 1919
Smith, R., *The Gorbals – Historical Guide and Heritage Walk*, 1999
Collins, K.E., *Second City Jewry: The Jews of Glasgow in the Age of Expansion, 1790–1919*, 1990
Hutt, C. and Caplan, H., *A Scottish Shtehl: Jewish Life in the Gorbals, 1880–1974*, 1974
Coveney, M., *The Citz: 21 Years of the Glasgow Citizens' Theatre*, 1990
Dunlop, A.C., *Hutchesons' Grammar: History of a Glasgow School*, 1992

Govan

Brotchie, T.C.F., *History of Govan*, 1905
Transactions of Old Govan Club, 1914–1934
Ritchie, A. (ed.), *Govan and its Early Medieval Sculpture*, 1994
Walker, F.M., *Song of the Clyde: A History of Clyde Shipbuilding*, 1984
Everitt, D., *The K-Boats*
Rountree, G., *A Govan Childhood: The Nineteen Thirties*, 1993
Twydell, D., *Rejected Football Clubs of Scotland*, vol. 2, 1993

Govanhill and Polmadie

Eunson, E., *Old Govanhill*, 1994
Edward, M., *Who Belongs to Glasgow*, 1993
Dow, D., *The Samaritan Hospital for Women*, 1989
Woods, P., *Third Lanark Football Club*, 1981
Nicolson. M. and O'Neill, M., *Glasgow: Locomotive Builder to the World*, 1987
Macmillan. N., *Locomotive Apprentice at the North British Locomotive Co.*, 1992

Hurlet and Nitshill

Taylor, C., *Levern Delineated*, 1831
Murray, R., *Annals of Barrhead*, 1942
Hughson, I. (ed.), *Bygone Barrhead*
Kinchin, J., *Tea and Taste, Glasgow's Tea Rooms, 1875–1975*, 1991

Langside

Marshall. I. and Smith, R., *Queen's Park – Historical Guide and Heritage Walk*, 1997
Greene, M., *From Langside to Battlefield*, 1993
Stamp. G., *Alexander 'Greek' Thomson*, 1999
Slater, S.D. and Dow, D.A., *The Victoria Infirmary of Glasgow, 1890–1990, A Centenary History*, 1990

Pollokshaws

Fraser, W., *Memoirs of the Maxwells of Pollok*, 1863
McCallum, A., *Pollokshaws Village and Burgh, 1600–1912*, 1925
Milton, N., *John Maclean*, 1973
McLean, I., *The Legend of Red Clydeside*, 1983

Strathbungo and Crossmyloof

Scott, A.M., 'Notes on the village of Strathbungo', in *Transactions of the Glasgow Archaeological Society*, 1885–90
Munro, J.M., *Strathbungo and its Kirk*, 1933
MacMillan, A., *Jeems Kaye, his adventures and opinions*, 1903
Steven, W., *Heroes of the Faith*, 1952 (Jane Haining)
Cowan, B., *Curling and the Silver Broom*, 1985

INDEX